D0927015

Interventions • Theory and Contemporary Politics
Stephen Eric Bronner, Series Editor

Freedomways Reader: Prophets in Their Own Country,
edited by Esther Cooper Jackson, with Constance Pohl

Business and the State in International Relations,
edited by Ronald W. Cox

Television and the Crisis of Democracy, Douglas A. Kellner

Notes from the Minefield,
Irene Gendzier

Freedomways
Reader

Prophets in
Their Own Country

edited by
Esther Cooper Jackson

Constance Pohl,
Assistant Editor

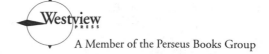
Westview
PRESS
A Member of the Perseus Books Group

To my husband
James Jackson
and my daughters
Harriet and Kathryn.

Copyright © 2000 by Westview Press, A Member of the Perseus Books Group

Published in 2000 in the United States of America by Westview Press, 5500 Central Avenue, Boulder, Colorado 80301-2877, and in the United Kingdom by Westview Press, 12 Hid's Copse Road, Cumnor Hill, Oxford OX2 9JJ

Visit us on the World Wide Web at www.westviewpress.com

Library of Congress Cataloging-in-Publication Data
Freedomways reader : prophets in their own country / edited by Esther Cooper Jackson, Constance Pohl.
    p. cm.
  Articles originally published in Freedomways.
  Includes bibliographical references and index.
  ISBN 0-8133-6769-7 (hc.)
  1. Blacks—History.   2. Afro-Americans—History.   3. Race relations—History.
4. United States—Race relations—History.   I. Jackson, Esther Cooper.   II. Pohl, Constance.
HT1581 .F735 2000
973'.0496073—dc21   99-048956

Design by Jeff Williams

The paper used in this publication meets the requirements of the American National Standard for Permanence of Paper for Printed Library Materials Z39.48-1984.

10   9   8   7   6   5   4   3   2

Contents

Part 2
Reports from the Front Lines:
Segregation in the South

J. H. O'Dell, 47

Part 3
International Solidarity

Esther Cooper Jackson, Constance Pohl, 108

THE ANTIWAR MOVEMENT

SOUTH AFRICA

Part 4
Moving North

LABOR

EDUCATION

WOMEN

PRISON AND THE COURTS

Part 5
Pioneers of Black Studies

Ernest Kaiser, 267

Part 6
Culture and the Cause of Black Freedom

Ruby Dee, 289

Photos

Foreword

JULIAN BOND

*Chairman, National Association for
the Advancement of Colored People*

Freedomways rightly believed that knowledge is power.

Its pages presented truths that seldom found an outlet elsewhere and arguments that suffered suppression more often than refutation.

It was born from the movement of the early 1960s, which in turn found its roots as much in the 1860s as the 1950s, 1940s, and 1930s. Importantly, *Freedomways* recognized that successful movements are built on the contributions and mistakes of the past. Its pages drew from yesterday while explaining today and predicting tomorrow.

In its opening announcement, *Freedomways* invited "historians, sociologists, economists, artists, workers, students—all who have something to contribute in this search for TRUTH—to use this open channel of communication that we might unite and mobilize our efforts for worthy and lasting results."

A veritable Who's Who of arts and letters—as well as workers and students—responded. The table of contents for each issue—as well as for this volume—lists a proud roster of aggressive participants, not just observers or recorders, of the movement for human rights.

What they wrote furthered the magazine's purposes: to "unite and mobilize our efforts." Contributors to *Freedomways* were distinguished by the high level of discourse they brought to their written work and also by their militant activism—these were writers with picket signs as well as pens in hand, scholars whose classrooms were the union halls, students who took instruction in the cotton fields or lunch counters, artists who brushed consciences as well as canvasses.

Each issue was eagerly awaited and its contents robustly debated. In these pages we found firm confirmation of our own unformed beliefs or challenges to what had been accepted wisdom; new ways of looking at the central problem of our time.

That the central problem was race, no one doubted. But *Freedomways* also argued that race was immensely complicated by greed, that prejudice and poverty were necessarily linked, and that it would take organized mass action to carry the day for freedom. *Freedomways* illuminated the "diversified and many-sided struggles of the Negro people."

We miss this forum today. I believe the world advanced because of *Freedomways* and would advance at a faster pace if the magazine were still here to prod us along, to spur thought and action.

Read these pages. Become envious of what was, and then become committed to bringing these pages alive again. As the editors urged, "Lift every voice and sing—of Freedom!"

Introduction

ESTHER COOPER JACKSON

The editorial in the very first issue of *Freedomways*, spring 1961, stated the purpose and goals of the collective of people who had founded *Freedomways*. We noted in part:

> Ours was always a multi-racial and multi-social land. There were, first, the Indians whom the newcomers did not wholly succeed in annihilating, then African slaves were brought. And the people who built the nation were drawn from many lands and backgrounds. The United States itself was born out of revolution and change. Founders of this country gave to the world the pronouncement which has served as a spark plug for every revolution which took place in the 19th and 20th century.
>
> "We hold these truths to be self-evident, that all men are created equal; that they are endowed by their Creator with certain inalienable rights, that among these are life, liberty, and the pursuit of happiness."
>
> A Civil War was fought and Amendments added to the Constitution with inconclusive results. In our own time decisions of the Supreme Court are flaunted and held in contempt.
>
> Now, we come to a national crossroad. Which way will we go? All who are deeply concerned know that this is a time for much serious thought, for careful balancing of ways and means. There is need for much discussion on every level.
>
> FREEDOMWAYS is born of the necessity for a vehicle of communication which will mirror developments in the diversified and many-sided struggles of the Negro people. It will provide a public forum for the review, examination, and debate of all problems confronting Negroes in the United States.

FREEDOMWAYS offers a means of examining experiences and strengthening the relationship among peoples of African descent in this country, in Latin America, and wherever there are communities of such people anywhere in the world. It will furnish *accurate* information on the liberation movements in Africa itself.

FREEDOMWAYS will explore, without prejudice or gag, and from the viewpoint of the special interests of American Negroes, as well as the general interest of the nation, the new forms of economic, political and social systems now existing or emerging in the world.

FREEDOMWAYS provides a medium of expression for serious and talented writers—for those with established reputations as well as beginners seeking a reading audience for the first time.

"You shall know the Truth—and the Truth shall set you free!"

This is our precept. We invite historians, sociologists, economists, artists, workers, students—all who have something constructive to contribute in this search for TRUTH—to use this open channel of communication that we might unite and mobilize our efforts for worthy and lasting results.

FREEDOMWAYS has no special interests to serve save those already clearly stated—no political, organizational or institutional ties. Those who commit themselves to its support become patrons only of a publication and an editorial policy designed to provide an open forum for the free expression of ideas. Sponsors of the publication will assume no responsibility for the particular views of any of its contributors; nor will contributors be constrained to abide by any editorial preference or bias of the publishers or editors.

FREEDOMWAYS offers all of us the opportunity to speak for ourselves.

Lift every voice and sing—of Freedom!

The Editors

In the 25 years of its publication, *Freedomways* had many outstanding moments. Three Nobel Prize laureates appeared in our pages: the poets Pablo Neruda and Derek Walcott, and the recipient of the Nobel Peace Prize, Dr. Martin Luther King Jr. The prize-winning authors James Baldwin and Alice Walker were contributing editors of *Freedomways*. Dr. King delivered one of his last speeches before his assassination at a *Freedomways*-sponsored centennial for W.E.B. Du Bois. African liberation leaders appeared in the quarterly: Kwame Nkrumah, Julius K. Nyerere, Agostinho Neto, Jomo Kenyatta, as did Caribbean leaders C.L.R. James and Cheddi Jagan. There were many firsts in the magazine, and many talented people who have since become well known started out in our pages. But above all, by lifting our collective voices, *Freedomways* helped advance the African American freedom struggle.

Initially, the idea of a Black literary and political quarterly had been the idea of Louis Burnham and his friend, youth leader Edward Strong, but on February 12, 1960, Louis Burnham died at the young age of 45 before his dream was realized. Then a number of us—writers, artists, activists—formed a collective to launch the magazine. Dr. Du Bois, who had edited the NAACP's magazine *The Crisis,* advised us on the difficulties of publishing a Black journal, and his wife Shirley Graham served as our first general editor.

As a founding editor of *Freedomways*, I spent a year prior to the publishing of the first issue in spring 1961—at Dr. Du Bois's advice—soliciting funds and consulting with writers, artists, educators, and others. We received some money from grants, but never any huge amounts. It was a plodding fund-raising effort. We didn't have any big foundation money, but we had our independence. It meant that more people participated and supported the journal, which was healthy and unique.

Dr. Du Bois, from his experience editing and publishing *The Crisis,* advised us not to bring out the first issue until we had enough money in the bank to publish for at least the first year. He also advised us not to work from a post office box but to get an office no matter how small; so I spent some time looking for an office and going to see people who might be interested in making contributions. Shirley Graham Du Bois had known some of the contributors during the McCarthy days of struggle, when Dr. Du Bois had been arrested with other leaders of the Peace Information Center. We became incorporated as Freedomways Associates Inc., established a board for the corporation, and we were in business.

In April 1961, we introduced the first issue at a reception for five or six hundred people at the Hotel Martinique on Thirty-fourth Street in New York. At the same time we had a more private event at the home of Dr. Du Bois on Grace Court in Brooklyn Heights. Most of the leading writers, artists, and activists of the day who wanted to see *Freedomways* succeed converged on the Du Bois home. We toasted the first issue with champagne as we read from the first editorial, which pronounced that we were going to struggle to see that this magazine continued. It was an inspiring evening.

Ossie Davis and Ruby Dee were associated with *Freedomways* for the full 25 years, as was Ernest Kaiser at the Schomburg Center for Research into Black Culture. The novelists John Oliver Killens and Julian Mayfield and the short-story writer Loyle Hairston were part of the collective as were Augusta Strong, J. H. O'Dell, W. Alphaeus Hunton, John Henrik Clarke, George B. Murphy, and Jean Carey Bond. Margaret G. Burroughs served as first art director; she was followed by John L. Devine, our only white editor and a trade unionist who was with us until the magazine ceased publishing. We started with a press run of only 2,000 copies but went up to 15,000 copies, particularly for special issues, which were read by many thousands more. Later editors included Angela Davis, Keith E. Baird, Brumsic Brandon Jr., Frank Chapman, Selwyn R. Cudjoe, Tom Dent, Edmund W. Gordon, and Leith Mullings. On the board were Dorothy Burnham and Calvin Sinnette; Mary Kaiser, Office Manager; and Norma Rogers, Special Events.

This anthology opens with articles published in the journal but written in the 1940s and 1950s that provide a historical context for the birth of the journal. The next five sections represent the main subjects covered by the journal: the Southern movement, international solidarity, the movement in the North, Black scholarship, and art and activism. The reader is able to follow the growth and change of the freedom struggle because the articles are placed generally in chronological order within the six sections.

Part I: Origins of *Freedomways*

The unique qualities of *Freedomways* flowed from the political philosophies of two extraordinary figures: Paul Robeson and W.E.B. Du Bois. Dr. Du Bois's speech "Behold the Land" to the Southern Negro Youth Congress (SNYC) in 1946 opens Part 1, Origins of *Freedomways*, which covers the period from the late 1930s to 1961, when the journal began publication. Many of us met in the Southern Negro Youth Congress—Louis Burnham, Dorothy Burnham, Augusta Strong, Edward Strong, James Jackson, and myself. Augusta Strong's article, "Southern Youth's Proud Heritage," provides the history of the Youth Congress, an organization of young Southern Blacks founded in 1937.

Dr. W.E.B. Du Bois with Esther Cooper Jackson at the Southern Youth Legislature of the Southern Negro Youth Congress, site of Du Bois's historic speech ("Behold the Land") at Columbia, South Carolina, October 20, 1946. Photo by Majestic Studio.

An article by Paul Robeson is included in the Origins section. Robeson was at the height of his career as a singer and actor when he gave his first concert in the South for the SNYC convention in 1942 at Tuskegee, Alabama. Even on the campus of Tuskegee, a Black college, the assembly hall was divided into sections for Blacks and sections for whites. Paul said he would only give the concert if it were not segregated, so that night the hall had an integrated audience. I remember many people from the surrounding farms coming to the campus and saying, "There's no segregation tonight; Mr. Robeson is to sing." He spoke in New Orleans that same year—twenty years before the thrust of the civil rights movement began—and said, "I find that I must come south again and again and yet again. It is only here that I achieve absolute and utter identity with my people." (I have a copy of the speech, entitled "We Must Come South.")

Henry Mayfield's article, "Memoirs of a Birmingham Coal Miner," published in *Freedomways* No. 1, 1964, tells of organizing Birmingham, Alabama, coal miners and steel workers in the 1930s and 1940s. At the union meetings, Blacks would sit on one side, and whites on the other. One summer, the folk singer Pete Seeger came to Birmingham to work with the SNYC and the League of Young Southerners, a white youth group of the Southern Conference for Human Welfare. James Jackson (my future husband) and Seeger attended union meetings of the steelworkers and coal miners to talk about voting rights and Black/white unity, and Pete would play his guitar and sing songs to inspire Black and white workers alike.

Louis Burnham, who had graduated from City College in New York, and his wife, Dorothy Burnham, a graduate of Brooklyn College (both were student activists), came to Birmingham in 1941, and during the years that I was with the SNYC we became very close friends. When I left the SNYC to live and work in Michigan in 1947, Louis Burnham took over as the executive secretary. Later, Burnham moved back to New York and became editor of the monthly newspaper *Freedom*, which Paul Robeson published in the early 1950s.

I think the SNYC would have continued in the South, despite the racism and segregation, if the national terror of McCarthyism had not been unleashed. But even though we had a very broad base—politicians, ministers, teachers, and others in the community—support for the organizations waned. This left a void, which *Freedomways* was all too eager and prepared to fill.

Part 2: Reports from the Front Lines

The following editorial appeared in the special issue "The Southern Movement" (No. 1, 1964):

> Many activists in the Freedom Movement, among them many of our readers, are keenly aware of the need for some instrument of communication and exchange of information between the various sections of the Movement, stretched across the south. *Freedomways'* format combines first-hand description of events, insight and analysis. Undoubtedly our readers will recognize the Names in the News who have contributed articles to this issue. What is really unprecedented is that while the American reading public has read a lot about these personalities and their leadership activities in the Freedom Movement, seldom has the story of these activities been told by the persons themselves. Each is writing about battle-fronts that he knows best: Birmingham, Alabama; Cambridge, Maryland; Savannah, Georgia; Mississippi and points south. . . . much of the subject matter represents a first in magazine coverage of the Negro Freedom Movement.

This editorial typified the approach of *Freedomways*, for often the writers reporting on the Black freedom struggle in the journal were also participating in the marches and the sit-ins. A typical writer of *Freedomways* wasn't someone sitting at a desk, analyzing reports back in New York City. The contributors were the people on the front line of the struggle. Jimmy McDonald, who wrote for the journal in 1961, was a Freedom Rider who was on the bus that was firebombed in Anniston, Alabama. In "Lorraine Hansberry at the Summit," James Baldwin recounted his and Lorraine Hansberry's 1963 meeting with Attorney General Robert Kennedy and her frustration at the government's refusal to act. (We have retained the word "Negro" in the earlier articles, which was the accepted usage of that time.)

The quarterly could be read in the libraries and was very inexpensive to buy, and as a result, many people had access to copies. Hundreds of school and public libraries subscribed to *Freedomways*, forming its base of support. (Friends in library science had given the founding editors lists of libraries to which they sent the first solicitations for subscriptions in 1961.) Libraries in a number of places in the South took bundles of *Freedomways*, and activists in the new

Student Nonviolent Coordinating Committee (SNCC) ordered large numbers of each issue. Julian Bond's name first appeared in *Freedomways* in 1962 in a letter to the Readers Column in which he explained the aims of the new youth group, SNCC. *Freedomways* had close ties with SNCC. (Because of space limitations, many of the articles by SNCC volunteers cannot be included in this anthology.)

The special issue in 1964, "The Southern Movement," provided, in the words of the editorial, "the most comprehensive coverage of the Freedom Movement in the south ever to appear in one issue of an American magazine." In the special 1965 issue, "Mississippi: Opening Up the Closed Society," young SNCC activists wrote about their experiences in the summer of 1964. Eric Morton explained the concept of "Mississippi Summer," and Staughton Lynd, the director of the Freedom Schools, described how that program began. Most of the contributors to the special issue were activists who had been arrested while they were on the picket lines. Not a few of the contributors were writing in jail. Lawrence Guyot and Mike Thelwell, founders of the Mississippi Freedom Democratic Party, published a two-part article in 1966 on the situation in Mississippi.

Part 3: International Solidarity

Part 3 opens with Dr. Du Bois's essay "The American Negro and the Darker World," written in 1957 and reprinted later in *Freedomways*. When we were starting the journal, Du Bois advised, "Make sure that you show the relationship of our struggle to people who are struggling all over the world, that we are not alone. These are our brothers and sisters." So, from the beginning *Freedomways* sought to include articles from people in anticolonial battles in emerging nations. Leaders of Africa and the Caribbean wrote for the magazine: Kwame Nkrumah, Agostinho Neto, and Cheddi Jagan, among many others. The pieces written by liberation fighters kept American readers informed about the liberation struggles in Angola and South Africa that were encouraged by the victories of newly free nations like Ghana and Guinea. *Freedomways* reported on all aspects of Africa and the Caribbean—literature and history as well as politics and analysis.

Many of the early African anticolonial leaders, such as Jomo Kenyatta, Kwame Nkrumah, and Nnamdi Azikiwe, called Du Bois the father of African liberation (as well as of African American struggle). In 1961 in New York, at our first public meeting to introduce *Freedomways*, the keynote speakers were Thomas Kanza, who represented Patrice Lumumba of the Congo at the United Nations, and Dr. Du Bois. President Kwame Nkrumah of Ghana had invited Du Bois to spend his last days in Africa, so after the second issue came out, he and Shirley Graham, his wife, moved to Ghana. Dr. Du Bois continued his interest in the magazine until his death in 1963, and the last articles that he wrote were for *Freedomways*. For some time Shirley Graham Du Bois was the general editor while in Africa, and she wrote many of the early editorials. We continued this close association until her death on March 27, 1977.

In addition to providing readers in the United States with news from abroad, *Freedomways* kept people abroad informed about the civil rights struggles taking place within the United States. Paul and Eslanda Robeson were living in London after Robeson's U.S. passport was restored and he was able to travel again (the U.S. government had denied Paul Robeson a passport from 1950 to 1958), and they immediately began to solicit subscriptions from foreign universities for *Freedomways*. The journal sought many subscribers outside the United States. Very few Black publications had this kind of worldview of the liberation struggle or this influence on the various national movements.

In the 1960s and early 1970s, *Freedomways* extended its solidarity coverage with reports on the antiwar movement as it related to Blacks. *Freedomways* was the first Black publication to take a firm stand against the Vietnam War. In 1965 Robert S. Browne, a former State Department official working for the U.S. foreign aid program, visited his wife's relatives in Vietnam. After Browne came back to the United States, he wrote a very important analysis for *Freedomways* of the doomed American effort in Vietnam. The first article of its kind, it got a tremendous reception.

In spring 1967 *Freedomways* reprinted Martin Luther King's address at Riverside Church, "A Time to Break Silence," in which he spoke out publicly for the first time against the Vietnam War. Because of the prestige King had acquired (he was by this time a Nobel Prize laureate), many people who had not taken a position on Vietnam until then listened and joined the opposition to the war. After that the right wing came down on Dr. King. J. Edgar Hoover was especially vehement in his attacks.

Then Diane Nash Bevel from SNCC toured North and South Vietnam with two other American women. When she returned from the trip, she wrote about it for *Freedomways*. We ran photographs with the article of the destruction in Vietnam alongside those of the firebombed Black churches in the American South. You could see that the same reactionary and racist forces were responsible for both the bombing of the churches and the bombing in Vietnam. (This article is not included due to space limitations.)

Looking back, I wish we had had an article by or about Malcolm X. I was on a radio talk show once with Malcolm, and we had a very pleasant relationship. My only criticism was that he was a fast talker and a fast thinker, and he often dominated the conversation. But he was very friendly toward the magazine then. Later he spent time with Shirley Graham Du Bois in Accra, Ghana. I think they had a warm exchange, and I'm sure his getting to know her and, through her, Dr. Du Bois must have been an influence.

A report on the African National Congress and the liberation struggle in Southern Africa appeared in the 1962 issue of *Freedomways*. To show the breadth of the journal, Part 3 closes with our editor Jean Carey Bond's account of a Black solidarity visit to Northern Ireland in 1982.

Part 4: Moving North

By the late 1960s, the freedom movement was taking on a broader range of issues—organized labor, affirmative action in the workplace and in education, the role of women, justice in the courts, and the death penalty, among others. These questions are still hotly debated today.

Parts 5 and 6:
Black Studies, Art, and Culture

The last two sections of the anthology are devoted to the political aspects of culture and scholarship. Dr. Du Bois's vast range of interests included pioneering investigations into the African American past and the history of Africa. Not surprisingly, some of the earliest research into Black history—which was eventually to be the basis of

Black studies departments in schools and universities—appeared in *Freedomways*, a sampling of which appears in Part 5.

As an active quarterly, *Freedomways* was unique in recognizing the role of art in the freedom struggle. It published literary works by some of the great writers and poets of the day, many of whom have since become quite well known. A special issue on the artist Charles White, which included reproductions of his art, was published in 1980. The artists Elizabeth Catlett, Tom Feelings, Joan Maynard, Cheryl Hanna, Romare Bearden, Jacob Laurence, Brumsic Brandon, Benny Andrews, Elton Fax, and Builder Levy were among the contributors. The works of two Nobel Prize laureates in literature, Derek Walcott and Pablo Neruda, appeared in its pages. Literature from the Caribbean and South America, the United States, and Africa reflected the international character of the magazine. We published some of Audre Lorde's first poetry and Alice Walker's early short story "The Diary of an African Nun." Later, Alice Walker became a *Freedomways* contributing editor and stayed with the journal until it ceased publication. I feel very proud of the number of people who wanted to be a part of the magazine.

Special Issues and Events

We often published issues devoted to a particular topic. Some of the subjects of our special issues were the Southern Freedom Movement; Mississippi: Opening Up the Closed Society; Lorraine Hansberry: Art of Thunder, Vision of Light; Charles White: Art and Soul; Paul Robeson: The Great Forerunner; The People of the Caribbean; W.E.B. Du Bois; Africa; and Southern Africa. John Henrik Clarke was very important in bringing out the special issue entitled "Harlem: A Community in Transition" in 1963, with poems by Langston Hughes and Sterling Brown, among others. The issue dedicated to Paul Robeson was later published as a book by Dodd Mead, titled *Paul Robeson, The Great Forerunner.*

The State Department had returned Paul Robeson's passport, which allowed him to travel again. On April 22, 1965, at the Hotel Americana in Times Square, *Freedomways*, at Robeson's suggestion, sponsored his welcome back to the United States. O'Dell and I met with him and his wife, Eslanda, to plan the event. Participating were Dizzy Gillespie, the actor Morris Carnovsky, jazz pianist Billy Taylor, Ruby

Dee and Ossie Davis, and many others. James Baldwin, whom I knew and admired very much as a brilliant thinker and writer, traveled from France to speak at this event. He became involved in *Freedomways* as a contributing editor shortly after it began. After the welcome-home celebration, some writers, artists, and political activists came up to Paul's room at the hotel, and we sat around talking until the wee hours of the morning. Baldwin sat on the floor, looking up and listening to Paul with much love and admiration. In an introduction to a *Freedomways* reader published in 1977, Baldwin wrote of the impact of *Freedomways* on his life.

Freedomways sponsored the centennial celebration of W.E.B. Du Bois's birth at Carnegie Hall in New York on February 23, 1968. Pablo Neruda and Pablo Casals were among the sponsors of the tribute. Casals and Du Bois were friends, and Du Bois often attended his musical celebrations in Puerto Rico. In its spring 1968 issue, *Freedomways* printed the speech Dr. Martin Luther King Jr. gave on that occasion. In his centennial address "Honoring Dr. Du Bois," King said, "We cannot talk of Dr. Du Bois without recognizing that he was a radical all of his life. Some people would like to ignore the fact that he was a Communist in his later years. . . . It is time to cease muting the fact that Dr. Du Bois was a genius and chose to be a Communist. Our irrational obsessive anti-communism has led us into too many quagmires to be retained as if it were a mode of scientific thinking." This was one of the last major speeches by Dr. King before his assassination.

On the staff and editorial board of *Freedomways* were people of various political views. Many different views were represented in the magazine, including those of communists. Sometimes we printed views we did not agree with, and we published letters from readers who took issue with previous articles. That was healthy—to have different points of view and have people react to them. I regret that because of space limitations some fine contributions have been omitted from this collection.

The last issue of *Freedomways* was published in 1985. In the editorial, we wrote: "In these twenty-five years worth of ink and paper have been wrought a rich legacy that will endure, a model that will instruct, and an example of commitment that will inspire the freedom fighters of tomorrow."

Our hope is that this anthology will also contribute to the future.

Freedomways
Reader

PART ONE

Origins of *Freedomways*

J. H. O'DELL

An editor of Freedomways

Freedomways magazine was born in a time of turmoil and change. Its founders were committed to the single purpose of assisting the mass assault on institutional racism and colonialism. The ideas that it popularized, the analysis that it contributed at various stages, and the voice it provided activists on the front lines were all directed to that end. The two decades preceding the founding of *Freedomways* in 1961 prepared the way for the popular uprising against racist practices to come. Those years of practical experience in activism also bore the seeds of the idea for such a journal.

Through most of the 1940s, especially when President Franklin Roosevelt was still alive, optimism about improvement in "race relations" ran pretty high. The Great Depression was becoming a memory. Millions of servicemen and -women were coming home from the war with plans to finish their education, thanks to the recently passed GI Bill of Rights, and get on with a peaceful life. The Black press kept our national community informed about the new United Nations, and we gathered hope from the fact that Dr. Du Bois was attached to the U.S. delegation meeting in San Francisco to establish the world body.

Duke Ellington captured that spirit of optimism when he introduced a jazz symphony entitled "New World a-Comin" at a concert
in Indianapolis in the summer of 1945. He said he was anticipating
the good things to come—to be enjoyed. Later that summer, Ho Chi
Minh announced that (in accordance with the Atlantic Charter) the
people of Vietnam were declaring their independence from France
after decades of colonial rule. A few weeks later, Indonesia launched
its struggle for independence from Holland.

In the late 1940s, National Association for the Advancement of
Colored People (NAACP) chapters grew rapidly in the South, in
both urban and rural areas. This leap in membership in the South,
combined with the long-established chapters in the rest of the country, clearly indicated that Black Americans looked to the NAACP to
carry forward the civil rights agenda. Black churches and Black fraternal organizations now spearheaded NAACP membership campaigns.

The Congress of Industrial Organizations (CIO) was the other
dynamic force emerging. Black labor was solidly in support of the
new industrial labor movement. Some 5 million workers, mainly
outside the South, had joined this union movement. The wave of
militant industrial strikes that swept the country in 1946 clearly expressed the mood. In a number of northern industrial states, a
coalition forged by the NAACP and CIO campaigned successfully
for the passage of legislation for fair employment practices in the
public sector. These "FEP" campaigns were directed at outlawing
racist hiring practices in state and local governments. They also set
an example of nondiscrimination in employment for the corporate
sector to follow.

The American Veterans Committee (AVC), an antiracist, multira-
cial group of World War II veterans, was formed. The AVC broke
with the Jim Crow traditions of the established veterans' groups like
the American Legion and the Veterans of Foreign Wars.

Two decisions by the U.S. Supreme Court in the 1940s also contributed to the changing mood. One ruling outlawed the Democratic Party's "white primary" elections in the South, thereby opening the electoral process to Black voters. Although it had only limited
effect at first, in the long term it was very significant. The other decision declared that "restrictive covenants" in the sale or rental of
housing were not enforceable in the courts. This opened up some of
the housing market to Blacks in a small way.

However, the harsh winds of the Cold War were rising to a menacing storm following Roosevelt's death. The new president, Harry Truman, and a segregationist administration were moving away from Roosevelt's "New Deal" vision. Step by step they were putting into place an apparatus of government repression and secrecy. The administration was attacking the New Deal and its adherents and creating a climate of fear to discourage any opposition.

President Truman had to give lip service to civil rights for Blacks in order to remain a viable candidate for the Democratic Party in the 1948 election, but his position on civil rights split the party. Segregationist Democrats in five southern states revolted against Truman's civil rights platform and formed the Dixiecrat party, with their own presidential candidate, Strom Thurmond. The 1948 presidential election took place in an atmosphere of lynchings and anticommunism. Truman's administration had promoted the fear of domestic communism. When the Dixiecrats bolted, the segregationists already had the weapon of anticommunism with which to fight any changes in the South. After anticommunism ceased to be effective in curbing the civil rights movement, it was still used against labor organizers.

By contrast, the newly formed Progressive Party's "Henry Wallace for President" campaign unequivocally supported civil rights. The party supported a restoration of the New Deal's vision of peace and a halt to the Cold War and the hysteria it had generated. In the South, a number of prominent Black southerners ran for office on the Progressive Party ticket. The Black community was largely disenfranchised in the South: only about 250,000 Blacks had been able to register to vote in the entire region. Nevertheless, Progressive Party candidates are remembered as pioneers in the effort to elect Black citizens to public office.

Few areas in the rest of the United States were accustomed to a Black man or woman running for elected office. The Progressive Party ran Black candidates in many other parts of the country as well.

The events at Peekskill, a small town in upstate New York, in the summer of 1949 marked the transition to the 1950s. Labor union people and the Civil Rights Congress had invited Paul Robeson to give a concert at their Labor Day picnic. Robeson was very popular among many CIO unions, and several had voted him an "Honorary Member." He was always a staunch supporter of labor's right to organize, a defender of the New Deal, and an uncompromising opponent of racism. Nor did he at all hesitate to express his belief that in the postwar world the United States and the Soviet Union should remain allies, as they had been in the war against fascism. The administration in Washington vilified all persons who held such "subversive" views, especially if they were influential public personalities like Robeson.

A mob attacked the Labor Day picnic in Peekskill, causing the concert to be canceled. Yet plans were made to return and hold the concert at a later date. The following week 25,000 people came to Peekskill to defend their right to peaceful assembly and Paul Robeson's right to sing a concert. The mob also returned to the scene in greater numbers, hurling rocks at the cars driving to the picnic grounds, smashing many car windows, and carrying insulting placards. Governor Thomas Dewey dispatched the New York State Police, but the police served as a shield for the mobs by literally turning their backs on them and instead waving their billy clubs at the concert-goers.

Peeksill was an omen of difficult days ahead. The nation would witness variations of this mob violence on many occasions. We would see it in Alabama, when Autherine Lucy attempted to enroll at the University of Alabama; and in New Orleans, when Black parents attempted to enroll their children in a "white" elementary school. It would occur at Little Rock, when Black students tried to enter Central High School; and again, in Anniston and Birmingham, Alabama, when the "Freedom Riders" attempted to travel interstate on nonsegregated public buses.

Most of the 1950s were as repressive as the 1940s had been hopeful. Senator Joseph McCarthy's demented rantings about communism grabbed the headlines, predictably, and for a while promoted his political ambitions. All of the mechanisms of the Cold War State were now in place. A presidential executive order required all federal employees to sign a loyalty oath. The attorney general's "Subversive List" was made fully operational through the formation of the Subversive Activities Control Board. Many states set up their own local House Un-American Activities Committees patterned after the one in Congress. In parts of the country, "Red Squads" formed within local police departments.

The defenders of segregation in the South moved (with all deliberate speed) to use whatever advantage the political climate offered them. The NAACP was outlawed in Alabama. Two NAACP officials who were leaders of the Right to Vote movement in Florida, Mr. and Mrs. Harry T. Moore, were murdered when their home was bombed on Christmas 1950.

This was the main feature of the political culture that African Americans and progressive whites faced as they labored to build a movement with the power to secure basic civil rights and abolish apartheid/segregation in the states of the Old Confederacy.

Then, along came Montgomery—one of those moments of awesome significance that mark the beginning of a new era. The Montgomery, Alabama, bus boycott demonstrated the power of community action in confronting the abuses of segregation. It was sustained by a joyful spirit of unselfish commitment mobilized around a proposition with universal appeal: "Better to walk in dignity than to ride in humiliation." Three hundred and eighty-five days later, it chalked up a victory for human rights.

The U.S. Supreme Court decision *Brown v. Board of Education* sounded the death knell of segregation. It affirmed the value of having a solid legal strategy, which the NAACP had developed over many years, even though its application was limited to the segregated public school system in the South. The Montgomery bus boycott provided a model for using mass direct action along with the courts to dismantle the segregation system. This style of disciplined, sustained mass mobilization inspired self-confidence in the participants and communicated our deep dissatisfaction with the status quo. It also made the issues being contested—in this case, segregated buses—visible to the larger public.

In 1957 the Southern Christian Leadership Conference (SCLC) was formed with Dr. Martin Luther King Jr. as its president. It adopted the modest goal of duplicating the Montgomery experience across the South. On May 17, the third anniversary of the Supreme Court decision, the SCLC convened a National Prayer Pilgrimage in Washington—a mass mobilization at which Dr. King articulated the theme "Give Us the Ballot." The right to vote for millions of people disfranchised by a variety of methods became a major dimension of the struggle to abolish segregation.

From Virginia to Texas, new local groups proliferated, and a new, dynamic leadership emerged, committed to the nonviolent direct action method of work. For the next decade and a half, the practitioners of mass action propelled the movement forward in an uncompromising assault upon institutional racism.

1

Behold the Land, No. 1, 1964

W.E.B. DU BOIS

Dr. Du Bois delivered this address at the closing session of the Southern Youth Legislature of the Southern Negro Youth Congress, in Columbia, South Carolina, October 20, 1946. That year, Dr. Du Bois foresaw that the South would be "the battleground of a great crusade." When Freedomways *published the speech in 1964, the editors stated: "Written almost twenty years ago, the text, for all its brevity, or possibly because of it, bears all the marks of a classic statement on the South. In slightly more than two thousand words, Dr. Du Bois, with the incomparably brilliant insight which characterizes all his works, illuminates the basic nature of the social, political and economic life of the South."*

The future of American Negroes is in the South. Here three hundred and twenty-seven years ago, they began to enter what is now the United States of America; here they have made their greatest contribution to American culture; and here they have suffered the damnation of slavery, the frustration of reconstruction and the lynching of emancipation. I trust then that an organization like yours is going to regard the South as the battle-ground of a great crusade. Here is the magnificent climate; here is the fruitful earth under the beauty of the southern sun; and here, if anywhere on earth, is the need of the thinker, the worker and the dreamer. This is the firing line not simply for the emancipation of the American Negro but for the emancipation of the African Negro and the Negroes of the West Indies; for the emancipation of the colored races; and for the emancipation of the white slaves of modern capitalist monopoly.

Remember here, too, that you do not stand alone. It may seem like a failing fight when the newspapers ignore you; when every effort is made by white people in the South to count you out of citizenship and to act as though you did not exist as human beings while all the time they are profiting by your labor, gleaning wealth from your sacrifices and trying to build a nation and a civilization upon your degradation. You must remember that despite all this, you have allies and allies even in the white South. First and greatest of these possible allies are the white working classes about you, the poor whites whom you have been taught to despise and who in turn have learned to fear and hate you. This must not deter you from efforts to make them understand, because in the past in their ignorance and suffering they have been led foolishly to look upon you as the cause of most of their distress. You must remember that this attitude is hereditary from slavery and that it has been deliberately cultivated ever since emancipation.

Slowly but surely the working people of the South, white and Black, must come to remember that their emancipation depends upon their mutual cooperation; upon their acquaintanceship with each other; upon their friendship; upon their social intermingling. Unless this happens each is going to be made the football to break the heads and hearts of the other.

White Youth Is Frustrated

White youth in the South is peculiarly frustrated. There is not a single great ideal which they can express or aspire to, that does not bring them into flat contradiction with the Negro problem. The more they try to escape it, the more they land into hypocrisy, lying and double-dealing; the more they become, what they least wish to become, the oppressors and despisers of human beings. Some of them, in larger and larger numbers, are bound to turn toward the truth and to recognize you as brothers and sisters, as fellow travelers toward the dawn.

There has always been in the South that intellectual elite who saw the Negro problem clearly. They have always lacked and some still lack the courage to stand up for what they know is right. Nevertheless they can be depended on in the long run to follow their own clear thinking and their own decent choice. Finally even the politicians must eventually recognize the trend in the world, in this country, and in the South. James Byrnes, that favorite son of this commonwealth, and Secretary of State of the United States, is today occupying an indefensible and impossible position; and if he survives in the memory of men, he must begin to help establish in his own South Carolina something of that democracy which he has been recently so loudly preaching to Russia. He is the end of a long series of men whose eternal damnation is the fact that they looked *truth* in the face and did not see it; John C. Calhoun, Wade Hampton, Ben Tillman are men whose names must ever be besmirched by the fact that they fought against freedom and democracy in a land which was founded upon democracy and freedom.

Eventually this class of men must yield to the writing in the stars. That great hypocrite, Jan Smuts, who today is talking of humanity and standing beside Byrnes for a United Nations, is at the same time oppressing the Black people of Africa to an extent which makes their two countries, South Africa and the American South, the most reactionary peoples on earth, peoples whose exploitation of the poor and helpless reaches the last degree of shame. They must in the long run yield to the forward march of civilization or die.

What Does the Fight Mean?

If now you young people, instead of running away from the battle here in Carolina, Georgia, Alabama, Louisiana and Mississippi, instead of seeking freedom and opportunity in Chicago and New York—which do spell opportunity—nevertheless grit your teeth and make up your minds to fight it out right here if it takes every day of your lives and the lives of your children's children; if you do this, you must in meetings like this ask yourselves what does the fight mean? How can it be carried on? What are the best tools, arms, and methods? And where does it lead?

I should be the last to insist that the uplift of mankind never calls for force and death. There are times, as both you and I know, when

> Tho' love repine and reason chafe,
> There came a voice without reply,
> 'Tis man's perdition to be safe
> When for truth he ought to die.

At the same time and even more clearly in a day like this, after the millions of mass murders that have been done in the world since 1914, we ought to be the last to believe that force is ever the final word. We cannot escape the clear fact that what is going to win in this world is reason if this ever becomes a reasonable world. The careful reasoning of the human mind backed by the facts of science is the one salvation of man. The world, if it resumes its march toward civilization, cannot ignore reason. This has been the tragedy of the South in the past; it is still its awful and unforgivable sin that it has set its face against reason and against the fact. It tried to build slavery upon freedom; it tried to build tyranny upon democracy; it tried to build mob violence on law and law on lynching, and in all that despicable endeavor, the state of South Carolina has led the South for a century. It began not the Civil War—not the War between the States—but the War to Preserve Slavery; it began mob violence and lynching and today it stands in the front rank of those defying the Supreme Court on disfranchisement.

Nevertheless reason can and will prevail; but of course it can only prevail with publicity—pitiless, blatant publicity. You have got to make the people of the United States and of the world know what is going on in the South. You have got to use every field of publicity to force the truth into their ears, and before their eyes. You have got to make it impossible for any human being to live in the South and not realize the barbarities that prevail here. You may be condemned for flamboyant methods; for calling a congress like this; for waving your grievances under the noses and in the faces of men. That makes no difference; it is your duty to do it. It is your duty to do more of this sort of thing than you have done in the past. As a result of this you are going to be called upon for sacrifice. It is no easy thing for a young Black man or a young Black woman to live in the South today and to plan to continue to live here; to marry and raise children; to establish a home. They are in the midst of legal caste and customary insults; they are in continuous danger of mob violence; they are mistreated by the officers of the law and they have no hearing before the courts and the churches and public opinion commensurate with the attention which they ought to receive. But that sacrifice is only the beginning of battle; you must re-build this South.

There are enormous opportunities here for a new nation, a new economy, a new culture in a South really new and not a mere renewal of an old South of slavery, monopoly and race hate. There is a chance for a new cooperative agriculture on renewed land owned by the state with capital furnished by the state, mechanized and coordinated with city life. There is chance for strong, virile trade unions without race discrimination, with high wage, closed shop and decent conditions of work, to beat back and hold in check the swarm of landlords, monopolists and profiteers who are today sucking the blood out of this land. There is chance for cooperative industry, built on the cheap power of T.V.A. [Tennessee Valley Authority] and its future extensions. There is opportunity to organize and mechanize domestic service with decent hours, and high wage and dignified training.

"Behold the Land"

There is a vast field for consumers' cooperation, building business on public service and not on private profit as the main-spring of industry. There is chance for a broad, sunny, healthy home life, shorn of the fear of mobs and liquor, and rescued from lying, stealing politicians, who build their deviltry on race prejudice.

Here in this South is the gateway to the colored millions of the West Indies, Central and South America. Here is the straight path to Africa, the Indies, China and the South Seas. Here is the path to the greater, freer, truer world. It would be shame and cowardice to surrender this glorious land and its opportunities for civilization and humanity to the thugs and lynchers, the mobs and profiteers, the monopolists and gamblers who today choke its soul and steal its resources. The oil and sulfur; the coal and iron; the cotton and corn; the lumber and cattle belong to you the workers, Black and white, and not to the thieves who hold them and use them to enslave you. They can be rescued and restored to the people if you have the guts to strive for the real right to vote, the right to real education, the right of happiness and health and the total abolition of the father of these scourges of mankind, *poverty*.

"Behold the beautiful land which the Lord thy God hath given thee." Behold the land, the rich and resourceful land, from which for a hundred years its best elements have been running away, its youth and hope, Black and white, scurrying North because they are afraid of each other, and dare not face a future of equal, independent, upstanding human beings, in a real and not a sham democracy.

To rescue this land, in this way, calls for the *Great Sacrifice;* this is the thing that you are called upon to do because it is the right thing to do. Because you are embarked upon a great and holy crusade, the emancipation of mankind, Black and white; the upbuilding of democracy; the breaking down, particularly here in the South, of forces of evil represented by race prejudice in South Carolina; by lynching in Georgia; by disfranchisement in Mississippi; by ignorance in Louisiana and by all these and monopoly of wealth in the whole South.

There could be no more splendid vocation beckoning to the youth of the twentieth century, after the flat failures of white civilization, after the flamboyant establishment of an industrial system which creates poverty and the children of poverty which are ignorance and disease and crime; after the crazy boasting of a white culture that finally ended in wars which ruined civilization in the whole world; in the midst of allied peoples who have yelled about democracy and never practiced it either in the British Empire or in the American Commonwealth or in South Carolina.

Here is the chance for young women and young men of devotion to lift again the banner of humanity and to walk toward a civilization which will be free and intelligent; which will be healthy and unafraid; and build in the world a culture led by Black folk and joined by peoples of all colors and all races—without poverty, ignorance and disease!

2

The Battleground Is Here, No. 1, 1971

PAUL ROBESON

The following is an address by Paul Robeson to the Annual Convention of the National Negro Labor Council, November 21, 1952, in Cleveland, Ohio.

I have been in many labor battles. It has seemed strange to some that, having attained some status and acclaim as an artist I should devote so much time and energy to the problems and struggles of working men and women.

To me, of course, it is not strange at all. I have simply tried never to forget the soil from which I spring.

Never to forget the rich but abused earth on the eastern coast of North Carolina where my father—not my grandfather—was a slave; and where today many of my cousins and relatives still live in poverty and second-class citizenship.

Never to forget the days of my youth—struggling to get through school, working in brick yards, in hotels, on docks and riverboats, battling prejudice and proscription—inspired and guided forward by the simple yet grand dignity of a father who was a real minister to the needs of his poor congregation in small New Jersey churches, and an example of human goodness.

No, I can never forget 300-odd years of slavery and half-freedom; the long, weary and bitter years of degradation visited upon our mothers and sisters, the humiliation and Jim Crowing of a whole people. I will never forget that the ultimate freedom—and the immediate progress of my people rest on the sturdy backs and the unquenchable spirits of the coal miners, carpenters, railroad workers, clerks, domestic workers, bricklayers, sharecroppers, steel and auto workers, cooks, stewards and longshoremen, tenant farmers and tobacco stemmers—the vast mass of Negro Americans from whom all talent and achievement rise in the first place.

If it were not for the stirrings and the militant struggles among these millions, a number of our so-called spokesmen with fancy jobs and appointments would never be where they are. And I happen to know that some of them will soon be looking around for something else to do. There's a change taking place in the country, you know. My advice to some of this "top brass" leadership of ours would be: *You'd better get back with the Folks—if it's not already too late.* I'm glad I never left them!

Yes, the faces and the tactics of the leaders may change every four years, or two, or one, but the people go on forever. The people—beaten down today, yet rising tomorrow; losing the road one minute but finding it the next; their eyes always fixed on a star of true brotherhood, equality and dignity—*the people* are the real guardians of our hopes and dreams.

That's why the mission of the Negro Labor Councils is an indispensable one. You have set yourself the task of organizing the will-to-freedom of the mass of our people—the workers in factory and farm—and hurling it against the walls of oppression. In this great program you deserve—and I know you will fight to win the support and cooperation of all other sections of Negro life.

I was reading a book the other day in which the author used a phrase which has stuck in my memory. He said, "We are living in the rapids of history" and you and I know how right he is. You and I know that for millions all over this globe it's not going to be as long as it has been.

Yes, we are living "in the rapids of history" and a lot of folks are afraid of being dashed on the rocks. But not us!

No, not us—and not 200 million Africans who have let the world know that they are about to take back their native land and make it the world's garden spot, which it can be.

In Kenya Old John Bull has sent in his troops and tanks, and has said Mau Mau has got to go. But Jomo Kenyatta, the leader of Kenya African Union, with whom I sat many times in London, has answered back. He says, "Yes, someone has got to go, but in Kenya it sure won't be 6 million black Kenyans. I think you know who'll be leaving—and soon."

And, in South Africa there'll be some changes made too. FREEDOM is a hard won thing. And, any time seven thousand Africans and Indians fill the jails of that unhappy land for sitting in "White Only" waiting rooms, for tearing down jim crow signs like those which are seen everywhere in our South, you know those folks are ready for FREEDOM. They are willing to pay the price.

The struggle in Africa has a special meaning to the National Negro Labor Council and to every worker in this land, white as well as Negro. Today, it was announced that the new Secretary of Defense will be Charles E. Wilson, President of the General Motors Corporation. General Motors simply happens to be one of the biggest investors in South Africa, along with Standard Oil, Socony Vacuum, Kennecott Copper, the Ford Motor Company, and other giant corporations.

You see, they are not satisfied with wringing the sweat and sometimes the blood out of ore miners in Alabama and Utah, auto workers in Detroit and Atlanta, oil workers in Texas and New Jersey. They want super duper profits at ten cents an hour wages, which they can get away with only if the British Empire, in one case, or the Malan Fascists, in another, can keep their iron heels on the black backs of our African brothers and sisters.

Now, I said more than three years ago that it would be unthinkable to me that Negro youth from the United States should go thousands of miles away to fight against their friends and on behalf of their enemies. You remember that a great howl was raised in the land. And I remember, only the other day, in the heat of the election campaign, that a group of Negro political figures pledged *in advance* that our people would be prepared to fight any war any time that the rulers of this nation should decide.

Well, I ask you again, should Negro youth take a gun in hand and join with British soldiers in shooting down the brave peoples of Kenya?

I talked just the other day with Professor Z. K. Mathews, of South Africa, a leader of the African National Congress, who is now in this country as visiting professor at Union Theological Seminary in New York.

Professor Mathews' son is one of those arrested in Capetown for his defiance of unjust laws. I ask you now, shall I send my son to South Africa to shoot down Professor Mathews' son on behalf of Charles E. Wilson's General Motors Corporation?

I say again, the proper battlefield for our youth and for all fighters for a decent life, is here; in Alabama, Mississippi, and Georgia; is here, in Cleveland, Chicago, and San Francisco; is in every city and at every whistle stop in this land where the walls of Jim Crow still stand and need somebody to tear them down.

3

Southern Youth's Proud Heritage, No. 1, 1964

AUGUSTA STRONG

Augusta Strong, a Freedomways *editor, had been a member of the Southern Negro Youth Congress. This is an excerpt from a longer article.*

. . . One summer in 1931, a frail tubercular youth was stopped on a Birmingham street by a cruising police car; an accusing finger within pointed him out as the man who had shot three white women, killing two. The sole mark of identification was the hat he was wearing. Guilt was a matter of course.

Only testimony by doctors that he was in the hospital ward bed at the time of the crime saved him from the death penalty. But before this point was reached, seventy Negro men and women had lost their lives, victims of white mob violence in the ensuing hysteria. As for the youth, his sentence was commuted to life imprisonment by his southern judges.

A few miles away in Paint Rock, Alabama, nine boys from fourteen to twenty-two were seized by police on a freight car they were riding, hoping to find work in another state. Two young white women were found on the same train several cars away. Inevitably, the police charged rape. Guilt again was a matter of course, and nine boys faced the electric chair, the beginning of the celebrated Scottsboro case which was to profoundly affect every Negro community in the north.

The Scottsboro case, symbol of continuing violence against Negroes, the rising power of reaction, the tremendous numbers of unemployed, discrimination in government and in labor unions roused communities of Negroes to action.

In the winter of 1935, the major Negro organizations came together in a national conference to consider united action to better their people. With the participation of major organizations and leaders in many areas of life, the National Negro Congress was formed in Chicago.

Numbers of militant youth came to the meeting. They felt at once that the acute problems of their people in the north were indissoluble from those of the south. . . .

All were agreed that a successful southern Negro youth movement would be a powerful force in winning equality and opportunity for all young Negroes and for raising their standards of life in general. The group voted enthusiastic approval of the suggestion to "go south" and selected some of their number to initiate a gathering of Negro young people in the unchartered regions of the south.

Over 500 delegates came to Richmond, Virginia, in February 1937 for the unprecedented assembly of southern youth. . . . The most spectacular achievement of the Congress during its first year was the organization of 5,000 tobacco workers of the city of Richmond into their first labor union [led by James Jackson]. These were among the most exploited workers in the city. The workers were grossly underpaid and worked under conditions of unbelievable filth for long hours . . . and pennies in pay. As a result of the efforts of the Youth Congress workers, the workers were able to almost double their yearly wages.

Volunteer organizers, none over 22 years old, helped organize other locals of the union, later, in Durham, Raleigh, and Winston-Salem. Classes to teach the workers reading and writing and elementary civics, to encourage an interest in voting were formed. At the same time, in some areas, efforts were made to form unions among women domestic workers. . . .

The Right-to-Vote Movement

In 1940, following a conference in New Orleans, a large-scale assault upon the poll tax was determined upon. A national campaign was considered to make Americans conscious of the 19 million southerners, 4 million of them Negroes, who were denied the vote in the south by the poll tax, white primaries and numerous voting restrictions. A National Anti-Poll Tax Week was initiated to rally support for an anti-poll tax bill blocked in the House Judiciary committee, and to lobby for a discharge petition to bring it to the floor. . . .

With most of the young men at war, the reins [of the organization] had been taken over by a young woman, Esther Cooper Jackson, whose native state was Virginia. Educated at Oberlin, and with a master's degree in sociology which she studied under Charles S. Johnson at Fisk, she came as a volunteer worker to the Southern Negro Youth Congress—and remained to become one of its leaders. High-principled, serious, fearless, she brought new fervor and imagination to the struggle for freedom.

During this period, the organizational secretary was Louis E. Burnham, who in his early twenties was already a tried and experienced youth leader. A talented writer and speaker, witty, popular, he was gifted with deep understanding of people. At New York's City College he had organized the Frederick Douglass Society, the first forum at the college for the serious consideration of racial concerns. He was a leader in the movement of northern white and student youth, and he had become widely known in the Harlem community when he ran for public office on a pro-labor platform. He left his middle-class home and the enticements of a career to join the youth movement in the south. . . .

The war years were spent in efforts to further the integration of Negro servicemen, in support of community soldier welfare programs, in efforts to secure Negro representation on civilian boards concerned with the war effort, and in continuing campaigns for equality in the armed services. War was still not won when the young people came together for their sixth southwide assembly in Atlanta. Dominating the conference discussions was the greeting President Franklin D. Roosevelt sent to the conference:

> I know that on the road to victory, hard at first and bloody still, the Negro youth of the south met, with other American young people, this challenge with a courage which has dignified their generation . . .

In the factories, on the farms, and in all fields of war activity, thousands of other Negro young people have given freely of their skill, their strength, their courage, their loyalty . . .

Their fight has been democracy's fight, and democracy's victory must be their victory—to cherish and extend as the men and women of tomorrow. . . . I send my best wishes to them and their cause.

. . . Outside of the major outlines of broad policy set by the south-wide conferences, the youth councils were independent bodies, each adopting and setting its program—a necessary thing where so many areas of the south varied in economic, cultural, educational, resources, and in quality and militancy of leadership.

The leadership of the national office gave special help in the formation of rural youth councils; self-help projects of quilting and basketry, products sold outside the area helped these groups establish educational and recreational programs for the youth in their areas, and to raise money for civil rights activities. Groups such as these carried on many campaigns incidental to their work, as when, for example, they secured the freedom of Nora Wilson, a 16-year-old Alabama country girl, sentenced to years at hard labor for the alleged theft of six ears of corn from a field. Rural councils aided the formation of sharecroppers' and farmers' unions—and often embraced whole families, parents as well as young people.

The Fairfield, Alabama, youth council opened a youth center and set up a library; the Birmingham council waged a successful campaign for the first swimming pool in the city for the use of Negroes; the Tuskegee council presented Paul Robeson for the first time in the deep south, in a non-segregated concert.

More than 115 councils, each representing a different city, town or rural area were active in such places as Irmo, South Carolina; Natchitoches, Louisiana; Hattiesburg, Mississippi . . . even a group in La Boca, Panama, requested to be chartered by the organization. All youth councils elected an educational director. . . .

The Columbia Conference

The Congress called a "Southern Youth Legislature" to meet in Columbia, South Carolina, in October 1946, to reassess the position of Negro youth in the south, and to plan further strategy for the vote . . .

Almost a thousand young people responded. Besides the voting issue, they asked the enactment of an FEPC law, adequate and equal housing, and an end to "white supremacy customs and practices" in all forms.

This was the most significant of the conferences, the most spectacular, the one which showed most clearly the role of the movement. National attention was focused on the gathering, and national figures joined to participate—among them Dr. W.E.B. Du Bois and Paul Robeson. Officials in Washington had sent government experts in agriculture, law, education, and health, as speakers and observers at the conference. . . .

The movement which had lived twelve glorious years came to an end with the emergence of McCarthyism which scattered the northern supporters and progressive and trade union allies of the young people and gave new strength to the native southern reactionaries like "Bull" Connor. Naked terror broke up the Congress. That was in 1949. But what the movement began, the seed it planted did not fall on barren ground. What has happened since, in the last several years especially, is ample testimony. For example, "Bull" Connor is gone from office and the Negro Freedom Movement is waxing ever stronger.

Moreover, as the young people who had initiated the movement had grown older, added responsibilities came their way. The new recruits to carry on could not adequately confront a situation where the allies were frightened away, were no longer at hand. Further, the problems the movement had tackled originally, as youth, had burgeoned into problems for the entire south. The anti-poll tax campaign, for instance, had become a national question; equality in education was heading to the point where it was to become the nation's number one issue, and similarly the other planks of the movement: jobs and equal opportunity in all phases of American life. For a dozen years the youth had carried the baton in this fateful race, they had influenced the perspective of a generation of southerners. Now they handed the baton on to the Negro people as a whole.

4

Memoirs of a Birmingham Coal Miner, No. 1, 1964

HENRY O. MAYFIELD

For more than twenty years, Henry Mayfield was a leading trade unionist in Alabama and a participant in civil rights struggles throughout the southern states. He completed this piece shortly before his death on December 31, 1963, when he was chairman of the board of Freedomways *Associates.*

In the basic industries in the south we had to work under the worst conditions and got the lowest wages.

Take the coal miners who worked for the Tennessee Coal and Iron Company (U.S. Steel). The conditions in the mines were very bad. Back in the early thirties we were loading coal by the ton. The company had handpicked men and gave them the contract which we had to work for the contractors. From week to week, or day to day, you never knew how much money you were going to make. Many days we stayed in the mines nine and ten hours and made only four or five dollars, sometimes less or nothing, because when you loaded a car you had no way of knowing how many tons of coal were in the car. You had to take the word of the company and the contractor. Many of the miners lived in the company's houses and had to trade at the company's stores because they seldom had any cash to trade at other stores. Clothes for the family were out of the question. The iron ore miners had to work under the same conditions as the coal miners.

The working conditions in steel and foundry were just as bad. But there was a difference in pay from the point of knowing how much you made at the end of the week. In steel and foundry the average hourly pay for Negro workers was about fifty cents an hour and you had to work from "can see to can't see . . . " (as long as the boss wanted you to work). If you asked the boss for pay for overtime, he would say that if you didn't like your pay, there were others willing to take it, or if you were a very good worker and the boss liked you, he would give you a few hours overtime and tell you not to tell the other workers.

I worked seven years in the biggest foundry in Birmingham, the Stockham Pipe and Fitting Company. Many of us worked twelve to fourteen hours daily. One of my fellow workers drove a mule hauling fresh sand into the foundry and cleaned up scrap metal. After the mule worked nine hours the worker had to take the mule to the stable and get a wheel barrow and finish the work. I remember one afternoon about 4:30 P.M. the foundry superintendent told the mule driver, "You can work all the overtime you want to but I don't want the mule working one damn minute overtime." The mule driver, Nash, said, "OK, Mr. Lynn." Nash pushed a wheelbarrow until about 9:30 that night. We don't have space in this article to deal with all the industry in the south but I am sure you get the point.

In 1932 the United Mine Workers of America (headed by John L. Lewis), and the Mine, Mill and Smelter Workers Union, started an organizing drive to organize coal and ore miners. When they started the organizing drive the bloody battle was on. We had to get a small group of workers together, sometimes meeting in the woods. The companies organized armed thugs to track us down and they would shoot to kill. The ore miners had shooting battles with the company thugs and men were shot on both sides.

Stickin' with the Union

The workers rallied to the union around the following demands: eight-hour day and five-day week, higher pay for tonnage or day labor, to do away with the contractors, two paydays a month (instead of one pay monthly), upgrading of Negroes as motormen, machine operators and crew leaders, union members to watch the weight of the company scale for those workers loading coal or ore by the ton and, last but not least, *recognition of the union*.

The company countered with a "company union" which appealed in the main to the white workers. The company told the white workers that the United Mine Workers of America and the Mine, Mill and Smelter Workers stood for *social* equality. They said that the Negro would come to your homes, eat, marry into your family and they blamed the Communists for trying to organize such unions.

We called the company union a "popsicle union" because when they started the organizing, they told the Birmingham families they would be served popsicles and watermelon. The company's popsicle and watermelon unions could not stop our organizing drive so the AFL took over the company union. We kept on fighting for the recognition of the U.A.W. and the Mine, Mill unions. Many Negro workers were fired because they were leaders in the union. After the company saw we were going to win, they wanted to make a deal with some of the Negro leadership. I worked in the largest coal mine of U.S. Steel in Birmingham. I took up grievances which cost the company thousands of dollars. The superintendent called me into the office and told me if I dropped the grievances, he would see that I made all the money I wanted. I told them I will starve with the other men until this condition is corrected. We won our demands.

(The organizing struggles of the Negro ore and coal miners laid the basis for the organizing of steel, foundry, packinghouse, laundry, textile, auto, dock workers, and construction workers.)

The 1941 Strike

We had to strike to win our demands before we won the Labor Board elections in 1941. Now I want to make the record very clear about the role of the Negro workers in organizing the basic industries in Birmingham. *The Negro workers were the main leaders in organizing unions in U.S. Steel, Republic Steel, and Sloss Iron Company.* The Negroes were the first to join the unions in the above mentioned industries. We elected all the local officers and grievance committeemen.

Sometimes we did not know how to vote on a motion or make a motion. Some of the men serving on grievance committees could not read or write; but they knew what to talk about when they met with the boss, and they were "tough" and would never back down. During contract time the Negro workers took the lead in working out the contracts. The few white workers in the locals were afraid to attend meetings or serve on committees.

The white workers only came forward after they found out that the Negroes were going to win without them because the Negro workers, at that time, were in the majority. The Negro workers trained the white workers in the struggle. Only because of the struggle and leadership of the Negro workers in the south was the union able to organize big industry.

The Negro women played a leading role in the organizing drive in the south. We organized women's auxiliaries in the coal and ore mines. When we were on strike the women would organize into groups and take baskets and go into stores asking for food for needy families and when they asked a storekeeper for help he knew not to say "No." We had some trouble in getting a few workers to join the unions. The women would send a committee to talk with the worker's wife or the worker and they would always win their point.

The youth, both boys and girls, played a leading role in organizing labor unions in the south. The young boys would be on the picket lines while the girls went out asking for food for the families. I think it is time for us to write some history about the role of the Negro in organized labor in the south.

There are many Negroes responsible for the labor movement in the south. Among them, Asbury Howard of the ore miners in Bessemer, Alabama, John Henry Hall of packinghouse, Willie Johnson in coal, Hosea Hudson in steel and foundry, Mrs. C. Foreman, and my mother, among the women—and many others. The white workers who fought alongside the Negro workers, during the first period of organizing, can be counted on one hand. After we got over the danger period, the white workers came in to take over the leadership.

The top district leadership told the Negro workers that to encourage the white workers to join the union, we must elect a white president and a white chairman of the grievance committee. The Negro workers didn't like it but they went along with the district in order to get the white workers into the union.

As soon as the white workers became active in the union, they started a campaign to kick out the most militant Negroes in the leadership who put up a real fight against racial discrimination in the factories.

Some white workers knew our position was correct but they were afraid to support us. We organized voter registration classes in our locals. Many whites would not vote for the local to support the classes. We sent thousands to register but the board of registrars would pass only a few. How do we stand today? Some small gains have been made but only because the Negro fought for them.

Income tables show the individual income of Negroes in the south is only about two-fifths that of comparable whites. The small gains we have made are in great danger of being wiped out because of job discrimination, automation and failure of the labor movement to fight for Negroes and for full employment. The backward white worker in the labor movement thinks it is OK for him to get better jobs and higher pay than his Negro brother. But what he doesn't know is that the basic policy of big business is to use one worker against the other; white against Negro. This is the way big business makes millions of dollars by keeping us fighting against each other. This the top leaders in the labor movement know as well as I do; but they are not going to fight for our rights without pressure from us.

The International Longshoremen's Association meeting in Miami, Florida, last July, incorporated some fine pledges into the resolutions about civil rights but the old forces in power retained control and defeated a Negro for the executive vice-presidency. George Meany, president of the AFL-CIO, refused to support the August 28th Civil Rights March on Washington. The International Union of Electrical Workers (Local 731) of Memphis, Tennessee, donated five hundred dollars to the White Citizens Council for legal aid in Greenwood, Mississippi, in the defense of Byron De La Beckwith, the accused murderer of Medgar Evers, leader of the NAACP in that state. Mr. Meany also said he would head a special Committee of Five to direct the AFL-CIO drive for biracial committees throughout the country to break down discrimination in all fields. Mr. A. Philip Randolph (one of the five vice presidents of the AFL-CIO) and the president of the Negro American Labor Council, has been fighting for years for the same program that Meany announced above. We must demand that the labor movement fight for the program adopted at the August 28th Washington March.

5

"Not New Ground, but Rights Once Dearly Won," No. 1, 1962

LOUIS E. BURNHAM

The following essay was first published in the National Guardian, *February 15, 1960.*

One hundred years would seem time enough and more for so rich and strong a nation as ours to redeem the promise of freedom made to an unoffending people it once held as slaves. That the promise was sealed in torrents of blood in the most bitter of wars could not but help, in ordinary circumstances, to guarantee its fulfillment. Yet the Negro today, while not a slave, is far from free, and none dares say how long, O Lord, how long before he shall cross the bar to equal and undifferentiated citizenship.

In Birmingham he may not rest for the night at the Thomas Jefferson Hotel or even the modest white hostelry. He may view the zoo animals in Memphis on Thursday, but no other day. In one city he may collect white men's garbage but not patrol their streets. In another he may be a policemen (provided he arrest only his "kind") but not a fireman (no matter whose house is burning). In some places he may deliver the mail but not sort it, while in others he may dig and pave the sidewalks but not build a house where a union card is required.

In great areas of the South his vote is restricted or entirely denied. Whenever he leaves one city for another, North or South, he does so with some trepidation, knowing that in some areas he may journey for hundreds of miles without assurance of even the meanest of accommodations and with the practical certainty of insult or assault should he request them.

Yet, when in his anguish and his anger he cries out, "Enough!" the rulers of the nation answer: "Time! Give us more time to right our fathers' wrongs. Do not doubt we have will: only give us time to find the way." President Eisenhower speaks, whenever he talks of Negroes at all, of the slow and tedious work to be done in changing men's hearts. Not that he has ever opened his mouth to challenge the racist to take his heel off the Negro's neck. What seems important to him is that we should never forget how difficult it is to persuade white men to accept Negroes as their equals.

A score of Senators echo this contention and assorted social soothsayers justify their complacency by reference to progress already made. Negroes were once 90 percent illiterate, they point out; now more than 90 percent of them read and write. Only a generation ago they were bunched on Southern peonage farms in abject poverty and misery; now two-thirds of all Negroes are city dwellers, the majority of them are industrial workers and 1,500,000 of them are in the unions.

Some few have become capitalists in insurance, banking, publishing and service industries and the Government is attaching the estate of one of their late cult leaders with a $6,000,000 tax lien. They are developing a consequential middle class; a few of their scholars even teach white youth, and the Negro intellectual today is a far cry from the unsophisticated ex-slaves who thronged academies and "colleges" during Reconstruction to study "a little Latin and a little less Greek."

Progress, we are cautioned, has been slow but sure and it will surely continue. Patience is needed, not agitation; rather than carping criticism, faith that democracy as it unfolds will spread its largess to the Negro, too.

There is a seeming plausibility in this reasoning and perhaps a majority of Americans accept it as a kind of gospel. Even some Negroes, themselves relatively comfortable, are disinclined to rock the boat or embarrass the nation in the eyes of a watching world.

But the argument is false and its consequences can be calamitous to the cause of Negro freedom. It is false on three counts.

First, much of what Negroes fight for today is not to gain new ground but to restore positions once dearly won and foully taken away. Four Negroes sit in Congress to speak for Northern constituencies, but not one from any of the Southern states which sent 22 Negroes to the House and Senate during Reconstruction and the Populist bid for power. For a brief time in our history more Negroes sat in the South Carolina legislature than now sit in all the legislatures of the 50 states. In 1896 the Negro vote in North Carolina was 120,000; today, though the Negro population of the state has trebled and women have won the franchise, Negro registration there stands at 150,000.

Is this progress? No, it is confirmation of a central lesson of Negro history: that the advance toward equality has not been a straight path, but a dreary zig-zag road; that the nation has undertaken to insure justice to the Negro only in fits and starts, but not with sustained enthusiasm for the project; that it has time and again let the slightest pretext turn it aside from the work at hand.

The lesson is there to learn, Du Bois and Carter G. Woodson, the founder of Negro History Week, made it plain in their writings many years ago. Younger historians—Herbert Aptheker, John Hope Franklin, and C. Vann Woodward—have underscored it in more recent works.

Are we then, in the thick of a second Reconstruction, as Georgia's Sen. Herman Talmadge recently complained in a protest against civil rights laws? Or have the forces of reaction already turned the tide toward restoration of their power to treat the Negro as their will or whim dictates? It may not be possible to tell, but this much is certain: the pace of progress has been slowed; the expectations of easy victory which sanguine men entertained on the heels of the 1954 Supreme Court decision have given way to a more sober estimate of the magnitude of the battle and the strength of the enemy; and Thurgood Marshall's year-end statement that all that remains in the legal fight against segregation is a "mopping up" process and "a little fast play around second base" was even more false than trite.

Tuskegee Institute in its annual survey on race relations in the South, came closer to the truth: "Race relations did not change appreciably in 1959. Despite the urgency of America's aspirations to promote peace . . . there was—on balance—little compelling evidence that America itself was able . . . to advance human understanding significantly within its own boundaries."

Nine Negro children entered Little Rock's Central High School in 1957. Today there are only five in former all-white schools. For two thousand others, segregation with all its deprivations is as much a fact of life as if the Supreme Court had never ruled against it. In Virginia, North Carolina, Tennessee, Florida and Texas massive resistance has given way to token integration, a tactic of resistance through "compliance."

Far from having assurance of victory in the fight for Negro rights, on every front the biggest battles lie ahead. But aside from this, the argument of those who would have the Negro "go slow" in light of former progress is false because it sees progress in absolute, but not in relative terms. To be sure, Negroes have moved from Southern farms to Northern cities, but whites have moved to exclusive suburbs in droves, leaving Negroes rotting slums. And a new set of problems—Northern Jim Crow, rising crime rates, persistent social disorganization, official neglect and abuse—have risen to take the place of the older, more typically Southern outrages.

The Negro can count his progress only as he closes the gap that separates him from his fellow citizens in opportunity and accomplishment. In good times and bad, unemployment among Negro workers remains twice as high as among whites. A recent government study revealed that of the 32,200,000 poorest family units of the nation, 6,400,000, or one-fifth, were Negro, though Negroes are but one tenth of the population. And these 6,400,000 families constituted more than a third of all Negro families in the nation.

The complaint is not that the Negro has stood still these past 100 years, but that he has not been able to close the gap. To do this he must move faster than others, not merely apace with them; he must have legal and social protections which others take for granted. This is the essence of the fight for "Negro" or "civil" rights. One way to accomplish this might be for the Government to indemnify its Negro citizens for the two-and-a-half centuries of slave labor exacted from their forebears' sweat and blood. The cost, while considerable, would be less than the price of a modern war and the rewards would be infinitely more worthwhile.

The third fallacy rises from a misunderstanding of the nature of the human quest for equality. One man cannot be more or less equal than another. One concession to a righteous demand merely provokes another demand, for the thirst for freedom grows on what it feeds on. The nation's task must be, then, not to discourage the Negro's demand for rights, but to grant them now and fully, even though doing so requires that the nation painfully revise its political and social structure. The change can only be for the better.

And the Negro's task must be to demand and fight for his rights no matter what the consequences. This becomes increasingly difficult to do in a prosperous time when the nation is conditioned by social "conflicts" in which nobody gets hurt. Even so staunch a fighter for equality as a veteran NAACP attorney of Atlanta recently told an Emancipation meeting that while Negroes "cannot compromise or retreat from their insistence upon equality under law" they are willing to work with others to determine the best means of equality "without any real detriment to any segment of our citizenry."

The attorney means well but is wrong. Negroes must never be content with only such rights as will not inconvenience anybody else. Their freedom is going to hurt somebody; otherwise their continued oppression would be inexplicable. What is encouraging about the prospect is that those who stand to suffer by the Negro's gain, though powerful, are but a numerically miniscule part of the whole American nation.

They take profit from the differential in the Negro's wages—profits measured in billions of dollars. Out of his disfranchisement they enjoy political preferment. On the basis of his social degradation they build a mannered aristocracy, pleasant to themselves but repugnant to the democratic vitality of the nation. They will be hurt by the Negro's forward surge, and the Negro must aim to hurt them. He must say to them, as Sojourner Truth once said, "You have got to give us house room or the roof will tumble in!"

But what of the white worker at the lathe and on the farm, the teacher, the doctor, the housewife; the cook in the restaurant, the seaman, the miner in the pit—the vast majority of Americans? Their prejudices? Yes. Their false sense of superiority? Yes. But, oh, how much to gain; nothing less than a nation to gain.

The Negro must say to them: Come, brother, let us hold hands and walk together; let us build together, on the foundation of my freedom, a new nation dedicated to the proposition affirmed at Gettysburg and waiting these many years for us to make it real.

That can be the Negro's greatest gift to this nation.

6

Honoring Dr. Du Bois, No. 2, 1968

MARTIN LUTHER KING JR.

Dr. King delivered the Centennial Address at Carnegie Hall in New York City on February 23, 1968, the one hundredth anniversary of Dr. W.E.B. Du Bois's birth. The International Cultural Evening sponsored by Freedomways *magazine launched an international year of celebration honoring the life and work of Dr. Du Bois. This was one of the last major speeches Dr. King gave before his assassination.*

Tonight we assemble here to pay tribute to one of the most remarkable men of our time.

Dr. Du Bois was not only an intellectual giant exploring the frontiers of knowledge, he was in the first place a teacher. He would have wanted his life to teach us something about our tasks of emancipation.

One idea he insistently taught was that Black people have been kept in oppression and deprivation by a poisonous fog of lies that depicted them as inferior, born deficient and deservedly doomed to servitude to the grave. So assiduously has this poison been injected into the mind of America that its disease has infected not only whites but many Negroes. So long as the lie was believed the brutality and criminality of conduct toward the Negro was easy for the conscience to bear. The twisted logic ran—if the Black man was inferior he was not oppressed—his place in society was appropriate to his meager talent and intellect.

Dr. Du Bois recognized that the keystone in the arch of oppression was the myth of inferiority and he dedicated his brilliant talents to demolish it.

There could scarcely be a more suitable person for such a monumental task. First of all he was himself unsurpassed as an intellect and he was a Negro. But beyond this he was passionately proud to be Black and finally he had not only genius and pride but he had the indomitable fighting spirit of the valiant.

To pursue his mission, Dr. Du Bois gave up the substantial privileges a highly educated Negro enjoyed living in the north. Though he held degrees from Harvard and the University of Berlin, though he had more academic credentials than most Americans, Black or white, he moved south where a majority of Negroes then lived. He deliberately chose to share their daily abuse and humiliation. He could have offered himself to the white rulers and exacted substantial tribute for selling his genius. There were few like him, Negro or white. He could have amassed riches and honors and lived in material splendor and applause from the powerful and important men of his time. Instead, he lived part of his creative life in the south—most of it in modest means and some of it in poverty and he died in exile, praised sparingly and in many circles ignored.

But he was an exile only to the land of his birth. He died at home in Africa among his cherished ancestors and he was ignored by a pathetically ignorant America but not by history.

History cannot ignore W.E.B. Du Bois. Because history has to reflect truth and Dr. Du Bois was a tireless explorer and a gifted discoverer of social truths. His singular greatness lay in his quest for truth about his own people. There were very few scholars who concerned themselves with honest study of the Black man and he sought to fill this immense void. The degree to which he succeeded discloses the great dimensions of the man.

Yet he had more than a void to fill. He had to deal with the army of white propagandists—the myth-makers of Negro history. Dr. Du Bois took them all on in battle. It would be impossible to sketch the whole range of his intellectual contributions. Back in the nineteenth century he laid out a program of 100 years of study of problems affecting American Negroes and worked tirelessly to implement it.

Long before sociology was a science he was pioneering in the field of social study of Negro life and completed works on health, education, employment, urban conditions and religion. This was at a time when scientific inquiry of Negro life was so unbelievably neglected that only a single university in the entire nation had such a program and it was funded with $5,000 for a year's work.

Against such odds Dr. Du Bois produced two enduring classics before the twentieth century. His *Suppression of the African Slave Trade* written in 1896 is Volume I in the Harvard Classics. His study *The Philadelphia Negro*, completed in 1899, is still used today. Illustrating the painstaking quality of his scientific method, to do this work Dr. Du Bois personally visited and interviewed 5,000 people.

He soon realized that studies would never adequately be pursued nor changes realized without the mass involvement of Negroes. The scholar then became an organizer and with others founded the NAACP. At the same time he became aware that the expansion of imperialism was a threat to the emergence of Africa.

He recognized the importance of the bonds between American Negroes and the land of their ancestors and he extended his activities to African affairs. After World War I he called Pan-African Congresses in 1919, 1921 and 1923, alarming imperialists in all countries and disconcerting Negro moderates in America who were afraid of this restless, militant, Black genius.

Returning to the United States from abroad he found his pioneering agitation for Negro studies was bearing fruit and a beginning was made to broaden Negro higher education. He threw himself into the task of raising the intellectual level of this work. Much later in 1940 he participated in the establishment of the first Negro scholarly publication, *Phylon*. At the same time he stimulated Negro colleges to collaborate through annual conferences to increase their effectiveness and elevate the quality of their academic studies.

But these activities, enough to be the life work for ten men, were far from the sum of his achievements. In the six years between 1935 and 1941 he produced the monumental seven hundred-page volume on *Black Reconstruction in America*, and at the same time writing many articles and essays. *Black Reconstruction* was six years in writing but was thirty-three years in preparation. On its publication, one critic said: "It crowns the long, unselfish and brilliant career of Dr.

Du Bois. It is comparable in clarity, originality and importance to the Beards' *Rise of American Civilization.*" The *New York Times* said, "It is beyond question the most painstaking and thorough study ever made of the Negroes' part in Reconstruction," and the New York *Herald Tribune* proclaimed it "a solid history of the period, an economic treatise, a philosophical discussion, a poem, a work of art all rolled into one."

To understand why his study of the Reconstruction was a monumental achievement it is necessary to see it in context. White historians had for a century crudely distorted the Negro's role in the Reconstruction years. It was a conscious and deliberate manipulation of history and the stakes were high. The Reconstruction was a period in which Black men had a small measure of freedom of action. If, as white historians tell it, Negroes wallowed in corruption, opportunism, displayed spectacular stupidity, were wanton, evil and ignorant, their case was made. They would have proved that freedom was dangerous in the hands of inferior beings. One generation after another of Americans were assiduously taught these falsehoods and the collective mind of America became poisoned with racism and stunted with myths.

Dr. Du Bois confronted this powerful structure of historical distortion and dismantled it. He virtually, before anyone else and more than anyone else, demolished the lies about Negroes in their most important and creative period of history. The truths he revealed are not yet the property of all Americans but they have been recorded and arm us for our contemporary battles.

In *Black Reconstruction* Dr. Du Bois dealt with the almost universally accepted concept that civilization virtually collapsed in the South during Reconstruction because Negroes had a measure of political power. Dr. Du Bois marshaled irrefutable evidence that far from collapsing, the southern economy was recovering in these years. Within five years the cotton crop had been restored and in the succeeding five years had exceeded pre-war levels. At the same time other economic activity had ascended so rapidly the rebirth of the south was almost completed.

Beyond this he restored to light the most luminous achievement of the Reconstruction—it brought free public education into existence not only for the benefit of the Negro but it opened school doors to the poor whites. He documented the substantial body of legislation that was socially so useful it was retained into the twentieth century even though the Negroes who helped to write it were brutally disenfranchised and driven from political life. He revealed that far from being the tragic era white historians described, it was the only period in which democracy existed in the south. This stunning fact was the reason the history books had to lie because to tell the truth would have acknowledged the Negroes' capacity to govern and fitness to build a finer nation in a creative relationship with poor whites.

With the completion of his book *Black Reconstruction,* despite its towering contributions, despite his advanced age, Dr. Du Bois was still not ready to accept a deserved rest in peaceful retirement. His dedication to freedom drove him on as relentlessly in his seventies as it did in his twenties. He had already encompassed three careers. Beginning as a pioneer sociologist he had become an activist to further mass organization. The activist had then transformed himself into an historian. By the middle of the twentieth century when imperialism and war arose once more to imperil humanity he became a peace leader. He served as chairman of the Peace Information Bureau and like the Rev. William Sloane Coffin and Dr. Benjamin Spock of today he found himself indicted by the government and harried by reactionaries. Undaunted by obstacles and repression, with his characteristic fortitude he fought on. Finally in 1961 with Ghana's independence established, an opportunity opened to begin the writing of an African Encyclopedia and in his 93rd year he emigrated to Ghana to begin new intellectual labors. In 1963 death finally came to this most remarkable man.

It is axiomatic that he will be remembered for his scholarly contributions and organizational attainments. These monuments are imperishable. But there were human qualities less immediately visible that are no less imperishable.

Dr. Du Bois was a man possessed of priceless dedication to his people. The vast accumulations of achievement and public recognition were not for him pathways to personal affluence and a diffusion of identity. Whatever else he was, with his multitude of careers and professional titles, he was first and always a Black man. He used his richness of talent as a trust for his people. He saw that Negroes were robbed of so many things decisive to their existence that the theft of their history seemed only a small part of their losses. But Dr. Du Bois knew that to lose one's history is to lose one's self understanding and with it the roots for pride. This drove him to become a historian of

Negro life and the combination of his unique zeal and intellect rescued for all of us a heritage whose loss would have profoundly impoverished us.

Dr. Du Bois *the man* needs to be remembered today when despair is all too prevalent. In the years he lived and fought there was far more justification for frustration and hopelessness and yet his faith in his people never wavered. His love and faith in Negroes permeate every sentence of his writings and every act of his life. Without these deeply rooted emotions his work would have been arid and abstract. With them his deeds were a passionate storm that swept the filth of falsehood from the pages of established history.

He symbolized in his being his pride in the Black man. He did not apologize for being Black and because of it, handicapped. Instead he attacked the oppressor for the crime of stunting Black men. He confronted the establishment as a model of militant manhood and integrity. He defied them and though they heaped venom and scorn on him his powerful voice was never stilled.

And yet, with all his pride and spirit he did not make a mystique out of blackness. He was proud of his people, not because their color endowed them with some vague greatness but because their concrete achievements in struggle had advanced humanity and he saw and loved progressive humanity in all its hues, black, white, yellow, red and brown.

Above all he did not content himself with hurling invectives for emotional release and then to retire into smug passive satisfaction. History had taught him it is not enough for people to be angry—the supreme task is to organize and unite people so that their anger becomes a transforming force. It was never possible to know where the scholar Du Bois ended and the organizer Du Bois began. The two qualities in him were a single unified force.

This life style of Dr. Du Bois is the most important quality this generation of Negroes needs to emulate. The educated Negro who is not really part of us and the angry militant who fails to organize us have nothing in common with Dr. Du Bois. He exemplified Black power in achievement and he organized Black power in action. It was no abstract slogan to him.

We cannot talk of Dr. Du Bois without recognizing that he was a radical all of his life. Some people would like to ignore the fact that he was a Communist in his later years. It is worth noting that Abraham Lincoln warmly welcomed the support of Karl Marx during the Civil War and corresponded with him freely. In contemporary life the English speaking world has no difficulty with the fact that Sean O'-Casey was a literary giant of the twentieth century and a Communist or that Pablo Neruda is generally considered the greatest living poet though he also served in the Chilean Senate as a Communist. It is time to cease muting the fact that Dr. Du Bois was a genius and chose to be a Communist. Our irrational obsessive anti-communism has led us into too many quagmires to be retained as if it were a mode of scientific thinking.

In closing it would be well to remind white America of its debt to Dr. Du Bois. When they corrupted Negro history they distorted American history because Negroes are too big a part of the building of this nation to be written out of it without destroying scientific history. White America, drenched with lies about Negroes, has lived too long in a fog of ignorance. Dr. Du Bois gave them a gift of truth for which they should eternally be indebted to him.

Negroes have heavy tasks today. We were partially liberated and then re-enslaved. We have to fight again on old battlefields but our confidence is greater, our vision is clearer and our ultimate victory surer because of the contributions a militant, passionate Black giant left behind him.

Dr. Du Bois has left us but he has not died. The spirit of freedom is not buried in the grave of the valiant. He will be with us when we go to Washington in April to demand our right to life, liberty and the pursuit of happiness.

We have to go to Washington because they have declared an armistice in the war on poverty while squandering billions to expand a senseless, cruel, unjust war in Vietnam. We will go there, we will demand to be heard, and we will stay until the administration responds. If this means forcible repression of our movement, we will confront it, for we have done this before. If this means scorn or ridicule, we will embrace it for that is what America's poor now receive. If it means jail we accept it willingly, for the millions of poor already are imprisoned by exploitation and discrimination.

Dr. Du Bois would be in the front ranks of the peace movement today. He would readily see the parallel between American support of the corrupt and despised Thieu-Ky regime and northern support to the southern slavemasters in 1876. The CIA scarcely exaggerates,

Dr. Martin Luther King Jr. with DuBois Williams, granddaughter
of W.E.B. Du Bois, at the celebration of the 100th birthday of W.E.B.
Du Bois, Feb. 23, 1968, at which Martin Luther King delivered this
historic tribute.

indeed it is surprisingly honest, when it calculates for Congress that
the war in Vietnam can persist for 100 years. People deprived of
their freedom do not give up—Negroes have been fighting more
than a hundred years and even if the date of full emancipation is un-
certain, what is explicitly certain is that the struggle for it will endure.

In conclusion let me say that Dr. Du Bois' greatest virtue was his
committed empathy with all the oppressed and his divine dissatisfaction with all forms of injustice. Today we are still challenged to be
dissatisfied. Let us be dissatisfied until every man can have food and
material necessities for his body, culture and education for his mind,
freedom and human dignity for his spirit. Let us be dissatisfied until
rat-infested, vermin-filled slums will be a thing of a dark past and
every family will have a decent sanitary house in which to live. Let us
be dissatisfied until the empty stomachs of Mississippi are filled and
the idle industries of Appalachia are revitalized. Let us be dissatisfied
until brotherhood is no longer a meaningless word at the end of a
prayer but the first order of business on every legislative agenda. Let

us be dissatisfied until our brother of the Third World—Asia, Africa and Latin America—will no longer be the victim of imperialist exploitation, but will be lifted from the long night of poverty, illiteracy and disease. Let us be dissatisfied until this pending cosmic elegy will be transformed into a creative psalm of peace and "justice will roll down like waters from a mighty stream."

7

Ode to Paul Robeson, No. 1, 1976

PABLO NERUDA

Pablo Neruda was awarded the coveted Nobel Prize for literature in 1971. The Chilean poet was universally acknowledged as the greatest poet of the century writing in Spanish. His death followed shortly after the bloody coup in Chile against the democratically elected government of Salvador Allende.

Once he did not exist.
But his voice was there, waiting.

Light parted from darkness,
day from night,
earth from the primal waters.

And the voice of Paul Robeson
was divided from the silence.

The darkness struggled to hold on.
Underneath roots were growing.
Blind plants fought to know the light.

The sun trembled.
The water was a dumb mouth.
Slowly the animals changed their shapes,
slowly adapting themselves to the wind
and to the rain.

Ever
since then
you have been the voice of man,
the song of the germinating earth,
the river and the movement of nature.

The cataract unleashed its endless thunder
upon your heart,
as if a river fell
upon a rock,
and the rock sang
with the voice of all the silent
until all things, all people
lifted their blood to the light
in your voice,
and earth and sky, fire and darkness and water
rose up with your song.

But later
the earth was darkened again.
Fear, war,
pain
put out the green flame,
the fire of the rose.

And over the cities
a terrible dust fell,
the ashes of the slaughtered.
They went into the ovens
with numbers on their brows,
hairless,
men, women,
old, young,
gathered
in Poland, the Ukraine, Amsterdam, Prague.

Again
the cities grieved
and silence was great,
hard
as a tombstone
upon a living heart,
as a dead hand
on a child's voice.

Then
Paul Robeson,
you sang.

Again
over the earth was heard
the potent voice
of the water
over the fire;
the solemn, unhurried, raw, pure
voice of the earth
reminding us that we were still men,
that we shared the sorrow and the hope.
Your voice
set us apart from the crime.
Once more the light
parted
from the darkness.

Then
silence fell on Hiroshima.
Total silence.
Nothing
was left:
not one mistaken bird
to sing on an empty window,
not one mother with a wailing child,
not a single echo of a factory,
not a cry from a dying violin.
Nothing.
The silence of death fell from the sky.

And again,
father,
brother,
voice of man
in his resurrection,
in hope
resounding
from the depths,
Paul,
you sang.

Again
your river of a heart
was deeper,
was wider
than the silence.
It would be small praise
if I crowned you king
only of the Negro voice,
great only among your race,
among your beautiful flock
of music and ivory,
as though you only sang for the dark children
shackled by cruel masters.

No,
Paul Robeson,
you sang with Lincoln,
covering the sky with your holy voice,
not only for Negroes,
for the poor Negroes,
but for the poor,
whites,
Indians,
for all peoples.

You,
Paul Robeson,
were not silent
when Pedro or Juan

was put out into the street,
with his furniture,
in the rain.
Or when the fanatics of the millennium
sacrificed with fire
the double heart
of their fiery victims,
as when
in Chile
wheat grows on volcanic land.
You never stopped singing.
Man fell and you raised him up.
Sometimes
You were a subterranean river,
something
that bore
the merest glimmer of light
in the darkness,
the last sword
of dying honour,
the last wounded fork of lightning,
the inextinguishable thunder.

You,
Paul Robeson,
defend man's bread,
honor,
fight,
hope.
Light of man,
child of the sun,
our sun,
sun of the American suburb
and of the red snows
of the Andes:
you guard our light.

Sing,
comrade,
sing

brother of the earth,
sing,
good father of fire,
sing for us all,
for those who live by fishing,
by hammering nails with battered hammers,
spinning cruel threads of silk,
pounding paper pulp,
printing.
Sing for all those sleepless in prisons,
awake at midnight,
barely
human
beings,
trapped
between two tortures,
and for those who wrestle with the copper
twelve thousand feet up
in the barren solitude of the Andes.

Sing,
my friend,
never stop singing.
You broke the silence of the rivers
when they were dumb
because of the blood they carried.
Your voice speaks through them.
Sing:
your voice unites
many men who never knew each other.
Now,
far away
in the Urals,
and in the lost Patagonian snow,
you,
singing,
pass over darkness,
distance,
sea,
waste land;

and the young stoker,
and the wandering hunter,
and the cowboy alone with his guitar
all listen.

And in his forgotten prison in Venezuela,
Jesús Faría,
the noble, the luminous,
heard the calm thunder
of your song.

Because you sing,
they know that the sea exists
and that the sea sings.

They know that the sea is free, wide and full of flowers
as your voice, my brother.

The sun is ours. The earth will be ours.
Tower of the sea, you will go on singing.

PART TWO

Reports from the Front Lines: Segregation in the South

J. H. O'DELL

From its beginning, *Freedomways* sought to provide the civil rights movement with a journal for the exchange of ideas and strategies forged in the actions of the day, in the tradition of Frederick Douglass, Ida B. Wells, and W.E.B. Du Bois.

The sixth decade of the twentieth century saw the growing use of "sit-ins" to integrate downtown lunch counters and other public facilities in the South. Largely organized by students attending traditionally Black colleges, the movement spread like wildfire. In the North, supporting actions mushroomed—for example, picket lines in front of Woolworths and other department stores that operated Jim Crow facilities in the South. Within a few months, dozens of southern cities had begun desegregating some public facilities. And the Student Nonviolent Coordinating Committee had been founded at Shaw University in Raleigh, North Carolina [in April 1960].

Running parallel to this activism was a routine presidential primary election campaign dominated by a lot of Cold War rhetoric about "missile gaps" and being "soft on communism." The civil rights denied to Black Americans was not a priority issue for the candidates. In the summer of 1960, with people still energized by the sit-ins, the movement held round-the-clock peaceful demonstrations at both the Republican and Democratic Party conventions. A picket line surrounded the convention meeting sites in Chicago and Los Angeles so that whoever received the nomination of each party would also get our message—"Freedom Now."

At that time the prevailing outlook in America was gradualism, which held that Black people would "gradually" be accorded the rights and privileges everyone else already had. America was now approaching the one-hundreth anniversary of the Emancipation Proclamation. In light of this, our growing movement decided that "gradualism" wasn't working for us. That was somebody else's agenda. We wanted Freedom Now. Every day it was denied was an unacceptable delay. Nevertheless, a steady stream of unsolicited advice admonished us not to "go too fast."

Freedom Now became the movement's new anthem. It was the slogan emblazoned on the signs and banners carried to the March on Washington and celebrated in the jazz suite "Freedom Now" composed by Max Roach. Its spirit was embodied in the Albany, Georgia, Movement; the Tallahassee Civic Association in Florida; the Petersburg Improvement Association in Virginia; and a dozen other local organizations that created a groundswell of antiracist resistance. The national organizations, the SNCC, the Congress of Racial Equality (CORE), and the SCLC, supported these local groups.

Getting rid of segregation once and for all was not the only motivation for this movement. People were also impatient with the condition of acute poverty that was the daily life of the African American. The 1960 census reported that the median income of Black families nationally was 57 percent of the median income of white families. Across the South, the median income of Blacks was less than 50 percent of whites, and in both South Carolina and Mississippi it was less than a third. A national unemployment rate among Blacks that consistently was twice the national average, whether in times of recession or of relative prosperity, aggravated the harsh economic reality. "The March on Washington for Jobs & Freedom" visibly expressed these concerns. The size of the mobilization on that hot August day in 1963 was unprecedented; the upbeat, confident joyous spirit was pervasive. People from every part of the country were there, many of them activists from across the color line, calling for Freedom Now!

More than a thousand youths participated in the SNCC's Mississippi Summer project in 1964, many coming from as far away as Minnesota, California, and even Europe. That summer they strengthened the base of the antiracist movement in Mississippi by training local residents in a range of community organizing skills. Through this project, a large contingent of young white activists acquired firsthand knowledge of the appalling conditions that an often-terrorized Black population lived under, sixty years into the twentieth century.

Congress passed the Voting Rights Act and President Lyndon B. Johnson signed it, with Dr. Martin Luther King standing behind him, looking on. But already a new movement was in the streets—the movement to end the Vietnam War.

8

The United States and the Negro, No. 1, 1961

W.E.B. DU BOIS

This article appeared in the inaugural issue of Freedomways.

In 1861 the legal status of the American Negro was something like thus: The Chief Justice of the Supreme Court, in an *obiter dictum*, had just said that, historically, the Negro had "no rights which a white man was bound to respect." Neither a horse, nor Frederick Douglass, could get an American passport for travel. Mules and men were sold at auction in Southern cities; and, while Bob Toomb's threat to auction slaves on Bunker Hill was unpopular, the act would not have been illegal. White Americans shuddered at miscegenation, yet in 1801 there were two million colored women who had no right to refuse sexual intercourse with their white owners. That these masters exercised this right was shown by 588,000 mulattos in 1860. Kidnapping of free Negroes in the North had been made easy by the Fugitive Slave Law. All agreed that the Constitution recognized slavery as a legal institution and that the government was bound to protect it. Abolitionists were considered as contemptible for consorting with impossible radicals and recognizing Negroes as equals. Lincoln had been elected President because the South and Border split on the slave trade: Lincoln was looked upon, not as the enemy of slavery, but as opposed to its expansion. He did not want slavery to come into competition with the free Northern white workers, and the workers hated Negroes as much as slavery. Lincoln did not believe that the Negro could be integrated into the nation. He would protect slavery in the South, but he would not encourage its expansion into the North. Lincoln undoubtedly did not like slavery, but he was no champion of freedom for Negroes.

In the nation as a whole, no considerable number of citizens objected to slavery or would fight for Negro freedom. When the war opened, everybody, North and South, declared it to be a "white man's war," that is, fought by whites for objects which whites had. The wishes of Negroes were not to be taken into account. Slavery was to be protected. Northern generals went out of their way to return fugitive slaves to their masters with apologies; and, on the other hand, when General Fremont tried to free slaves in his area, he was promptly slapped down.

On the other hand, there were certain difficulties that arose. What about the slave who served his master as a servant or laborer, and helped him drive back the Northern armies? And, especially, what about the slave who ran away and took refuge in the Northern armies? The single slave might be returned; but then the slaves poured by the thousands into the Northern armies. Butler was right in considering them "contraband of war," that is, property owned by the enemy which the Union Army should at least sequester, if not use themselves.

The enthusiasm of the North for the war was not to be counted on. After all, what was the North fighting for? Certainly not to free Negroes, also, not to subdue the South. The Northern laborer, especially the foreign-born; the civil servant; farmer and small merchant, had no taste for going South for murder and destruction. The well-to-do bought their way out of the draft, which did not endear them to the laborers nor increase their general popularity. As the draft began to pinch the poor, they turned on the Negroes, who were not drafted, and who were willing to take the jobs of those whites who were. They hanged Negroes to lampposts in New York, and mobbed them in Cincinnati, and declared that they were not going to fight for "niggers."

This was a serious matter, especially, as many of the Negroes were willing to fight for themselves. Their leaders were begging to bear arms, but the government was adamant: no Negro soldiers. Moreover, Lincoln laughed. "If we put arms into their hands," he said, "next day they would be in the hands of our enemies." Then, again, things happened whether we would or no. Down in South Carolina, for instance, we had driven a wedge into the Southern armies. We needed soldiers to guard our gains, but the War Department had no soldiers to spare. The draft was failing. So General Hunter put guns in the hands of freed slaves, drilled them in their use, and told them to shoot intruders. Congress boiled with rage. But Hunter answered: "What else could I do?" "I am not arming slaves, but, since there are no white troops, I have put guns in the hands of free Blacks to guard what we have gained." Congress burst into laughter, and the first colored regiment was sworn into the army. That was but a beginning. Systematically, wherever the Northern armies appeared, the slaves stopped work and joined them. The generals pretended to be greatly annoyed. Here were thousands of mouths to feed, space had to be provided, and sickness cared for. They usually forgot to mention that cooking, cleaning, hard labor, and menial service were being furnished free, and in abundance, without search or wage, to armies invading a strange and hostile land. More than this, every inch of the land, every tree and river, every person and town, was known intimately to this writhing mass of people who did this work willingly, because they thought it was their own salvation. What would Alexander and Caesar have said; what would Frederick the Great and Napoleon have done, if God had sent them a gift like this?

The Federal government, for the most part, laughed, jeered and complained. They told funny stories about the "darkeys" as they ate their biscuit and sent them on as spies. Then, too, the South was having difficulties. There was no "solid South." The South was a small group of rich and near rich slave owners and landowners. The majority of poor whites had nothing, neither land or employment, and were now asked to fight for slavery, when they hated the slaves, who got the work and food that belonged to them. Also, they hated the masters who got everything; and they began to desert from the Southern armies. Then, too, the plight of the elegant slave owner before the world was not happy. England, after fostering the slave trade for a century, found it wise and more profitable to free the seized African and stop the African slave trade to America. France had carried on a revolution for freedom, equality and brotherhood, but did not propose to include among her brothers the Black slaves of Haiti. So the slaves killed the French and ran them off the island. Now, Britain and France needed the cotton raised in the southern United States. The South tried to appease them. It promised not to revive the slave trade, at least, not at once. But Frederick Douglass, talking in England and Ireland, told the factory workers how the Black slaves were suffering, and the British workers refused to recognize the slave South.

On the other hand, the northern United States, refusing still to fight for abolition, nevertheless, began to use Negroes as troops and workers and spies, and explained that they were working for the "Union," and by Union they meant control of slavery's cotton crop and its sale to France and Britain at the highest possible price. Otherwise, the South, itself, would sell the crop abroad, and the Northern factories would close. Here a curious contradiction was seen as the war went on. The Northern armies cut the South in two, but they did it only by using the teeming Negro slaves of the Mississippi Valley. They marched from Atlanta to the sea, but only with the help of the Black throngs of Georgia who cleared the path and stole the food for them. The grateful Northern armies, when they reached the sea, gave the Negroes land, but the Federal government, when it later gained full control, took this land away and gave it back to its former slave-holding owners. The Negroes sang in the sea-swept darkness, "Nobody knows the trouble I've seen." General Howard wept.

The war reeled on. Black men were used as shock troops and slaughtered by the thousands to make way for victorious white feet. In the end, 300,000 Negroes were used as servants, stevedores and spies. There were 200,000 armed Negro troops, and in the background, peering from the sidelines, were three million more Negroes, ready to fight for freedom. No wonder freedom came.

The Southern leaders were frightened. If Black soldiers continued to be drafted and fought as they had fought at Fort Wagner, Port Hudson and Petersburg, then the North with its supplies, and ships, and the hesitation of Europe, would beat the South to its knees. The South tried every expedient, even seeking to enlist the slaves on their side; and, failing, surrendered.

Meantime, the North had had a vision, not the whole North, but the North of thinkers, dreamers, abolitionists and free Negroes.

Uncle Tom's Cabin had done its work. "John Brown's Body" was a-moldering in the grave, and the eyes of poets had seen the "Coming of the Lord." At last, then, there was a reason for this senseless war, and that was the freeing of the slaves. Lincoln came to a decision. He would try to make the border states agree to a gradual emancipation; and he would challenge the recalcitrant South with immediate freedom of the labor which was supporting it.

It was a wise brave word which Karl Marx and his First International Workingmans Association sent Lincoln in 1864:

"When an oligarchy of 300,000 slaveholders dared to inscribe for the first time in the annals of the world 'Slavery' on the banner of armed revolt, when on the very spots where hardly a century ago the idea of one great Democratic Republic had first sprung up, whence the first declaration of the rights of man was issued, and the first impulse given to the European Revolution of the eighteenth century, when on those very spots counter-revolution, with systematic thoroughness, gloried in rescinding 'the ideas entertained at the time of the formation of the old Constitution' and maintained 'slavery to be a beneficial institution,' indeed, the only solution of the great problem of the 'relation of capital to labor,' and cynically proclaimed property in man 'the cornerstone of the new edifice'—then the working classes of Europe understood at once, even before the fanatic partisanship of the upper classes, for the Confederate gentry had given its dismal warnings, that the slaveholders' rebellion was to sound the tocsin for a general holy war of property against labor, and that for the men of labor, with their hopes for the future, even their past conquests were at stake in that tremendous conflict on the other side of the Atlantic . . . They consider it an earnest sign of the epoch to come that it fell to the lot of Abraham Lincoln, the single-minded son of the working class, to lead his country through the matchless struggles for the rescue of the enchained race and the reconstruction of a social world."

The Emancipation Proclamation of 1863 sounded like more than it was. Negroes were not "henceforward and forever free." But Emancipation certainly began. The abolitionists gave up. Since the Negro was free what more was there to be done? The *Liberator* stopped publication. Lincoln saw a way out. He proposed a further step toward complete emancipation by enfranchising the élite of the Negro mass; the rich, the educated, the soldiers; small in number, but encouraging in prospect. The South bluntly refused.

Then, after Lincoln's death, came a poor white from Tennessee, who, after being cajoled by the former masters, agreed to hurry them back in the saddle with full control over their former slaves. A series of Black Codes were adopted which made the nation gasp. Stevens and Sumner came forth with plans which made sense, but they could not command a majority in Congress. Stevens said: give the Negro a Freedman's Bureau, give each slave 40 acres and a mule, and give them special legal protection. Sumner said and reiterated: give them the vote, nothing else is democracy; the Negro must have the vote.

Meantime, the mass of Northerners were neither in favor of freedom for Negroes nor votes for freedmen, and least of all, for any distribution of capital among them. What the conventional North saw, and the farmers and the factory builders, was the South walking back into Congress, threatening to lower the tariff, to attack the monopoly of gold, and to bring down prices. On top of this, they saw the spawn of war, thieves and grafters, like Tweed, start on a rampage of public theft. Industry and reform got together, and the conquered slave aristocracy got their ear. They made many of them believe that the theft and graft which was sweeping the North, was also rampant in the South because of the emancipated slaves. This was untrue, and everybody who really studied the situation knew it was untrue. Schurz and Trowbridge and others who looked at the South saw the truth. It was the educated free Negro of the North, working hand and glove with the freed Negro leader of the South, who, together, tried desperately to rescue the South from the accumulated disasters of war. The Negroes wanted free popular education. It was their talisman, their star of hope. Probably never in the world have so many oppressed people tried in every possible way to educate themselves.

The best conscience of the North rose to help them. The 8th Crusade of School Marms sent an endless column of teachers into the South. The white South reviled them, and spit upon them. When it could it drove them out and killed them. But they, the Negro politicians and the Negro masses, established the first system of free, popular education which the South ever saw, and they welcomed to the door of the school room, white and Black, men, women, and children, rich and poor. Beyond that, they took over the social uplift which the South had left to the slave plantations and the whim of the slave barons. They established a system of hospitals which still exists. They built decent jails, poorhouses. They began to build orphanages and insane asylums. But the landholders refused to pay the increased taxation and felt justified in stealing and cheating governments carried on by the help of their former slaves. To these were added "carpet-baggers" who were lured South by the high price of cotton and cheap labor. The thieves and grafters came, and the white South pretended to see no difference between the uplifter and robber; but they quickly made friends with the railroad manipulators and "financiers" and the white carpet-baggers, shook hands with the Negro leaders; and, in the end, when land had been stolen and debts piled up for railroads, Negroes were blamed for the financial disaster that fell on the nation in 1873; and freedmen suffered for all the disaster that followed in the South.

The few Negro leaders did, for the most part, a splendid job. Even the slave South praised men like Cardoza of South Carolina, Dunn of Louisiana, Lynch of Mississippi and Gibbs of Florida. These men led reform in South Carolina. They led reform in Louisiana. They fought graft it Florida and Alabama. But, instead of getting the sympathy and cooperation of the Northern leaders of reform, they got obloquy and contempt or concerted oblivion; while Northern industry and religion and the Southern aristocracy blamed every misfortune which came from the attempt to abolish slavery in the United States upon the slaves who were freed.

It was a contemptible transaction. Because, after all, it was the Negro, and the Negro alone, who restored the Union after the violence of 1861 to 1864. Indeed, who else but the Negro could have restored the Union? The mass of the Southern white population was too poor and ignorant to be of use, and they had no leaders. Their leaders had become slave owners and their ambition was to destroy the Negro whom they hated and feared. On the other hand, the Negroes had leaders. The best of the house servants, the educated free Negro from the North, and the white Northern teachers and missionaries. The enfranchisement, then, of the Negroes, was not an act of grace on the part of the North; it was the only thing they could do. If the Southern freedmen, with their leadership, could carry on the functions of the state, they could, if protected by military force and legal guardianship, restore the Southern states to their seats in Congress on such conditions as the victors laid down. This was done; and, instead of the anarchy and failure which the white South expected and the North was prepared to see, the South staggered to its feet; and what the leaders of the whites feared, was not the failure of these freedmen's governments, but their increasing success. They, therefore, offered the North, and especially its business leaders, a compromise. They would accept tariffs on imports, which soon reached the highest in the nation's history; they would let the national war debt be paid in monopolized gold; they would drop the demand for payment of the Southern war debt and for emancipated slaves. One thing they insisted on was the complete control of labor and the disfranchisement of the freedmen, and that they easily got from a complacent North, now on the way to immense wealth and power. Calmly, the North withdrew military protection, winked at the mob violence of the Ku Klux Klan, and promised to let the freedmen be disfranchised with only token opposition. They even gave up control and oversight of Southern voting for federal officials. This will destroy democracy, said some. Others answered: democracy is already dead.

Lynching and mob law now swept the South, and, of course, could not be allowed to continue. By 1880 the leaders of the nation began to look about to see how far they could get the Negroes themselves to assent to a caste condition in the United States based on color and race. They found, at last, such a leader in Booker Washington. Not that Washington believed in caste, not that Washington wanted anything less than other Negro leaders; but that he assented to compromise because he saw no other way. He was willing to let the whites believe that Negroes did not want social equality or the right to vote or education for the higher professions, but ask only for whatever the whites offered, and would be patient and quiet under a caste system. Industry poured millions into their propaganda; and, as a result came disfranchisement and color caste. There followed the Niagara Movement of Negroes in 1905 and the establishment of the NAACP in 1910. The Southern states and some of the Northern states passed laws forbidding intermarriage, limiting employment, establishing ghettos, discriminating in transportation, and taking away the vote of most of the Negroes in the United States. It was an impossible condition to which no people, if they were really human, would consent. The NAACP was established by radical whites, reinforced by an increasing number of thinking Negroes, and it finally made a frontal attack upon lynching and mob law which brought the nation to its feet.

After all, a civilized nation could not continue publicly to murder one Negro each week without giving him a trial. It looked as if the chief industry of white women in the South was that of being raped by burly Negroes. The white women, themselves, at last, protested, and an anti-lynching law was nearly forced through Congress, but finally failed.

Then the front of attack changed. Trusts appeared and organized wealth disguised in corporations began to take over control of the nation. They seized the West Indies, Central and South America. They consorted with imperial Europe. When imperial colonialism drove Europe to war, the United States found it could make money by following. The First World War came and posed the fundamental question of Negro citizenship. The Supreme Court, after years of hesitation, sustained it. But the Negro was allowed to go into war as a stevedore, rather than as a soldier, and was treated with every indignity. After this war came wild speculation and severe depression. Franklin Roosevelt, with Harry Hopkins, began to socialize the nation, in order to beat back the power of the trusts and industrial monopolies. They did not wholly succeed; but they began just as the unexpected Second World War burst on civilization.

In this Second World War the Negro was registered in the ranks of the Army and the Navy and in the Air Corps, and their success only made clearer their caste condition in the nation. This, in the succeeding cold war, became so threatening a phenomenon that the Supreme Court in 1954 declared race discrimination, especially in schools, unconstitutional. The former slave South was furious, but was soon appeased by the assurance that the decree would not be enforced. The South could use "deliberate speed" which meant do little or nothing. That, again, aroused the Negroes. It led to bus strikes like that in Montgomery, and to, student sit-ins, where the Negroes began to assert rights which had never been taken from them by law, but only yielded to in custom. This still goes on.

The world regards us with amazement: we are leading the "Free World." We champion "Democracy" and for this we stage Little Rock, drive Negroes from the polls, chase Black students with bloodhounds and throttle free speech. On top of this Africa arises and our FBI trains a "Peace Corps" to guide it.

9

A Freedom Rider Speaks
His Mind, No. 2, 1961

JIMMY McDONALD

The Supreme Court had ruled in 1961 that bus terminal restaurants could not discriminate against interstate travelers. The Freedom Riders set out to test the enforcement of the federal law in the terminals in the South. A member of the Congress of Racial Equality (CORE), Jimmy McDonald was in the first group of seven Black and six white Freedom Riders. Segregationists bombed and burned their bus when it reached Anniston, Alabama.

Civil Rights in the past seven years have become the rallying point of Negro students of the South. The sit-ins were just a prelude to the Freedom Rides. But what are these Freedom Rides, and why are they being employed at just this time?

The interstate Commerce Commission had, some time before the first such ride, declared that interstate travel should flow freely without anyone engaged in it having to suffer the humiliation of racial discrimination of any kind. Thus it is only fitting that a group of twenty-one persons should have left Washington on May 4, 1961, on an integrated bus ride through the South, merely to see if the dictum of the United States government was being adhered to or not. These people were not breaking any laws, or "trying to take the law into their own hands"; they simply were doing what the federal government had told them they could do and that no one could stop them from doing.

In spite of Southern cries of Northern agitation, it has become evident to all of us familiar with the struggle of the Negro people to make a reality out of their legal rights to equality that it is impossible for the Negro to make any effective progress towards this seemingly modest goal unless they receive equal support and encouragement from the North.

The people who participate in these rides come from a variety of backgrounds. Some are school administrators; others are doctors, students, practitioners of the arts and sciences, and, of course, many are ministers. Yet all have one thing in common: a feeling that was expressed eloquently by one of them: "As long as I travel around the world and people ask me about Little Rock, Emmett Till, and Charles Mack Parker, I feel that I have an obligation to myself and to the Negro people to contribute something worthwhile." Yet, even if no uncommitted European, no underfed African being exposed to the lures of Communism no embarrassed friend of the United States in the united Nations had asked these questions—so difficult to answer—the moral obligation "to contribute something worthwhile" would still exist. It seems horribly ironic that a perfectly peaceful, and legal, bus ride should turn out to be that "something worthwhile," and that it should result in the imprisonment and vilification of the riders.

Trade Unions: Could Help, but Lag Badly

In many of the Southern states where the trade union movement has been active, these unions have made very few and very weak attempts to organize a full civil rights program, even within the limited framework of the union. In some cases, there is discrimination in the membership, while the leaders preach the brotherhood of man from their lofty perches on top of white ivory towers in the North. But these people, as well as several elected and appointed local, state, and national officials, have made no attempt to aid in an effective, organized campaign, while just the use of their names would have had an important positive effect on the already existing movements.

James Farmer (second from left) and James Peck (third from left), both of the Congress of Racial Equality (CORE) with fellow Freedom Riders in 1961.

Governor Patterson, of Alabama, in his "dignified" statement refusing to accept any responsibility for the "disgraceful behavior of rabble-rousers," who showed, he maintained, their true colors by allowing themselves to be unmercifully beaten by a mob of "law-abiding Alabama citizens," was just such a case. Here we can see how, if state executive officers, or just the chief of police, were to use their positions in a responsible manner, there would be a complete change of atmosphere. Instead of being thrown into segregated jails, the Freedom Riders could peacefully—and lawfully—sit together in integrated waiting rooms. And no one Southern white would lose the slightest shred of dignity by it. In fact, he would gain immeasurable stature by simply acknowledging the law of God and, incidentally, that of the United States of America.

Now, I have been asked on many occasions, "Do you hate these people?" And as pathetic as it sounds, I do not. In order for me to hate them, they must do something to me which harms me—and this they cannot do. But what I do hate is the society that produces such people, a society in which the white man has set himself up as the undisputed spokesman for the Negro. After all, if only the white can speak for the colored, how can the Negro object to this arrangement? All this, of course, disregards the obvious biological fact that the Negro has a mind and a mouth of his own and is as capable of using them as anyone else. Not to mention what also should be evident: only the Negro knows what the Negro wants and, at last, although he still can not say it at the polls, he is letting the world know what it is to be treated like a human being.

Who Needs to Cool Off?

In spite of this, we find responsible people demanding "cooling off" periods and moderation. This is not a new request, and we often have complied with it. I would be happy if they would moderately respect me as a human being and afford me the same dignities that are the right of every one of us to expect and receive—which include the right to life, liberty, and the pursuit of happiness. But according to these so-called moderates, I already am going too fast. They would rather I did nothing to secure the civil rights that have been denied me and my people since the first Negro slave was brought here in the seventeenth century. For 300 years we have been cooling off. More recently, we were cooling off when they lynched our mothers and fathers. And did we not cool off when they raped and jailed Mrs. Rose Lee Ingram? Perhaps she, too, was disturbing the peace and refusing to obey an officer. We also were prepared to cool off when they told the Jim Crow school boards to let us get a decent education "with all deliberate speed," and Miss Autherine Lucy discovered which word they valued most. But after a while, a cooling-off becomes a deep freeze. Now we are trying to take a bus ride, on an interstate carrier, through several Southern states, and the Ku Klux Klan, White Citizens Councils, and their brethren bomb our buses, board them, and bust us; all with the semiofficial blessing of the governor of Alabama and the chief of police of the city of Birmingham. It is not the Negro people who should cool off—they are cool enough already. Those who should cool off are the bomb throwers and their legalistic counterparts, the constabulary and judiciary of Anniston, Alabama, Birmingham and Jackson, Mississippi.

I am tempted to say, so far, so good. But, although we have made appreciable gains while remaining cooled-off, several rights remain for us to reclaim. Things are not so good. We intend to remain cooled-off—we can count on the Klan and the Council for all the heat we shall need; but we will not become docile. We will keep sending Freedom Riders down South—and these are not "so-called" Freedom Riders; they are exposing themselves to all sorts of danger to insure the freedom not just of the Negro, but of every American. Segregation is a dangerous precedent, and if we accept it—shall we say, "sitting down"—not one American is free. Least of all those who segregate. We will continue to ride for freedom, in the bus terminals and in the rest of our country!

What other areas must be freed? We must see effective integration, and by that I do not mean one and two percent integration, both in New Orleans and in New Rochelle. We must be able to ride in any part of any bus going anywhere. And this includes taking a local bus to our homes, which can be in any part of any city—not just above 110th Street in New York or across the railroad tracks in Prince Edward County. We must be able to get any job we are qualified to hold—qualified to hold not just because we are Negroes and it looks good for the company to hire a few of us.

We know that we have the same capacities as anyone else. We know that we just want to use these capacities without interfering with the right of the white man to use his capacities. We do not want to take way his home, or his job, or his wife—we are happy enough with our own women. But we do not want our women to have to work for the white women because our men are denied the right to a well-paying and challenging job. We are tired of being porters with college degrees.

Desegration—or Integrated Hell?

How can free, Christian Americans believe that many of their fellow-citizens must be born in a Jim Crow hospital, raised in a Jim Crow ghetto, educated in a segregated school, told to eat only in certain restaurants, wait in separate waiting rooms (which cannot be equal), be forced to take an inferior job, die, and be buried in a segregated cemetery, and then go on to an integrated heaven? What will happen is that we all will go to an integrated hell—whether in this world or the next.

We have already gone far in changing this pattern. Student action groups have shown the way. They now must be followed by private citizens, both white and colored. They must be encouraged by the federal government, whose duty it is to see that the rights and privileges of all its citizens are respected. While the attorney general admitted, on June 14, "They [the Freedom Riders] have a legal right to travel," he added that since "the Justice Department has taken action, I don't see that the rides accomplish anything." Well, for one thing, they will force the Justice Department to implement, in deeds as well as words, the law of the land. Even its words so far have been discouragingly vague and vacillating. As long as the attorney general so refused to take a position, we must continue in our uncompromising efforts to see that the full force of law is placed in back of the laws.

The sit-in movement has proved itself a success. The Freedom Rides now add an exclamation point to that statement. Our next movement towards full equality will be an exclamation point to the success of the Freedom Rides. And a success they will be!

10

What Price Prejudice? On the Economics of Discrimination, No. 3, 1962

WHITNEY M. YOUNG JR.

When Whitney Young delivered this address to the National Conference of Social Welfare in New York City, he was the executive director of the National Urban League. Young pointed to the destructive effects of economic inequality on the Black family. Soon civil rights activists would look beyond the "de jure" segregation of the South to the "de facto" segregation and poverty imposed on black people throughout the United States.

. . . Is there any relationship between the economic condition of Negro citizens and the amount of family disorganization? I said to the person, as I say to you, with, a restraint and a patience that is as long as my answer was brief, the answer to your erudite question is yes.

Let us for a few moments put it in its simplest terms. What does being without money mean in a society whose values are highly materialistic, whose consumer production everywhere displayed are without precedent, and where the acquisition of everything in that society, both tangible and intangible, requires money?

In these terms it means little food, little housing, little health, little education, little culture, little status, and little citizenship.

I suppose the all-embracing terms we use in the profession to describe this situation is insecurity and frustration. The adult members of a family not only feel a personal sense of failure, but with their children this is further aggravated by a deep sense of guilt. The conscious feelings of inferiority experienced by many Negro citizens and suggested by all of the outside world for a time in history placated the ego and provided at least surface rationalization. But this avenue of escape is no longer open to the adult members of a family. Almost without exception, whatever the role the Negro may be playing at a given moment, he knows that his condition, his status and his role are man-made. Too much has happened; the world is too small; communication too sophisticated, and examples, though few, are still enough to make him know that the only thing really unique about him is the color of his skin and the unusual reaction it engenders in most white Americans.

This reaction may take the form of patronizing condescension, bland indifference, subtle prejudice, overt hate or violence. Most often the Negro is just ignored. This is best described in Ralph Ellison's book "Invisible Man" and James Baldwin's "Nobody Knows My Name."

To get back to the subject—the effects of economic inequality on family functioning—the most immediate is a denial of not luxuries, but just basic things, such as food, clothing and shelter. Even a record, a book, or an ice cream cone for a child—to say nothing of a theatre ticket, a bicycle, or summer camp. A trip to the hairdresser for mother, or membership in a bowling club for father—even these are out of the question. It forces a family into a physical environment in terms of house and neighborhood that guarantees the worst health standards, most inadequate schools, fewer recreational facilities and the least police protection. They pay more for less shelter, because the demand for housing for Negro citizens is many times the available supply. Poverty does not lend itself to making political contributions like exploiting landlords and absentee slum owners do, so improvements demanded under city codes or services required by city laws are oftentimes overlooked. Public day-care centers are likely to be non-existent, and so the 2- or 3-year-old is left with the 6-year-old or with an 80-year-old woman down the block. Many services are available if you can get to them, or are willing to wait and can make an appointment for between 9-and-5 from Monday through Friday. Public assistance can be secured if you can get rid of your husband, or if he is agreeable to only coming around during odd hours of the night.

This is, of course, nothing new to you. Most of us have learned to observe this manifestation of economic inequality in a pretty detached and "objective" fashion more becoming to a professional. Much more interesting would be the psychological impact of economic inequality upon family functioning. Let me, therefore, touch briefly on this aspect. So far as the Negro male is concerned, modern economic deprivation is viewed as part of his age-old story of humiliation and abuse. In slavery, the system was designed to keep him in his place; later, as a source of cheap labor. His present high unemployment, low skills and inadequate earnings tell us more about the conscious and unconscious injustices of the past than they do about the present. The effects on family functioning and role performance are, however, what you might expect. Both as a husband and as a father he is made to feel inadequate, not because he lacks love and affection, intelligence or even a grey flannel suit, but because in a society that measures him by the size of his paycheck he just doesn't stand very tall. He reacts to this situation with withdrawal, bitterness toward the society, aggression both within the family or racial group, self-hatred, crime and/or escape through a variety of ways which would allow him to be lost in fantasy or compensated through a variety of exploits.

For the Negro mother, her functioning is that dictated more by necessity than through choice. As a major breadwinner—if not the only breadwinner of the family, she assumes roles and responsibilities far beyond her ability to perform any of them too well. But, contrary to what most social scientists and even some social workers speculate about, she knows quite well and resents very deeply the forces responsible for her fate.

As for the children, they, too, often suffer from the absence of a strong male image and a mother too tired and bitter to give time, supervision and, sometimes, though not often, love. They experience on the one hand bitterness and hostility toward a society which mistreated their parents. On the other hand, they feel humiliation, shame and wounded pride. They feel frustration and hopelessness.

It is this situation that produces our statistics on broken homes, dependency, delinquency, drop-outs, crime, illegitimacy and other social disorganization. It is this situation which has presented us with a tension unprecedented in our history. Time is not our ally. The time has passed for studies and committees. Unless there is a major crash program now to drastically change this situation, we shall all be sorry as human beings and shall all suffer as American citizens. . . .

As for you I ask several things:

1. That what you seem to observe and identify as the problem of Negro citizens or the mal-functioning of Negro families will be best understood and corrected if seen and treated as a problem of cities and society-at-large;
2. That you reject any notion of this as a single-facet problem— economic, housing, education, etc.—for in reality it is all of these. You can't secure a decent job without a good education, and a good education can today only be secured in good neighborhoods with good schools and wholesome social and cultural surroundings;
3. That immediately we begin giving special attention, both in terms of services, facilities, and personnel to the low socio-economic areas of our communities;
4. And, finally, we must give recognition to the fact that all artificial barriers erected to keep ethnic groups separate must be removed. We must see this not as a problem, but as an opportunity. For the minority group member it means expanded horizons, better housing, and educational opportunities. For the white citizen it means finally a way to get rid of some of the drab sameness that leads to stagnation and so ill prepares their children for the world today and certainly of tomorrow. Only through diversity and inclusiveness do people become creative and secure human beings.

President Kennedy, in his "Alliance for Progress" speech made the statement that "if peaceful revolution is impossible, violent revolution is inevitable."

Our revolution at this point with American Negro citizens is a Revolution of Expectation that seeks only his birthright as an American citizen.

May we move with speed, perception and intelligence to assure the success of this revolution and to justify the heritage which is ours as social workers.

11

The Southern Youth
Movement, No. 3, 1962

JULIAN BOND

*When this letter appeared in the Reader's Forum, Julian Bond was one of the
leaders of the Student Nonviolent Coordinating Committee.*

It was with great interest that I read *Reader's Forum* by Wilfred Cal-
lender (FREEDOMWAYS, Spring 1962). I was a little distressed that
there was no mention in his piece of the Student Nonviolent Coordinating Committee, the organization I work for.

SNCC, or "snick" as Attorney Len Holt calls us in his article *A
Southern Lawyer Speaks of Freedom* (FREEDOMWAYS, Spring 1962),
was founded at a conference of student sit-in leaders in Raleigh,
North Carolina, in April 1960. Called by SCLC, the gathering was a
needed one, for although the chief virtue of the student protest
movement has been its spontaneity, there was a need for communication between the students, a need for an exchange of techniques,
and a need for a coordination of effort.

At Raleigh, a committee was formed with one representative from
each state. Marion Barry, then a student at Fisk University, was

elected chairman. We established a small office in Atlanta, hired an executive secretary, and began the tedious business of trying to coordinate a movement, inform others about the goals and aims of the struggle, and to raise funds to provide scholarship aid for students expelled from school.

By the early spring of 1961, however, it became clear that something more was needed. Too many students had been interested only in lunch counter integration; when this goal was reached, their movements became dormant. Someone would have to breathe new life into these areas, and someone would have to take the gospel of the movement into areas where there had been no action.

Members of the Coordinating Committee volunteered. They were on the Freedom Rides last summer. They were in McComb, Mississippi, and helped to begin the first action movement in that state. They began a voter registration drive in rural Mississippi counties, and were shot at, beaten, and jailed. They were in Albany, Georgia, as long ago as October 1961, and were there to go to jail with 737 Albanites. They are still there, working in Georgia's "terrible" Terrell County, registering voters in an area where 6 new Negro names on the voter's list is a victory. They were in Talladega, Alabama, when 200 students were beaten two blocks through the city by state troopers. They were in Huntsville and Tuscaloosa, and they will be in other small towns as well. They were in Baton Rouge, Louisiana, when Southern University was closed down, and they suffered for their presence there. Three SNCC staffers—two Negroes, one white—were arrested there for "criminal anarchy." One spent 59 days in jail.

These young people—20 in all—three white, are sitting in, registering voters, and giving instructions in the all-important "how" in small towns and back counties all over the South. When workers for most civil rights organizations receive salaries which equal the dangerous work they do, these youngsters receive only what we laughingly call "subsistence" pay. Three staff members, who are married, receive $60 a week. Thirteen others get $40 a week. Four are working full time in Mississippi for only $20 a week. Our office is located on Atlanta's Auburn Avenue, and has been given us rent-free. We exist on contributions from "interested friends."

I think it is a grave mistake for Callendar to say that "by their very nature the sit-ins could not have the benefit of coordination." This past weekend we have had a meeting, in Atlanta, of 45 student leaders who represent their local protest groups in 6 Southern states. These students make up SNCC's Coordinating Committee, and they are able to coordinate the activities of student groups in their areas.

In April of this year we held a conference in Atlanta, and over 300 students attended. We discussed the value of jail versus bail, got legal advice from talented lawyers, made plans for coordinated efforts against segregation, and pledged to send representatives to SNCC Coordinating Committee meetings.

We issue a monthly newsletter, the *Student Voice,* which gives news of student activity in the South. It is available to your readers for the asking, by writing to our office, 135 Auburn Avenue, Atlanta 3, Georgia.

SNCC is an independent organization. We work with local citizens and groups in an attempt to initiate direct action and voter registration programs. SNCC does not speak for the movement, for no one does, and no one can. But SNCC is working in the South in areas no other civil rights group has ever been to, with farmers, domestics, laborers, and people who really want to be free.

12

Nonviolence: An Interpretation, No. 1, 1963

JULIAN BOND

We are holding nonviolent workshops in the smaller Delta towns. Several people in Shaw have on their own asked us to tell them how to go about registering. We have mentioned voting only [in] passing. We have been working on the theory that if you can make a man feel like a whole person and realize his own worth and dignity and if you make him understand his plight better, he will want to vote on his own account.

— *from a SNCC secretary in the Mississippi Delta*

The adherents of nonviolence as a means to achieve social change fall into two categories. One group, containing most of the activists working in the south today, believes in and has seen the proof of nonviolent direct action as an effective means of protests and as a method of achieving change. The other group, smaller in number, believes in nonviolence not only as a tactic, but as a way of life and a philosophy of living. (Let us realize here that no social action method in and by itself is sufficient to successfully integrate the nation's

Negro masses. The power of the boycott, legalistic procedures, and mediation are all employed by America's protesting Negroes.)

Opponents of the nonviolent method have yet to offer a suitable alternative. Many point with pride to Robert Williams, ex-President of the Monroe, North Carolina NAACP branch, who was hounded from the United States by racists after he encouraged Negroes in Monroe to defend their homes against night raiders. But what they fail to recall is that Williams believed in nonviolence, participated in nonviolent demonstrations in Monroe, and was charged with kidnapping a white couple he had taken into his home—in the spirit of nonviolence to protect them from a Negro mob.

A statistical listing of the successes of nonviolence as typified by the student sit-in movement, which began in February 1960, is impressive. The number of facilities integrated, jobs secured and oppressive laws lifted is great. But the believers in nonviolence say it goes further than 'just a hamburger.' The critic of the students' methods who thinks that these young militants are interested only in dime store lunch counters and movie theaters is seriously mistaken.

"I was in New York the other day," one student said, "and read the inscription on the Statue of Liberty. 'Give me your tired, your poor, your hungry masses yearning to breathe free,' it read. Well baby, I thought, here we are."

The young nonviolent protestors who are working in the rural counties of Mississippi's Delta, Alabama's Negro Belt, and Georgia's cotton country are not aiming at a world where all men can eat together at the same lunch counter. Their aim is to change a society that lets some men keep others from eating where they choose, to develop the 'beloved community' they speak of. To these students, nonviolent protest methods serve two purposes. The method and technique of nonviolence integrates a given lunch counter or a movie theater, and the philosophy of nonviolence affords men—those involved in the rights struggle and those opposed to it—a chance at confrontation and exchange of ideas that will certainly make the former stronger and will perhaps convert the latter. "I know that the person who has a real commitment to nonviolence will never leave the movement," William Porter said. Porter, who headed the youth group of the Albany, Georgia, movement, said that Albany's success "cannot be measured with Montgomery's, where nonviolent protests and the Supreme Court brought segregated busses to an end. Our victory here has been over the minds and hearts of Albany's Negro masses, who now not only know how to get their rights, but are determined to do so."

Porter is one of forty-five college-age young people, Negroes and whites, who make up the staff of the Student Nonviolent Coordinating Committee SNCC. They are all former participants in student sit-in demonstrations in their own home and college towns, but they have all left their schools, families, and in some cases, their jobs to work for SNCC at a $15 a week subsistence wage. They work in Arkansas, Mississippi, Alabama, Georgia, and South Carolina on direct action and voter registration projects designed, as *Saturday Evening Post* writer Ben Bagdigian put it, "to upset the social structure of the deep South and to change party politics in the United States." The historic alignment of Southern Dixiecrats and Northern Republicans, the hypocrisy of both parties in dealing with civil rights, and the lack of any real advancement for Negroes beyond the 1954 Supreme Court decision motivate these students.

Through their nonviolent workshops in the cotton towns of the rural south, they are spreading a message that transcends lunch counter integration. SNCC staff member Mrs. Diane Nash Bevel, expecting her first child last summer, surrendered herself to a Mississippi judge who had charged her with "contributing to the delinquency of minors" because she had encouraged young Negroes in Jackson, Mississippi, to join the Freedom Rides. Mrs. Bevel said, "I refuse to cooperate any longer with what I consider to be an immoral court system." The judge, perhaps aware of the hue that would arise were he to sentence an expectant mother to a three-year jail term, refused to sentence her. Her refusal to cooperate with Mississippi's segregated and prejudiced courts stems from her readings and training in nonviolence.

Just as the students consider it wrong to inflict harm on another, they consider it evil to participate in any way with a system built on wrong. For this reason the workers in the SNCC Atlanta office refuse to shop in any of the city's Woolworth stores. Although the Woolworth branches here integrated a year ago, students in Pine Bluff, Arkansas, are currently staging sit-ins at a Woolworth there.

For this reason several have registered as conscientious objectors with their draft board; at least one student working in the North has refused to register at all. "This movement is bigger than a civil rights fight," one of SNCC's Southwest Georgia staffers said. "We're fighting for basic civil liberties. That's what the whole Albany move-

(Left to right) John Lewis and Gene Young of SNCC and Jerome Smith and David Dennis of CORE, 1963, Greenwood, Miss. Unidentified child stands between Lewis and Young.

ment is about, whether the First Amendment applies in Albany or not."

Ruby Doris Smith, a former Freedom Rider who worked on SNCC's first voter registration campaign in Amite county, Mississippi, in 1961 says that nonviolence helped build up the courage of the rural Negroes she worked with. "They had never heard of Martin Luther King or the movement boycott," she said. "But one young girl told me that she wasn't afraid of the police in McComb when she and 112 of her classmates staged a protest march through the town. The older people too are deeply religious and find courage in nonviolence. We reminded them that Christ had been nonviolent on the cross and I think that now the kids and their parents believe that not only can they do something to change the system, but that they have an obligation to change it."

One of the tragedies of nonviolence is that the biggest critics are those who understand it least. Some northern liberals look upon the students as a bunch of modern 'Uncle Toms' praying for deliverance while white mobs ravish and beat them. The reverse is true. The students who are working today in Dawson and Leesburg, Georgia, in Leland and Greenwood, Mississippi, and in Gee's Bend, Alabama, are daily placing their lives on the line. When trouble threatens, as it does with unsettling certainty every day, they draw upon an inner courage which wells from practicing what they preach: that every man has his own worth and that all men must strive together to build the 'beloved community.'

To a northerner reading of arrests and beatings such a statement may sound trite or even naïve, but to the young militants who know it to be true, it is a simple statement of fact.

13

Lorraine Hansberry at the Summit, No. 4, 1979

JAMES BALDWIN

James Baldwin describes here a meeting with Attorney General Robert Kennedy that took place in 1963. A noted essayist and novelist, Baldwin was a contributing editor to Freedomways.

I must, now, for various reasons—some of which, I hope, will presently become apparent—do something which I have very deliberately never done before: Sketch the famous Bobby Kennedy meeting. I have talked about it or around it, and a day is coming when I will be compelled to deliver my entire testimony. But, for the moment, I want merely to suggest something of Lorraine Hansberry's beauty and power on that day; and what the incomprehension that day's encounter was to cause the nation and, presently, and until this hour, the world.

Let us say that we all live through more than we can say or see. A life, in retrospect, can seem like the torrent of water opening or closing over one's head and, in retrospect, is blurred, swift, kaleidoscopic like that. One does not wish to remember—one is perhaps not *able* to remember—the holding of one's breath under water, the miracle of rising up far enough to breathe, and then, the going under again; or the tremendous difference between the light beneath the water, and the light when one comes up to the sky.

Lorraine would not be very much younger than I am now if she were alive. She would be 49, and I am 55. But she was very much younger than I when we met—she being 29 then, and I being 34. At the time of the Bobby Kennedy meeting, she was 33. That was one of the very last times I saw her on her feet, and she died at the age of 34. The fact that I would not now be much older than she if she were alive is one of the reasons I miss her so much—we could have such times together now!

People forget how young everybody was. Bobby Kennedy, for another, quite different example, was 38. His father had been Ambassador at the Court of St. James—among other quite stunning distinctions—and it goes without saying (nor was it his fault) that he had not the remotest concept of poverty. I doubt that poverty can be imagined, and the attitudes of the American middle class, or the middle class anywhere, are proof that the memory obliterates poverty with great speed and efficiency.

In a sense, therefore, the meeting took place in that panic-stricken vacuum in which Black and white, for the most part, meet in this country. I am not now speaking of conscious attitudes, but of history. White people do not wish to be reminded whence they came by the poverty which is, they hope, behind them. Neither do they wish, for the most part, to enter into Black suffering—it was Bobby Kennedy, after all, who, referring to the Irish past, said that a Negro could become president in 40 years. He really did not know why Black people were so offended by this attempt at reassurance. But a Black woman pointed out that she resented and rejected such encouragement from the son of an Irish immigrant, who had arrived on these shores long after she had been auctioned here.

It is to be remembered that, at the time of the meeting, Medgar Evers had but lately been blown away at the age of 37. Malcolm and Martin (both to be murdered at the age of 39) are still with us. Birmingham, Alabama, has already had its effect on, among others, Julian Bond, a youngster, and Jerome Smith, not much older, and Angela Davis. Angela had known the children blown away in that Birmingham Sunday school. This event invested her with a resolution which was eventually to land her on the FBI's *Most Wanted List*.

Telescoping, severely now, the details, I had just come off the Southern road and, principally, from Birmingham when Bobby Kennedy asked me to throw this meeting together. I had met Bobby Kennedy once at a White House function and had told him, with some vehemence, that I wanted to talk to him about the role of the FBI in the Deep South. He had looked at me as though he was thinking that it might not be a bad idea to hand me over to the FBI but was very cordial—I suppose; anyway this encounter had something to do with his reason for calling me. I called, among others, Miss Lena Horne, who said that she "never" flew. She, nevertheless, arrived the next day. I found her wearing a beige suit sitting in Bobby Kennedy's lobby and complaining that she had a "hole" in her shoe from guiding this plane across the continent. She had just driven in from Idlewild—soon to be renamed Kennedy [Airport].

The meeting had been called so swiftly that I had not been able to find Lorraine or Jerome. I think that it was my brother, David, who managed to find them both; but anyway, here they were: Lorraine, Jerome and David.

And here came Burke Marshall and Bobby Kennedy, and we went on up to the suite.

There were many more people than I can name here. Let us say that I simply called Black or white people whom I trusted, who would not feel themselves compelled to be spokesmen for any organization or responsible for espousing any specific point of view. I called the people who had, I knew, paid some dues and who knew it. Rip Torn, for example, a white Southerner, though that does not describe him, was here; and the Black sociologist Kenneth Clark; and Harry Belafonte, a very good man on the Southern road and a very good man, indeed; and Ed Berry of the Chicago Urban League; and others, but I am trying to talk about Lorraine.

The meeting began quietly enough until Lorraine responded to Bobby's failure to understand or reply to Jerome's passionate query as to the real role of the U.S. Government in, for example, Birmingham. Bobby—and here I am not telescoping but exercising restraint—had turned away from Jerome, as though to say, "I'll talk to all of *you*, who are civilized. But who is *he?*"

Lorraine said (in memory, she is standing, but I know she was sitting. She towered, that child, from a sitting position), "You have a great many very accomplished people in this room, Mr. Attorney General, but the only man you should be listening to is that man over there. That is the voice," she added, after a moment during which Bobby sat absolutely still staring at her, "of twenty-two million people."

As Mr. Kennedy did not appear to understand this, Miss Horne eventually, and as the afternoon wore on perpetually, attempted to clarify it—saying, for example, "If you are so proud of your record, Mr. Attorney General, *you* go up to Harlem into those churches and barber shops and pool halls, and *you* tell the people. *We* ain't going to do it, because *we* don't want to get shot."

I think I was watching everything. But I know I was watching Lorraine's face. She wanted him to *hear*. Her face changed and changed, the way Sojourner Truth's face must have changed and changed or, to tell the truth, the way I have watched my mother's face change when speaking to someone who could not hear. Who yet, and you know it, will be compelled to hear one day.

We wanted him to tell his brother, the President, to personally escort to school, on the following day or the day after, a small Black girl already scheduled to enter a Deep South school.

"That way," we said, "it will be clear that whoever spits on that child will be spitting on the nation."

He did not understand this either. "It would be," he said, "a meaningless moral gesture."

"We would like," said Lorraine, "from you, a moral commitment."

He did not turn from her as he had turned away from Jerome. He looked insulted—seemed to feel that he had been wasting his time.

But he reacted very strongly to Jerome's answer to his question, "Would you take up arms to defend this country?" The answer was, "Never! Never! Never!"

Bobby Kennedy was surprised that any American could feel that way. But something got through to him when this same answer was reiterated later—by a Black voice shouting, "When I pull the trigger, kiss it goodbye!"

Well, Lorraine sat still, watching all the while and listening with a face as still, as beautiful and as terrifying as her face must have been at that moment when she told us, "My Lord calls me. He calls me by the thunder. I ain't got long to stay here." She put that on her tape-recorder in her own voice at the moment she realized that she was about to die.[1]

---

[1]The quoted words are heard in the film *Lorraine Hansberry: The Black Experience in the Creation of Drama*, Films for the Humanities, Inc., Princeton, N.J. 08540.

The meeting ended with Lorraine standing up. She said, in response to Jerome's statement concerning the perpetual demolition faced every hour of every day by Black men who pay a price literally unspeakable for attempting to protect their women, their children, their homes, or their lives, "That is all true, but I am not worried about Black men—who have done splendidly, it seems to me, all things considered."

Then, she paused and looked at Bobby Kennedy who, perhaps for the first time, looked at her.

"But I am very worried," she said, "about the state of the civilization which produced that photograph of the white cop standing on that Negro woman's neck in Birmingham."

Then, she smiled. And I am glad that she was not smiling at me. She extended her hand.

"Goodbye, Mr. Attorney General," she said and turned and walked out of the room.

We followed her. Perhaps I can dare to say that we were all, in our various ways, devastated, but I will have to leave it at that.

I had forgotten that I was scheduled to be interviewed by Dr. Kenneth Clark, and we were late.[2] We were hurried into the car. We passed Lorraine, who did not see us. She was walking toward Fifth Avenue—her face twisted, her hands clasped before her belly, eyes darker than any eyes I had ever seen before—walking in an absolutely private place.

I knew I could not call her.

Our car drove on; we passed her.

And then, we heard the thunder.

---

[2] *Freedomways* published Dr. Clark's interview with James Baldwin.

14

"We're Moving!"
No. 1, 1971

PAUL ROBESON

On August 28, 1964, the first anniversary of the historic March on Washington, Paul Robeson issued a statement to the African American press, from which the following was excerpted.

While I must continue my temporary retirement from public life I am, of course, deeply involved with the great upsurge of our people. Like all of you, my heart has been filled with admiration for the many thousands of Negro freedom fighters and their white associates who are waging the battle for civil rights throughout the country and especially in the South. Along with the pride has been the great sorrow and righteous wrath we all shared when the evil forces of white supremacy brutally murdered the Birmingham children and some of our finest heroes, like Medgar Evers and the three young men in Mississippi.

For me there has also been the sorrow that I have felt on returning home and experiencing the loss of persons who for many long years were near and dear to me—my beloved older brother, Rev. Benjamin C. Robeson, who passed away while I was gone; and my long-time colleague and co-worker, Dr. W.E.B. Du Bois, foremost statesman and scholar of our people, who died last year in Ghana. And now has come deep grief at the death of Benjamin J. Davis, a precious friend whose indomitable courage and dedication to the fight for freedom has always been a glowing inspiration for me.

Many thousands gone ... but we, the living, are more firmly resolved: "No more drivers lash for me!" The dedicated lives of all who have fallen in our long uphill march shall be fulfilled, for truly "We *shall* overcome." The issue of *freedom now* for Negro Americans has become the main issue confronting this nation, and the peoples of the whole world are looking to see it finally resolved.

When I wrote in my book, *Here I Stand*, in 1958, that "The time is now," some people thought that perhaps my watch was fast (and maybe it was a little), but most of us seem to be running on the same time—now. The "power of Negro action," of which I then wrote, has changed from an idea to a reality that is manifesting itself throughout our land. The concept of mass militancy, of mass action, is no longer deemed "too radical" in Negro life.

The idea that Black Americans should see that the fight for a "Free World" begins at home—a shocking idea when expressed in Paris in 1949—no longer is challenged in our communities. The "hot summer" of struggle for equal rights has replaced the "cold war" abroad as the concern of our people.

It is especially heartening for me to see the active and often heroic part that leading Negro artists—singers, actors, writers, comedians, musicians—are playing today in the freedom struggle. Today it is the Negro artist who does *not* speak out who is considered to be out of line; and even the white audiences have largely come around to accepting the fact that the Negro artist is—and has every right to be— quite "controversial."

Yes, it is good to see all these transformations. It is heartening also to see that despite all the differences in program and personalities among Negro leadership, the concept of a united front of all forces and viewpoints is gaining ground.

There is much—much more—that needs to be done, of course, before we can reach our goals. But if we cannot as yet sing: "Thank God Almighty, we're free at last," we surely can all sing together: "Thank God Almighty, we're *moving!*"

15

Birmingham Shall Be Free Some Day, No. 1, 1964

FRED L. SHUTTLESWORTH

Reverend Shuttlesworth was a long-time leader of the Birmingham, Alabama, movement. This piece appeared in a special issue, No. 1, 1964, devoted to the Southern freedom movement.

. . . Years ago, only a few Negro citizens dared to speak out, and there could be no consistent challenge to segregation; the Ku Klux Klan saw to that, and back of them were the police. The unwritten rule was "if the mobs don't stop Negroes, the police will." Not only was there no vociferous clamor for civil rights; the Negro's existence depended upon his keeping quiet and upon the white man's paternalism.

Dialogue between the white and Negro community was non-existent, except that between servant and master; and City Hall's communication was with crooks and racketeers Indeed, men were arrested for holding interracial meetings. Did not "Bull" Connor brag of arresting ex-Senator Glen Taylor? And when a reporter interviewed "Bull" Connor about his attitude and obedience to law, the commissioner was quoted in the *Afro-American* newspaper as saying "Damn the law; down here I am the Law.". . . .

Against this background, several years ago the Negroes organized the Alabama Christian Movement for Human Rights (ACMHR) [in 1958].

At the inception of the "Movement," it was common practice for police to issue a hundred or more parking tickets on meeting nights. We have been used to police attending mass meetings since 1958; but they came many times with sirens screaming, lights flashing, fire axes, rushing into buildings hunting "fires" which were not there—but failing to stampede Negroes, or to extinguish the fire that wouldn't go out.

We have challenged segregation so thoroughly that a few days ago [in 1963] in federal court the city claimed to have no barriers now at all. The challenges have indeed been costly. The KKK castrated Mr. Judge Aaron, a common, ordinary Negro citizen, just like a man would a hog. They beat Rev. Charles Billups with chains. In the early days of our Movement countless Negroes went to jail and lost their jobs. Some even lost homes and many left for other cities. Time would fail to tell of the personal involvement of my family and myself. The thousands of crank and very real telephone threats, the mobs at Terminal Station, and at Phillips High School, before which I was dragged and beaten in the streets and my wife stabbed in the hip; the two dynamite explosions, through which we lived by the grace of God; the agonies of having to crusade almost alone, at first; the brutal tactics unleashed upon us by the city—all these things did not move us, nor deter us from our goal.

They rather proved the mettle of the Birmingham Negro; and laid the basis for the massive assault which took place last summer. . . .

These things happened and many more in Birmingham before last spring. I like to feel, despite the vacillations of the new city council, that the massive demonstrations, led by the illustrious Dr. Martin Luther King, Reverend Ralph Abernathy, Reverend Wyatt Walker, and others who assisted me, have brought Birmingham to her senses; and that further persistence by our Movement will finally make it a City of Brotherhood.

I look back to the 3,300 who went to jail, and take pride in my people. And I think way back to the dark, dismal days of 1956 to 1963, and see Negroes trekking through snow and cold, rain and heat, persecution and peril, sacrifice and hardship, and then I say "thank God for knowing them, and the power of Faith."

America shall be free, some day!

16

Tremor in the Iceberg: The Mississippi Summer Project, No. 2, 1965

ERIC MORTON

This article appeared in the special issue devoted to the Mississippi Freedom Summer 1964, titled "Mississippi: Opening Up the Closed Society." Eric Morton was the materials coordinator for the Mississippi Summer Project.

The Mississippi Summer Project was a wide range of educational, political and social programs designed to reach down into every Black community to organize and train the people to lead themselves. Some of the programs were the Freedom Schools, the Community Centers, the Adult Literacy Project, the Work-Study Project, the Mississippi Student Union, the Freedom Vote, the Mississippi Freedom Democratic Party, the Food and Clothing, Welfare Program, the Freedom Libraries, and the Voter Registration Campaign.

What had begun with only a few SNCC workers and a "mock election" vote to educate the disenfranchised Negro's of Mississippi to the use of the ballot had grown into a radical, grassroots movement to develop alternative organizations and institutions which would be more responsible to the needs of the local Negro communities, existing outside the white society.

Implicit in the building of this movement was the idea of a counterstructure composed of institutions and groups bound by deeper understandings of inter-relationships, organization, work, identity and aims—facts which would more realistically meet the needs of the vastly neglected Black people of Mississippi. The primary aim was not to integrate the Negro's into the existing white power structure but to organize them into a durable structure of their own which could enable them to achieve the kind of changes they needed and desired.

A project of this nature was dependent for its development on a number of factors, not the least of which was the commitment of thousands of people, inside and outside the state, either by direct involvement in the project itself or by the indirect involvement of being a contributor in one way or another. This widespread participation was necessary because of the wide range and scope of the Mississippi Summer Project; from the beginning, it was a developing movement, and only incidentally an organizational effort. It was a movement committed to certain ideals (e.g., the refusal to accept the Convention's compromise at Atlantic City), rather than to a set of fixed goals achieved through conventional direct action protest. Therefore, it was necessary for the rest of America to be brought into the struggle with something more than a verbal commitment: they had to be willing to work from the bottom and be ready to involve themselves in the movement's evolving ideals.

To this extent, it was not the usual type of civil rights drive; and for this reason, it was one of the most significant developments in the history of the civil rights movement. The movement which was started in Mississippi to transform that state didn't confine itself to the geographical limits of the state. It created an intense involvement among thousands of people, inside and outside the state, with a growing concern for social justice and political change, to an extent that no other "movement" had ever involved them. The furor created in Mississippi during the summer of 1964 erupted at the Democratic Convention in Atlantic City, led to the Congressional challenge in Washington, D.C., and ignited similar student activists on college campuses throughout the country.

Several obvious factors were instrumental in making the project the unique achievement it was. The first one which comes to mind is that 85 per cent of the hard core staff were members of the youthful; militant, uncoordinated Student Nonviolent Coordinating Committee who gave to the project their dynamic character and approach. Secondly, I should point to the fact that it was an unusual coalition of the national civil rights organizations with the local civic, religious, social and political groups in the state working together in the name of the Council of Federated Organizations (COFO). This fact had an attractive influence upon the people of Mississippi and the general public-at-large, especially among the middle classes. I give most of the credit to the total impact of the thousands of student volunteers, artists, skilled workers, laborers, professional people, educators, politicians, and others who went to Mississippi to work, to see, and to investigate. Over 1700 persons worked in the state who came from every region in the United States, including some who came from foreign countries as far away as England, France, and Germany. They worked with one condition: every volunteer and staff worker would train a Mississippian to do whatever work he was doing and eventually *work himself out and the Mississippian in.*

Within the state over 100,000 local people participated in the civil rights movement, including a few whites. Throughout the state, Black communities formed voter registration groups, such as the Ruleville Voters' League, the Tupelo Progressive Democratic Club, and the Hattiesburg Voter Registration League to educate themselves to the responsibilities and rights of democratic citizenship. At their regular political meetings you would hear enthusiastic discussion on decision-making in a democracy: who decides? where should the ultimate decision-making power reside?; in the people, or at the top? In most of the project areas local Negro's did their best to organize forms of assistance for the project workers to provide them with shelter, food and protection. In Jackson, Mississippi, a group of Negro women formed an organization called Women's Power which provided clothing for the small number of Negro children who integrated public schools for the first time in that city. Also, they provided the Jackson project workers with one free meal every day for several months which they cooked and served in two different churches. The most dramatic sign of all was their response to the Freedom Election: over 80,000 people voted in that election, casting their "mock ballots" for the leaders of the MFDP, the party they formed and led. They responded with the attitude that *theirs was the real election* and the regular election was the *mock* election.

Working side by side with the local people were the volunteers, who learned as well as taught; the relationship was one of reciprocal stripping and discovery. Many of them returned home to form pockets of concern and activity for the civil rights movement within their communities. One young volunteer urged her parents and the people in her community to form a Pittsburgh Friends of COFO to support the project, which, subsequently, shipped several trucking vans of food, clothing, office supplies and other useful equipment to Mississippi. A group of artists in Pittsburgh, inspired by the Friends of COFO, raised a large sum of money for the project work. A Union County, N.J., teacher who taught at the Freedom School in Holly Springs, Mississippi, was the impetus for her home county which adopted Benton County in Mississippi, and they provided funds for the teacher in order that she might continue her work there. A group of teachers from New York City returned home and organized assistance within the United Federation of Teachers in New York State.

One of the most interesting examples of sacrifice and dedication was shown by a man who was not a volunteer in the usual sense of the word as I have been using it here. He was a Catholic priest from White Plains, New York, who desired to do whatever he could. Located in the basement of his home was a small, complete print shop which he offered to donate to COFO. We accepted. Not only did he crate each piece of equipment and pay for its shipping, but he voluntarily went to Mississippi to install the equipment and to train several young Negroes to operate the shop. Later, he was instrumental in organizing several fund-raising affairs to raise money for larger printing equipment and a year's supply of paper. He helped form the Mississippi Assistance Project, one of the most massive contributing organizations of its kind. They contributed money and shipped several railroad boxcars of every conceivable item the project could use. MAP sent eleven of its people to Memphis, Tennessee, from which point the railroad shipment was distributed by five Hertz trucks to all the Freedom Projects in Mississippi, over a period of three days. Included in the group of eleven were a dentist, a writer, a lawyer, a banker, several students, and a doctor.

Another large and well-organized assistance group was the Minnesota Task Force which included in its membership the State Attorney General, the Mayor of St. Paul and Minneapolis, State Senators and Representatives, businessmen, rabbis and clergymen. They suc-

A scene from organizing days in the Southern Freedom Movement, 1964.

ceeded in raising a substantial amount of money and supplies, including vehicles.

Other individual people and organized groups expressed their commitment by giving whatever they had to offer. A fight promoter sent a large carton of boxing headgear. A pharmaceutical company sent several cartons of vitamin pills and a crate of first-aid kits.

A seafarer's union in California offered to provide free shipping to any coastal area in Mississippi. Several Teamster locals gave free trucking to various projects in the state. Rae Branstein, Secretary of the National Committee for Rural Schools, sent boxes of new dungarees and lumber shirts to be distributed among the children of Mississippi. Many national magazines donated subscriptions to each Freedom project, and some newspapers regularly sent great quantities of each issue. Bookstores donated multiple copies of specific titles requested. The Committee of Concern, set up by Quakers and representatives from the National Council of Churches, organized to rebuild burned and bombed churches. A group of college students spent their Christmas vacation rebuilding a burned church. A carpenter raised enough funds in California to go to Mississippi and build a Community Center, from the ground up, in Holmes County, A Negro electrician from Chicago did the electrical wiring in the Holmes County Community Center, and installed fluorescent lights in the Jackson headquarters. Even foreign embassies, mostly African, sent materials pertaining to their countries, such as books, maps, records, etc.

These were some of the more conspicuous forms of commitment which I have detailed, but people in cities all over the country responded to the struggle to crack the citadel of racism in America. Many northern colleges had organized assistance projects functioning on their campuses. . . .

We can cite a few achievements, both tangible and intangible [of the summer of 1964]. For instance, some of the volunteer workers and some of the staff workers saw the need for other forms of social action, either in the south or on their campuses or in their communities. One volunteer returned to the Berkeley campus and was instrumental in starting the Free Speech Movement. Other volunteers are working in the growing protest movements on other campuses. *Others have become part of the growing Southern Student Organizing Committee,* a group of southern white students who have patterned themselves after SNCC. Some have returned to northern cities to do grassroots organizing in the ghettos; former Freedom School teachers are now in the process of developing Freedom Schools in New York City.

Three SNCC workers left the state to develop the Free Southern Theatre to provide real theatre for those in the Black Belt who have no theatre. In the way of legislation, there is the Civil Rights Bill, the pending Voting Bill, and the pending legislation curbing the activities of the Ku Klux Klan, with the possibility of getting Federal protection for civil rights workers.

The participating organizations themselves were stimulated to extend themselves into other areas, and into other forms of action. The Medical Committee for Human Rights has expanded considerably and has started recruiting more doctors and nurses. They have purchased mobile hospital units to use in the Deep South; and plans have been discussed for the building of clinics in Mississippi. More lawyers are entering into the struggle. The Southern Christian Leadership Conference and the National Association for the Advancement of Colored People are expanding their base of operations. The Congress of Racial Equality staff working in Mississippi submitted plans to the National Action Council for the creation of a Southern Regional Office which would operate over a wider area in the Deep South. SNCC has started the new year with plans for a Blackbelt Project and a People's Conference to discuss new methods and goals.

The Mississippi experience raised some important questions which need to be answered. Do we continue working inside of, or outside of the existing institutional structure? Can a similar program be activated in northern ghettos? What is the future of the FDP idea and the Freedom Schools? How can we further expand and utilize direct action and civil disobedience as they were used in Atlantic City and Washington, D.C.? How can we force the public into a critical reexamination which will extend into every phase of human endeavor? What is the future role and direction of the entire civil rights movement, beyond the present attack on racism?

Perhaps, as in Mississippi, the thing to do is enter into every block, every neighborhood, every community and ask the people; get them to speak for themselves. If nothing else, Mississippi has shown that a real grassroots movement is possible, if it has its base in those who have been neglected the most.

17

The Freedom Schools: Concept and Organization, No. 2, 1965

STAUGHTON LYND

Professor Lynd directed the Freedom Schools during the 1964 Mississippi Summer Project. He continues an active life in Youngstown, Ohio.

. . . Before presenting the program of the Mississippi Freedom School Convention, let me try to convey a little of the feel of the occasion. Delegates were to arrive in Meridian the evening of Friday, August 7. On Thursday I drove up from Jackson with Luis Perez, who was trying to start a Freedom School in Neshoba County, where the three men had been killed. The housing committee placed us in a home just across the street from the Meridian Freedom School. It had no bathroom of any kind. At one in the morning we were awakened by Mark and Betty Levy, the able and indefatigable coordinators of the school, and members of the student planning committee. This was the week that the bodies of the three missing men were found. The Negro community of Meridian, we learned, had planned a funeral Friday night for James Chaney. Groups of silent marchers would leave a number of churches at dusk and walk to the church where the service would be held. This was just the time when delegates to the Freedom School Convention would be arriving. There might very well be a riot in response to the funeral. In the shadowy office of the Freedom School we tried to decide what our responsibility was to the delegates and their parents. We decided that they should come and participate in the funeral if they wished.

They came. As I drove groups of late-arriving delegates from the bus station to the Freedom School, we passed the lines of silent marchers converging at the church. Some wore dark suits and ties. Some did not. It made no difference for all one noticed was their faces.

Saturday morning the Convention began. Over the front of the room was a large handpainted sign: "Freedom Is A Struggle." At one side was another neatly lettered sign with the times and places of workshops and plenary sessions. At lunch we gathered around Roscoe Jones and sang and sang. That evening the Holly Springs Freedom School presented "Seeds of Freedom," a play based on the life of Medgar Evers. At the end, the girl playing Mrs. Evers said she would carry on her husband's struggle, and each member of the cast ("students" and "teachers") told why they had come to Freedom School. Then the Free Southern Theater, a group of professional quality, organized by SNCC's John O'Neal and Gilbert Moses (no relation to Bob), presented Martin Duberman's *In White America*. It too had an interpolated ending. Susan Wahman, wife of Tom Wahman who helped me with Freedom School administration, spoke the words which Rita Schwerner had said to President Johnson: "I want my husband."

Half a program had been adopted Saturday afternoon, the rest Sunday afternoon, after a second round of morning workshops. A. Philip Randolph addressed the youngsters on the need for economic as well as political programs, something their program showed that they already knew. Jim Forman, SNCC's Executive Secretary, talked about the students of Africa who went on to higher education but came back to their people to put this education to work. Bob Moses, characteristically, asked the Convention questions. Did they want to carry on Freedom Schools in this winter? Why? Did they want Freedom School *after* public school, or *instead* of public school? Why? What about the problem of graduating from an unaccredited school?

Most of the delegates favored returning to public school and at-tempting to improve them (here was the seed of the idea of boycott).

At the end of Sunday afternoon all were exhausted, as always at conventions. We struggled on to the end of the program. With a joy-ful shout, the program was declared adopted. Then one young man asked for the floor. "Wait," he said, "I move that copies of this pro-gram be sent to every member of the Mississippi legislature, to Pres-ident Johnson, and to the Secretary General of the United Nations [tumultuous applause], and—wait, wait—a copy to the Library of Congress for its permanent records [pandemonium]. . . . "

18

Life in Mississippi: An Interview with Fannie Lou Hamer, No. 2, 1965

J. H. O'DELL

This article is from the special issue on the Mississippi Freedom Summer, "Mississippi: Opening Up the Closed Society." At the time of this interview, Mrs. Fannie Lou Hamer was vice chairman of the Mississippi Freedom Democratic Party (MFDP) and a candidate for Congress from the Second Congressional District of that state. J. H. O'Dell, an editor of Freedomways, *was director of the SCLC's voter registration program in the South.*

...*O'Dell:* Mrs. Hamer, it's good to see you again. We want to talk about some of your early childhood experiences which helped to make you the kind of person you are and provided the basis for your becoming so active in the Freedom Movement.

Hamer: I would like to talk about some of the things that happened that made me know that there was something wrong in the south from a child. My parents moved to Sunflower County when I was two years old. I remember, and I will never forget, one day—I was six years old and I was playing beside the road and this plantation owner drove up to me and stopped and asked me "could I pick cotton." I told him I didn't know and he said, "Yes. You can. I will give you things that you want from the commissary store," and he named things like crackerjacks and sardines—and it was a huge list that he called off. So I picked the 30 pounds of cotton that week, but I found out what actually happened was he was trapping me into beginning the work I was to keep doing and I never did get out of his debt again. My parents tried so hard to do what they could to keep us in school, but school didn't last but four months out of the year and most of the time we didn't have clothes to wear. My parents would make huge crops of sometimes 55 to 60 bales of cotton. Being from a big family where there were 20 children, it wasn't too hard to pick that much cotton. But my father, year after year, didn't get too much money and I remember he just kept going. Later on he did get enough money to buy mules. We didn't have tractors, but he bought mules, wagons, cultivators and some farming equipment. As soon as he bought that and decided to rent some land, because it was always better if you rent the land, but as soon as he got the mules and wagons and everything, somebody went to our trough—a white man who didn't live very far from us—and he fed the mules Paris Green, put it in their food and it killed the mules and our cows. That knocked us right back down. And things got so tough then I began to wish I was white. We worked all the time, just worked and then we would be hungry and my mother was clearing up a new ground trying to help to feed us for $1.25 a day. She was using an axe, just like a man, and something flew up and hit her in her eye. It eventually caused her to lose both her eyes and I began to get sicker and sicker of the system there. I used to see my mother wear clothes that would have so many patches on them, they had been done over and over and over again. She would do that but she would try to keep us decent. She still would be ragged and I always said if I lived to get grown and had a chance, I was going to try to get something for my mother and I was going to do something for the Black man of the south if it would cost my life; I was determined to see that things were changed. My mother got down sick in '53 and she lived with me, an invalid, until she passed away in 1961. And during the time she was staying with me sometime I would be worked so hard I couldn't sleep at night. . . .

O'Dell: What kind of work were you doing?

Hamer: I was a timekeeper and sharecropper on the same plantation I was fired from during the time she was with me, if there was
something I had to do without, I was determined to see that she did
have something in her last few years. I went almost naked to see that
my mother was kept decent and treated as a human being for the first
time in all of her life. My mother was a great woman. To look at her
from the suffering she had gone through to bring us up—20 children: 6 girls and 14 boys, but still she taught us to be decent and to
respect ourselves, and that is one of the things that has kept me
going, even after she passed. She tried so hard to make life easy for
us. Those are the things that forced me to try to do something different and when this Movement came to Mississippi I still feel it is
one of the greatest things that ever happened because only a person
living in the State of Mississippi knows what it is like to suffer; knows
what it is like to be hungry; knows what it is like to have no clothing
to wear. And these people in Mississippi State, they are not "down";
all they need is a chance. And I am determined to give my part not
for what the Movement can do for me, but what I can do for the
Movement to bring about a change in the State of Mississippi. Actually, some of the things I experienced as a child still linger on; what
the white man has done to the Black people in the south! . . .

19

The Politics of Necessity and Survival in Mississippi, No. 2, 1966

LAWRENCE GUYOT and MIKE THELWELL

Following are excerpts from a two-part article by two leaders of the Mississippi Freedom Democratic Party (MFDP). Lawrence Guyot was at the time chairman of the MFDP, and Mike Thelwell was director of its Washington office during the "challenge." The term "relocation of population" used by the Mississippi legislature, is sadly familiar in 1999. It is also interesting that according to this article, the Mississippi Welfare Agency distributed leaflets "extolling the generosity of welfare and wage rates in northern cities."

The New Mississippi Plan: Gradual Depopulation

. . . The posture of the Government of Mississippi towards the Negro population did not change significantly from 1890 up to the 1950s. At this time, the rumblings caused by the Supreme Court school decision, and the spreading wave of Negro demands for justice caused the State to rethink their plan. One extremely significant change had taken place since the end of the Second World War. Whereas, in the past, it had been necessary, even to the extent of violence and fraud, to keep Negroes in the State for economic reasons, technological changes in the cotton fields were beginning to make large concentrations of Negroes unnecessary.

In the early sixties, the first modern voter registration drives, which is to say the first signs of sustained political activity in the Negro community, were begun. At that time, there was an attitude prevalent in the older Civil Rights groups, notably the NAACP, that Mississippi had to be changed from outside pressure. Inherent in this attitude was the belief that it was not possible for Negroes in Mississippi to organize for political action without a disproportionate cost in human life. What was established, under federal conditions, by that first small group of Student Nonviolent Coordinating Committee (SNCC) organizers, and the local Negroes, is that it was possible to organize politically and to survive. And, as far-fetched as this may sound today, the right to organize politically in Mississippi was really in the balance during those violent months in 1962. That the Mississippi Freedom Democratic Party (MFDP) exists today is due to the determined heroism of the small group who fought and won that first battle.

It is at this point where even the most hide-bound racist could recognize that the Movement in Mississippi was not to be driven out by violence and economic reprisal, that the change in the State's policies began to be evident. This change focused on the fact that there were just too many potential voters in the Negro community, and that Mississippi had the highest percentage of Negroes of any State in the Union. (Later, during the debate over the 1964 Civil Rights Bill, the Dixiecrats were to express this fear of the large Negro population, by their advocacy of a program of "equalizing the proportional Negro population of all states," in which they challenged the nation to undertake a program of relocating the Negro population so that each state would have the same proportion of Negroes.)

In Mississippi the State began a program that can best be characterized as one of gradual genocide, the goal of which was to effect the dispersal or extinction of the Negro population.

The White Citizens Councils were organized, and in Mississippi received financial support for their programs from the State through the Sovereignty Commission. Richard Morphew, Public Relations

Director of the Councils, admitted to receiving $90,000 from the State. In communities touched by the movement the Citizens Councils launched counter programs designed "to make it impossible for Negroes involved in agitation" to get work, credit, in short to remain in the community.

This was particularly true in the Second Congressional (Delta) District, where the densest concentrations of Negro population are to be found. It is in this area where the huge plantations are located and where the large reservoir of Negro labor had to be maintained. In this area the Negro population is predominantly agricultural laborers, who live either on plantations, sharecrop a small "section," or else are herded together into tar-paper and clap-board shanty towns from which they are fetched in trucks and busses to their work on the plantations. To a person going through one of these towns the dominant impression is of large numbers of people who are *waiting*. That is precisely their condition, they have been *kept* available, in a kind of perpetual waiting for the times when their labor would be needed on the plantations. So long as they were needed they were given credit, welfare, or some form of subsistence during the winter months. Even in the best of seasons, families that worked full season in the fields—an increasingly rare occurrence—would be forced as a matter of course to go on welfare during the winter. It was in this manner that their economic dependence was maintained as a matter of political and economic policy.

However, with Negroes clamoring for the ballot and the mechanization of the cotton fields rendering Negro labor more and more unnecessary, an entirely new situation came into being in Mississippi.

These changed conditions precipitated a kind of grim race between the Negro community and the State. It has been our necessity to militate for the franchise before the new conditions forced so many Negroes out as to render the franchise meaningless in the depleted community. The State's policy was to delay and obstruct Negro voting until the community had been thinned out. There have been specific acts that the State has taken against the Negroes that are illustrative of this warfare.

Welfare payments to entire communities, and particularly persons who have attempted to register, have been severely cut back. In the same communities the Welfare Agency has distributed leaflets extolling the generosity of welfare and wage rates in northern cities like Chicago.

The State has steadfastly maintained that it is unable to afford the cost of distributing free federal surplus food to needy Delta communities. This despite the fact that it can afford to subsidize Citizens Council propaganda broadcasts, appropriated $50,000 to lobby against the 1964 Civil Rights Bill, has undertaken the cost of the legal defense of any County Clerk indicted under the 1957, '64 or '65 Civil Rights Bills for failing to register Negroes, and which could in 1964 afford to double the manpower of the Highway Safety Patrol, and purchase thousands of dollars worth of military weaponry to use against the Summer Project.

In 1961, the Congressman from the Delta, Jamie H. Whitten, in his capacity as Chairman of the House Sub-committee on Appropriation of the Agriculture Committee, killed a measure that would have provided for the training of 3, 000 tractor drivers in Mississippi. Two-thirds of the applicants for this program were Negro.

These actions by the State represent essentially a changing of the rules, an alteration of the economic arrangement in which winter credit and subsistence to agricultural workers was central. Viciously effective, it leaves thousands of Negroes with the alternatives of starving or leaving. It poses a serious crisis to the Negro community, especially since those affected have been deprived of all opportunity to develop skills which would enable them to adjust to the requirements of an industrial society.

As 1966 opens, the economic interests in Mississippi have moved against the Delta population with a new ferocity. What appears to be the beginning of an organized wave of evictions has begun and some 250 families—about 2200 human beings—have already moved or have been informed that there will be no work for them this spring. It has been estimated that between 10,000 and 12,000 persons will lose their homes and livelihood this current season. These families are not eligible for social security, unemployment compensation or any state or federal welfare program. The plantation owners are not required to give prior notice or compensation to those displaced. On one plantation in Bolivar County the owner gave notice to nearly 100 workers by giving them ten dollars each and advising them to go to Florida. Many of the evictees are active in the MFDP and the Civil Rights Movement, but the evictions represent the bulk dismissal of unskilled workers on the large plantations. Only skilled workers—tractor drivers, cultivator and cotton picking machine operators are being retained. This situation is aggravated by the actions of the Mississippi Economic Council, an association of planters and business men which has been campaigning for the rapid mechanization of cotton production as a means of spurring the Negro exodus, and by the fact that this year, the Federal acreage allotments for cotton production have been cut by 35 percent.

The economic squeeze is undoubtedly the most effective and cruel of the State's weapons, but the full force of the "embattled minority" neurosis, that guides the actions of white rulers of Mississippi, was most fully reflected by the legislation introduced, and in many cases passed in the legislative session in the spring of 1964.

When SNCC announced the plans for the Summer Project of 1964 a special session of the State Legislature was called and the legislative record shows clearly that Mississippi's attitudes towards the Black population has remained remarkably free of change since the 1840s. Introduced and passed were: a bill outlawing economic boycotts; two bills outlawing the picketing of public buildings (courthouses are the scenes of registration attempts). Both bills were almost identical but the second was to be used in the event the first was declared unconstitutional by the federal courts. A series of police oriented bills was introduced; these provided for extra deputies, for security and patrol personnel for public institutions, for placing the Safety Patrol at the disposal of the Governor and doubling its manpower, providing for a curfew which could be enforced at the discretion of local police authorities, providing for the sharing of municipal police forces during civil disturbances, providing for juveniles arrested for civil rights activities to be treated as adults, and finally a bill to prohibit the summer volunteers from entering the State.

On the question of education, bills were passed to prohibit the establishment of freedom schools and community centers and to revoke the charter of the integrated Tougaloo College. The pattern of the "Old Plan" [immediately following Reconstruction] of control by military force and restriction of educational opportunities can be clearly recognized in these legislative proposals.

Two pieces of legislation introduced in this session deserve special comment, as they are symptomatic of a species of desperate hysteria that is completely unpredictable and therefore dangerous.

The first provided for the sterilization of persons convicted of a third felony. This was introduced by Rep. Fred Jones of Sunflower County in which there is a Negro majority. Jones was then a member of the Executive Committee of the Citizens' Council. While not specifically mentioning Negroes, the bill contained a clause placing the ordering of sterilization at the discretion of the all-white trustees of Parchman Penitentiary and since Negroes are more subject to criminal conviction in Mississippi courts, the intent of the proposal was clear.

A similar bill was introduced and *passed*, though with amendments. This bill provided for the sterilization of parents of the second illegitimate child, with the alternative of a prison sentence of from three to five years. In introducing this, Rep. Meeks of Webster County clearly indicated that it was intended towards the Black population. After passing the House the bill went to the Senate where it passed with amendments deleting sterilization and making the birth of the second illegitimate child a misdemeanor rather than a felony and lessening the sentence. When it came back to the House for ratification, the proponents of sterilization argued for its inclusion, Rep. Ben Owen of Columbus saying, as reported by the *Delta Democratic Times* of May 21, "This is the only way I know of to stop this rising black tide that threatens to engulf us." The bill finally passed as amended by the Senate.

We have been at pains to delineate this background of social, economic and political attitudes, actions and conditions in some detail. It is only from this perspective—not one of individual and irrational acts of racism, but one of rational, organized, and programmatic oppression on the part of the power machine of the State, that the plight of Mississippi's Black population, and the MFDP response to it can be understood.

The Political Movement in Mississippi

In the light of the conditions we have outlined, the Movement in Mississippi recognized the need for effective and speedy political changes in the State before most of the Negro population had to face the choice of starvation or migration. The answer to the prevalent northern question, "Why stay?" is simply, where is there for an agricultural Negro to go?

It was evident that the resources of education, training, medical facilities, housing, food and employment that the community needed could only come from massive government programs which the State was not prepared to participate in. The federal government, while possessing these resources, was not inclined to initiate any such program in Mississippi for a number of reasons, foremost among which is its traditional and scrupulous respect for the right of the State government to conduct the affairs of its concentration camp as it sees fit. There is hardly one federal program, including the Poverty Program, which does not require the approval of the State Governor. The obvious answer is to change the composition and thus policies of the State government.

However, in 1963, this kind of thinking was the most rarified and remote kind of theory. What kind of effective political participation and what kind of organization were possible for a people whom the entire apparatus of government operated to exclude and disperse. The concept of parallel elections or "freedom ballots" provided a partial solution. Its operation was simple. While most Negroes could not vote, a Negro could stand for election, and the Negro community could unofficially cast their votes in a parallel election. . . .

[In 1963,] over 80,000 votes were cast in the Negro community for Dr. Henry for Governor and Rev. King as his Lieutenant Governor.

Even from this first freedom election, it must be noted, the underlying concept of challenging the illegal state structure, outside that structure, was present. Our intention was to file a suit calling for the voiding of election results on the basis of the voting section of the 1957 Civil Rights Bill and a Reconstruction Period statute, providing for the challenging of state elections for reason of racial discrimination. Although this particular challenge never materialized, the challenge *concept* persisted. This was based on a need to demonstrate some kind of political effectiveness, which could not be accomplished inside a State where you could not vote, and on the fact that the government of Mississippi, and all elections it conducted were, and had been since 1890, in clear and indefensible violation of the Constitution. . . .

Although the "challenge" to the gubernatorial elections of 1963 never materialized, perhaps the most significant practical consequence of the King-Henry campaign was the statewide nature of the campaign. It took the Movement, for the first time, beyond activities affecting a single town, county, municipality or electoral district, and placed us in the area of statewide organization. This consideration is now a basic tenet of MFDP organization and operation, that the entire Negro community, all 45 percent of the vote it represents, must be united in an independent, radically democratic organization so as to be able to act politically from a position of maximum strength. Without this kind of solid community organization the vote, when it comes, will be close to meaningless as an implement of necessary social change. It is the beginnings of this organization that emerged from that campaign, and in the summer of 1964, the statewide organization was formalized by a series of precinct, county, and district meetings, culminating in a State Convention of the Mississippi Freedom Democratic Party.

PART THREE

International Solidarity

ESTHER COOPER JACKSON

CONSTANCE POHL

At the close of World War II, revolutionary "winds of change" swept across Africa and transformed the continent. Africans revolted against the European empires and created independent nations where there once had been colonies. Many of the leaders of these anticolonial revolutions wrote for *Freedomways,* among them Kwame Nkrumah, Julius Nyerere, Jomo Kenyatta, and Agostinho Neto.

Freedomways disseminated the writings of the African leaders in the United States, and it informed readers in Africa and Asia about the civil rights movement. By promoting the exchange among activists internationally, the journal advanced the liberation of all peoples.

The influence of W.E.B. Du Bois was evident in the journal's solidarity with Africa. Du Bois organized the Pan-African Conferences from 1919 to 1945, wrote many articles and books on African history and culture, and initiated the project of the *Encyclopedia Africana*. It is little wonder that leaders like Nkrumah called him the father of African liberation. Appropriately, Du Bois's "The American Negro and the Darker World" opens this section. In this article Du Bois described the legacy shared by all people of African descent, because of slavery and the European colonization in Africa. No one said it better than the Caribbean scholar and author of *The Black Jacobins*, C.L.R. James, in the memorial issue for Dr. Du Bois: "Far in advance of all the official politicians and publicists of his time, in his pan-African conferences and his writings, he made the world aware that the emancipation of Africa and the life, liberty and the pursuit of happiness by Africans was an international responsibility. The League of Nations and now the United Nations pursue the paths he charted. Here there is no American whose head reaches near his massive shoulders."

Du Bois warned in *The World and Africa* (reprinted as an editorial, "The Giant Stirs") that Black Americans "have a chance to trade wide breaks in the American color line for acquiescence in American and West Europeans' control of the world's colored peoples. They are being bribed to trade equal status in the United States for the slavery of the majority of men."

Freedomways editors addressed the concerns of "people of the Caribbean area and the Caribbean communities of New York and London" in several special issues. The poetry of the future Nobel laureate Derek Walcott and articles by President Cheddi Jagan of Guyana appeared, as well as short stories and political analyses by Caribbean writers.

Freedomways made major contributions to the movement to end the war in Vietnam. Black leaders like Paul Robeson recognized that the Vietnamese were rebelling against the French colonial empire in Indochina and so opposed the U.S. entry into that war. Robeson's clarity of vision is evident in the articles first written in the 1950s and reprinted in *Freedomways,* "Ho Chi Minh Is Toussaint L'Ouverture" and "Playing Catch-Up." In retaliation for Robeson's solidarity with the peoples of the emerging nations, the American cold warriors accused him of treason and deprived him of his passport. But Robeson predicted correctly that American politicians should not expect African Americans to pick up the gun against their "darker brothers." Indeed, this cry surfaced in the antiwar movement of the 1960s as many young men in the United States refused, like Muhammad Ali, to be drafted to kill Vietnamese people.

Two other major contributions of African Americans to the peace movement are included as well: Robert Browne's in-depth analysis of the Vietnam struggle, the first article of its kind in a Black journal, and Martin Luther King's clear-sighted denunciation of the inhumanity of the war, "A Time to Break Silence." With this speech, Dr. King brought together the civil rights and antiwar movements and had a stunning effect on the nation.

In its 1962 issue, *Freedomways* embraced the struggle against South African apartheid with the article "Three African Freedom Movements." By the end of the 1970s the movement had galvanized Americans, particularly Black Americans, as can be seen in "The African-American Manifesto on Southern Africa" by the Black Congressional Caucus. *Freedomways* ceased publishing several years before the magnificent triumph of Nelson Mandela and the African National Congress that the journal had aided since 1962.

20

The American Negro and the Darker World, No. 3, 1968

W.E.B. DU BOIS

This speech was originally delivered April 30, 1957, in New York City on the occasion of the celebration of the second anniversary of the Asian-African (Bandung) conference and the rebirth of Ghana. Freedomways *reprinted the article in the centennial year of Dr. Du Bois's birth, 1968.*

From the fifteenth through the seventeenth centuries, the Africans imported to America regarded themselves as temporary settlers destined to return eventually to Africa. Their increasing revolts against the slave system, which culminated in the eighteenth century, showed a feeling of close kinship to the motherland and even well into the nineteenth century they called their organizations "African," as witness the "African Unions" of New York and Newport, and The African Churches of Philadelphia and New York. In the West Indies and South America there was even closer indication of feelings of kinship with Africa and the East.

The planters' excuse for slavery was advertised as conversion of Africa to Christianity; but soon American slavery appeared based on the huge profits of the "sugar empire" and the "cotton kingdom." As plans were laid for the expansion of the slave system, the slaves themselves sought freedom by increasing revolt which culminated in the 18th century. In Haiti they won autonomy; in the United States they fled from the slave states in the south to the free states in the north and to Canada. Here the Free Negroes helped form the Abolition Movement, and when that seemed to be failing, the Negroes began to plan for migration to Africa, Haiti and South America.

Civil war and emancipation intervened and American Negroes looked forward to becoming free and equal citizens here with no thought of returning to Africa or of kinship with the world's darker peoples. However the rise of the Negro was hindered by disfranchisement, lynching, and caste legislation. There was some recurrence of the "Back To Africa" idea and increased sympathy for darker folk who suffered the same sort of caste restrictions as American Negroes.

This brought curious dichotomy. In our effort to be recognized as Americans, we American Negroes naturally strove to think American and adopt American folkways. We began to despise all yellow, brown and black peoples. We especially withdrew from all remembrance of kinship with Africa and denied with the white world that Africa ever had a history or indigenous culture. We did not want to be called "Africans" or Negroes and especially not "Negresses." We tried to invent new names for our group. We began to call yellow people "chinks" and "coolies"; and dark whites "dagoes." This was natural under our peculiar situation. But it made us more easily neglect or lose sight of the peculiar change in the world which was linking us with the colored peoples of the world not simply because of the essentially unimportant fact of skin color, but because of the immensely important fact of economic condition.

In the latter part of the eighteenth century, Europe had begun to expand its trade and to import raw materials to be transformed into consumer goods. Machines and methods for manufacture of goods increased tremendously.

When the revolt of the slaves, especially in Haiti, and the moral revolt in England, and America, led to the emancipation of slaves, the merchants who had invested in slave labor began to change the form of their investment; they seized colonies in Asia and Africa and in-

President Ben Bella, leader of the Algerian Liberation Movement (left, seated), W.E.B. Du Bois (center, seated), and Shirley Graham Du Bois (left, standing). Four aides traveled with Ben Bella to Ghana to meet with Dr. Du Bois where this photo was taken.

stead of exporting native labor used the land and labor on the spot and exported raw materials to Europe for consumption or further manufacture. Immense amounts of wealth for capital were seized by Europeans in India and China, in South America and elsewhere; and thus colonial imperialism arose to dominate the world. Most of the exploited peoples were colored, yellow, brown, and black. A scientific theory arose and was widely accepted which taught that the white people were superior to the colored and had a right to rule the world and use all land and labor for the benefit and comfort of Europeans.

While the emancipation of slaves in America involved great losses for European investors, the simultaneous seizure of wealth of Asia and the new control of colonial labor enabled new rich employers in Europe and North America to accumulate vast sums of capital in private hands and to start the factory system. This method of conducting industry used new inventions and sources of power so as to drive laborers off the land, herd them in factories and reduce them to semi-slavery in Europe, by a wage contract.

This brought the labor movement. In the more advanced European countries labor and its friends fought for more political power, public school education, higher wages and better conditions. These things they gradually secured by union organization and strikes. On the other hand, in Eastern Europe there was little education and wages remained very low. Political power rested in the hands of an aristocracy which became rich through encouraging and protecting western investment. This semi-colonial status of labor was even worse in South and Central America and in the West Indies, while in most of Asia and Africa the condition of colonial labor approached slavery.

Thereupon, arose the doctrine of socialism which demanded that the results of the manufacture of goods and the giving of services go to the labor involved and not mainly to the capitalists. This doctrine was in essence as old as human labor. Primitive labor got all the results of what it did or made. Many early societies like the first Christians and tribes in Africa lived as communal groups, sharing all results of work in common.

Slavery intervened, so that some workers were owned by others; then came aristocracy where a few took the results of the work of the many and the nation became the abode of a rich idle and privileged class who were served by the mass of laborers. Protest against this and the doctrine that income should in some degree become the measure of effort became an increasing demand from the ancient world through the mediaeval world and was studied and scientifically stated by Karl Marx in the first half of the nineteenth century. He proposed that capital belong to the state and that workers run the state. Capitalists vehemently opposed this but were compelled partially to meet the demands of labor by raising wages. In the capitalist nations this raise was more than compensated for by increased profits due to exploitation in colonial and semi-colonial lands. Also, the spread of democratic control was counterbalanced by hiring white labor to war on colonial labor, and using public taxation for war rather than social purposes.

From the defeat of Napoleon in 1815 to the first world war there was continuous struggle led by white troops armed with the most ingenious weapons to keep colonial peoples from revolt, and most of the peoples of the world in subjection to Western Europe.

This was the situation at the beginning of the twentieth century. British, French, and American capitalists owned the colonies, with the richest natural resources and best controlled and lowest paid labor. By 1900, they were reaching out for other colonies elsewhere: other nations with fewer or no colonies, led by Germany, demanded a reallotment of colonial wealth. This brought on the First World War.

But, it brought more than this; the assault of Germany and her allies was so fierce that Britain and France had to ask help from their colored colonies. They needed Black manpower and without it France would have been overthrown by Germany in the first few months of war. Britain needed food and materials from Asia, Africa, and the West Indies. The United States needed American Negroes who formed an inner labor colony as laborers and stevedores. This meant an increase of wages and rights for colonial peoples. In the United States, it brought the first recognition since 1876 of the equal citizenship of Negroes.

The workers of Eastern Europe, South and Central America were not as badly off as the American serf and Chinese and Indian coolies, but they were sunk in poverty, disease, and ignorance. They were oppressed by their own rich classes working hand in glove with white western investors. When war came they starved and died. The situation became so desperate that Russians and Hungarians refused to fight. Their rulers sought compromise by trying to replace imperial rule with Western European democracy. But the Russian leaders, students of Karl Marx and led by Lenin, demanded a socialist state.

The western world united to forestall this experiment. It said that no socialist state could succeed, but lest it should and lower the profits of capitalists, the effort must be stopped by force of arms. Sixteen capitalist nations, including Britain, France, Germany, the United States, and Japan, invaded Russia and fought for ten years by every means, civilized and uncivilized, to overthrow the plans of the Soviet Union. However, the worldwide collapse of capitalism in 1930, made this attack fail and the world witnessed the founding of the first Socialist State

Then came a new and even more unexpected diversion. The depression which was the partial collapse of capitalism, was so bad in Germany, Spain, and Italy that those states fell into the hands of two dictators, Hitler and Mussolini. Backed by capitalists, they seized power and demanded control not only of the colonial world then dominated by Britain, France, and North America, but domination of the whole world. The west tried to compromise, and offered practically everything demanded, but Hitler's greed and German ambition grew by what they fed upon. They were so convinced of their superior power over the west that Hitler started a Second World War; like the first, aimed at control by part of the white race over the resources, land, and labor of the rest of the world, he began a wild career. He killed six million Jews, accusing them of being the main cause of the depression and of being an inferior race. He conquered France, and chased the British off the continent. They huddled on their own small island to make a last stand. But, here Hitler paused. He had a new vision. If instead of wasting his power on a desperate England he turned east and seized the semi-colonial lands of the Soviet Union and the Balkan states, then from this central heartland he could win Asia and Africa and after that turn back to deliver the *coup de grace* to Britain and America. Hitler thereupon scrapped his treaty with the Soviets, which they, spurned by the west, had been forced to accept, and to the relief of Britain and the United States, Hitler turned to conquer Russia. Englishmen and Americans said with Truman, "Let them kill as many of each other as possible." So, although Hitler's rear was exposed, the western powers held off attack for a year and when they did attack went to the defense of their African colonies and not to aid the Soviet Union. The west was sure that the Soviets would fall in six weeks and thus rid the world of socialism and Nazism at one stroke.

The result was astonishing. The Soviet Union, almost unaided, conquered Hitler, saved the Baltic States and the Balkans. Roosevelt, Churchill, and Stalin faced a world in which the Soviet Union, Britain, France and the United States must go forward toward a world in which socialism would grow; not perhaps as complete communistic states like the Soviet Union, but in states like the United States and England where social progress under the New Deal and the Labor government would advance together along paths leading to the same ultimate goal.

This co-operation American business repudiated when it invented the atom bomb. After Roosevelt died, our capitalists determined to drive communism from the world and push socialism back. The crusade failed. India became independent and adopted modified socialism; China conquered the stool pigeons whom we paid to stop her revolution and became a Communist state. The Soviet Union, instead of failing as we predicted, became one of the foremost nations of the earth, with the best educational system and freedom from church domination and second only to this nation in industry. Also the Soviet Union took a legal stand against the color line and stood ready to oppose colonialism. We tried to re-conquer China during the war in Korea and to help France retain Indo-China. But again we failed. Meantime we formed the greatest military machine on earth and spent and are still spending more money preparing for war than ever any other nation on earth at any time has spent.

The excuse for our action is that communism is a criminal conspiracy of evil-minded men and that private capitalism is so superior to socialism that we should use every effort to stop its advance. Here we rest today and to sharpen our aim and concentrate our strength, we starve our schools, lessen social service in medicine and housing, curtail our freedom of speech, limit our pursuit of learning, and are no longer free to think or discuss.

Where now does that leave American Negroes? We cannot teach the peoples of Africa or Asia because so many of them are either communistic or progressing toward socialism, while we do not know what socialism is and can study it only with difficulty or danger. After the First World War we Negroes were in advance of many colored peoples. We started in two ways to lead Africans. In the West Indies, Garvey tried to have Negroes share in western exploitation of Africa. White industry stopped him before he could begin. In the United States Negro churches carried on missionary effort and a few Negroes in 1918 tried to get in touch with Africa so as to share thoughts and plans. Four Pan-African Congresses were held in 1919, 1921, 1923, and 1925, which American, African, and West Indian Negroes attended, and a few persons from Asia and South America. They made a series of general demands for political rights and education. The movement met much opposition. However, it encouraged similar congresses which still exist in all parts of Africa and it was the inspiration back of the mandates commission of the League of Nations and the trusteeship council of the United Nations.

After a lapse of twenty years, a fifth Pan-African Congress was held in England in 1945. It was attended by Negro labor leaders from all parts of Africa and from the West Indies and one from the United States. Especially prominent were the delegates from Kenya and from Ghana, the first independent Black dominion of the British Commonwealth. The resolutions adopted here had a clear socialist trend, and further Pan-African Congresses were envisioned to be held in Africa.

Whither now do we go? We American Negroes can no longer lead the colored peoples of the world because they far better than we understand what is happening in the world today. But we can try to catch up with them. We can learn about China and India and the vast realm of Indonesia rescued from Holland. We can know of the new ferment in East, West, and South Africa. We can realize by reading, if not in classrooms, how socialism is expanding over the modern world and penetrating the colored world. So far as Africa is concerned we can realize that socialism is part of their past history and will without a shade of doubt play a large part in their future.

Here in our country, we can think, work and vote for the welfare state openly and frankly; for social medicine, publicly supported housing, state ownership of public power and public facilities; curbing the power of private capital and great monopolies and stand ready to meet and cooperate with world socialism as it grows among white and Black.

21

Address to the United Nations, No. 1, 1961

OSAGYEFO DR. KWAME NKRUMAH
President of the Republic of Ghana

Kwame Nkrumah considered Dr. Du Bois his greatest teacher. In 1961 President Nkrumah warned in this speech to the United Nations that there could be long-term consequences of neocolonial interference in the Congo. He proved right, and the effects are still with us today.

Mr. President, Distinguished Delegates:

I appear before you today on a sad and solemn occasion, the first meeting of the General Assembly since the murder of the Prime Minister of the Congo, Patrice Lumumba. . . .

I believe we must stand foursquare on what is one of the most important principles of international law and basic to the whole conception of the United Nations.

A government which comes into power as a result of a genuine revolution is entitled to international recognition. Otherwise a way is left open for interference in the internal affairs of member states. But an intervention from outside aimed at fomenting a revolution in a member state is as illegal as is an intervention aimed at suppressing a genuine revolution. If, as I believe, Mobutu's rebellion in Leopoldville, Tshombe's rebellion in Katanga and Kaloji's rebellion in South Kasai were engineered from outside, then any assistance to these rebels or any recognition of them in any form is intervention in the internal affairs of the Congo.

It is for this reason that Ghana so strongly deplored the decision of the United Nations to seat the so-called Kasavubu delegation. This action was not supported by any single country which had a contingent in the Congo, and it is, in my view, a glaring example of how universally accepted principles of international law are sacrificed to the exigencies of the cold war.

What has been done is not only to recognize in the United Nations a faction whose recognition is contrary to every principle of international law, but also to recognize as the Government of the Congo, a group which does not even claim to speak for the whole of the country.

The tragic fruit of this recognition is seen to-day in the fact that the so-called Government which was recognized by the United Nations, has made an armed attack at Matadi on the forces of the United Nations.

Even as I speak, the lives of soldiers of the United Nations contingents are threatened by the undisciplined mutineers enlisted by Kasavubu and Mobutu.

The significance of the Congo situation is that it gives the United Nations an opportunity to reassert its authority. If speedy and effective action is taken now in the Congo, the United Nations will have that prestige and moral backing which it must have if it is to tackle other even graver world problems. I have in mind the problems bound to arise over Angola, Mozambique, the Union of South Africa, Ruanda-Urundi, South West Africa, Algeria, the Rhodesias and any other African colonial territories. These are all potential problems for the United Nations, and the United Nations must work out now the machinery which can be used to solve such problems should the necessity arise. . . .

I would like to say a few preliminary words about how Ghana regards the Congo situation in general.

The murder of Patrice Lumumba is not merely the murder of an individual. It is the murder of that principle of legality which the United Nations has been advocating in the Congo. It is the grossest affront to the whole conception of collective action through the United Nations, and it marks the most cynical disregard of the authority of the United Nations by a puppet regime maintained in power by outside assistance in flagrant disregard of the Security Council resolutions.

Indeed, the murder is the culminating event which proves what Ghana has long contended, namely, that the United Nations cannot restore law and order in the Congo if it takes a neutral position between order and disorder, if it permits Parliament to be suppressed by mutineers and the constitution of the Republic disregarded and ignored.

The position at present is that though the Security Council resolutions have insisted that the integrity of the Congo must be preserved, Katanga is, under the very eyes of the United Nations, being detached from the Republic. The Security Council has repeatedly called for the removal of foreign troops, yet war is being waged by Belgian-led bands of mutineers supplied with arms from Belgium and equipped with Belgian military aircraft. An end must be made to this situation. As I said when I last addressed this Assembly, the Congo is the heart of Africa; any wound inflicted upon the Congo is a wound to the whole of Africa. Outside interference in the Congo is a threat to the independence of every African State and a further extension of the cold war.

It is with these considerations in mind that I put my proposals before you. The are:

First: A new and strengthened United Nations civil and military Command should be established in the Congo;

Second: This Command, and the contingents under it, must be primarily African and should take over complete responsibility for law and order in the Congo;

Third: All Congolese armed units should be disarmed; this disarming will involve their return to barracks and the surrender of their weapons to the new United Nations Command:

Fourth: The disarming and handing-over should be voluntary and should lead to the reorganization and re-training of the

Congolese National Army; but if certain factions will not cooperate, force must be used;

Fifth: All non-African personnel serving in the Congolese Army
must be expelled immediately;

Sixth: The United Nations Command should control the major
air and sea ports in the Congo so that the flow of arms and
equipment to warring factions may be stopped and adequate
support for United Nations troops be guaranteed;

Seventh: All foreign Diplomatic Missions and Representatives
should immediately leave the Congo for the time being in
order to give this new United Nations Command a fair
chance and to eliminate the cold war from the Congo;

Eighth: Once the military situation has been brought under control on these lines, all political prisoners must be released by
the new United Nations Command, and the new Command
should then convene Parliament under its auspices; those responsible for the murder of Patrice Lumumba and his close
associates should then be brought to justice.

It is self-evident that the first task of the United Nations is to allow
the Congolese people to be ruled by a government of their own
choice. The Congolese constitution provides a means by which such
a government can be chosen, and we support the Gizenga Government because it was chosen by this means and was the government
that invited the United Nations to the Congo.

The duty of the United Nations is not to force on the Congolese
people this or that government because the other states of the world
think that any particular government would be a suitable one for the
Congo. This is colonialism. I therefore do not understand the emphasis which a number of powers lay on recognizing this or that government. Ultimately, it must be the Congolese people who choose
their government and not the United Nations. What the United Nations must do is to see that the Congolese people have the opportunity to choose the government which they want.

One of the greatest sons of the United States of America, Thomas
Jefferson, laid down this principle, namely, that before recognizing a
government, that government must be supported by "the will of the
Nation, substantially declared."

The "will of the Nation substantially declared" can only be, under
modern conditions, obtained by the free exercise of representative in-

stitutions. Under the constitution of the Congo the representative institution charged with choosing the Government of the Congo is the Congolese Parliament. The President's duties consist of formally appointing to office Parliament's nominees. Unfortunately, with the murder of Patrice Lumumba and other prominent parliamentarians, the existing Parliament of the Congo is no longer likely to be fully representative. Further, so much has occurred since it was originally elected that the mandates upon which various members were chosen now bear little relation to the needs of the present situation. My proposal is, therefore, that there should be, as soon as the United Nations have established law and order, a new general election conducted under United Nations supervision and under conditions where every political party can freely canvass for its policy without fear, without force or without intimidation.

Before, therefore, accepting a decision of the present Congolese Parliament as an expression of the will of the nation, the United Nations must first satisfy itself that Parliament is not meeting under duress and that the balance of political forces has not been changed by organized murder.

The murder of Senators and Members of the Chamber, including that of Joseph Okito, the Vice President of the Senate killed at the same time as Patrice Lumumba, suggest that Kasavubu, Tshombe, Mobutu and Kalonji realized they would not be able indefinitely to resist pressure for a meeting of Parliament and determined to secure a majority by assassination.

What we need in the Congo is not a solution that is a compromise or seeks to reconcile the divergent views between East and West. What we want is a solution acceptable to the Congolese people and which ensures peace and stability in Africa and thus excludes the cold war from the continent. . . . We in Africa have a vested interest in peace. What is taking place in the Congo today could lead to serious conflagration which would set us all ablaze and spare no one. Unless this unhappy and ominous trend is arrested at once, a major wall will descend upon us. . . .

The Force Publique [of the Congo] was founded some seventy years ago by King Leopold II of the Belgians in his capacity as personal ruler of the Congo, and its object was to enforce what was known as "King Leopold's System." This system, which was described by the United Kingdom Foreign Secretary of the day, Lord Landsdowne, as "bondage under the most barbarous and inhuman conditions and maintained for mercenary motives of the most selfish character." This army of King Leopold was allowed to live on the land in return for assisting him to enforce such tyranny.

I have in my possession an old copy of the "St. Louis Post-Dispatch" dated the 26th July 1908. It contains Mark Twain's famous cartoon about the Congo—a huge pyramid of skulls flanked by mutilated skeletons on the top of which stands the Belgian King Leopold. There is also a long interview with a Mr. William Lange who was a former river captain in the employ of the Congo Government. There are photographs taken by Mr. Lange showing children with their hands cut off by the Force Publique and he described in detail how Belgium deliberately trained these troops in brutality. To use his own words, the Belgians "used to pat them on the back and praised them when they had committed some especially horrible piece of cruelty or had brought in as trophies of the day, the largest number of hands, feet or other parts of the human body."

It is only necessary to turn to the official document published by the Belgian Government in July 1960 to realize that the Force Publique still continued to behave in the same fashion. The Belgian officials' enquiry into the assaults, raping and murdering of Belgian in the Congo shows that, almost exclusively, these acts were committed by members of the Force Publique. It should be remembered that it was these same soldiers who had, only the year before, fiercely repressed the popular demonstrations for liberty in Leopoldville and who had a seventy year history of brutality behind them.

Let me put the issue clearly. Up until now, in effect, the United Nations has supported the mutinous Force Publique against the democratically elected Government of the Congo. The policy which I am putting to you now is that no Government can exist on such support. The Force Publique was a colonial army, trained in brutality and inhumanity and with a long and consistent history as the subservient tool of the Belgian colonial oppressor. Such a force, in the view of the Government of Ghana, can never be the basis upon which to build a government. . . .

It has been said that history repeats itself first as tragedy and then as a farce. We must make certain that we do not repeat as a farce the tragedy which befell Africa as the result of the Berlin Conference of 1885. This Conference was called to solve the problems of the

Congo. It ended by drawing up a set of rules to regulate the division of Africa among the great powers. This Berlin Conference was a gathering of the fourteen most important nations of the world at that time and they included the United States, the United Kingdom, Czarist Russia and France, whose successors in title provide four out of the five Permanent Members of the Security Council. The only interested parties not represented were the inhabitants of Africa whose welfare and progress it was the ostensible object of the Conference to assist. From the point of view of the powers attending, it would be impossible to quarrel with the proposals of the Conference which were to exclude colonial rivalry—the cold war of those days—from Africa by friendly agreement on how the continent should be divided up. Slavery was to be suppressed, trade promoted, missionary endeavor encouraged and Africa opened up to commerce and industry. Nevertheless, there is an important lesson for us to-day in the criticism which was made in the United States Congress at that time. A United States Congressman, Perry Belmont, after reciting the many advantages which Africa would supposedly receive as a result of the agreement reached between the Great Powers, thus concluded:

> Certainly all these are beneficial and desirable objects. But at least for us in the United States, these were and are, when worked out in Berlin for Africa, *European objects.*

Ghana's criticisms of the United Nations action are identical with those made long ago by this United States Congressman. The objects attempted are all beneficial and desirable but, at least for us in Africa, they are, when worked out in the Security Council and in the Secretariat of the United Nations, not essentially African objectives. They are primarily objectives aimed at halting the cold war by achieving a compromise between the great powers and they reflect, in all their imperfections, the struggle of the great powers over issues which do not affect the Congo or Africa.

The settlement arrived at by the Conference of Berlin was of course no settlement of the African problem. It split up the continent arbitrarily, dividing peoples of the same ethnic or historical background and drew frontiers through old established lines of trade and communications. It ushered in for Africa an era of unparalleled colonial oppression. . . .

In the same way as Africa was broken up into colonies by the great powers in their own interests at the Conference of Berlin, so today the Congo is in danger of being fragmented into small states—the clients of one or other of the great powers. There is danger of this being done either directly as in the case of the separatist movement in Katanga, or indirectly by means of federation imposed through outside pressure which might dismember the Congo as effectively as if it had been formally partitioned into separate states. . . .

22

What Happened in Ghana? The Inside Story, No. 3, 1966

SHIRLEY GRAHAM DU BOIS

Shirley Graham Du Bois was a founding editor of Freedomways. *In 1966 at the time of the overthrow of President Nkrumah's government, she was living in Ghana, where she had moved with her husband in 1962.*

It would be inaccurate to designate what happened in Ghana the last week in February 1966, as a *coup d'état*. None of the elements for this classic type of counter-revolution existed in Ghana. There was no revolution going on, no crumbling away of Government; the people were not groaning under the heel of tyranny and oppression and no Strong Man emerged from the Army bringing order and tranquility to a torn country. Far from it!

These are the proclaimed justifications for the historic *coup d'état*. But the *coup* of our decade is something quite different. Under the manipulation of imperialists and neo-colonialists it has been employed as the surest and most effective offensive against the freedom and independence of emerging peoples. In Latin America, in the Middle East, in Asia and now in Africa, the *coup* has operated successfully. For the moment the exploiters of Africa are breathing easier; they see the threat of African unity and ultimate strength receding. They have brought down Ghana! They think they have eliminated that worldwide symbol of African unity—Kwame Nkrumah!

Men of goodwill everywhere were shocked and bewildered. How could this happen in Ghana? Why? *Where* was the opposition? Visitors coming to Ghana for the past several years have been amazed by the evidence of progress which greeted them on every hand: the wide, well-paved roads traversing the country; the hospitals, free schools, housing developments, technical training colleges; the new industrial city of Tema with its busy, modern harbor and rising factories; the straight-legged village children, free from diseases and scourges seen in so many parts of Africa and Asia; the beauty of Accra's planned construction. They often remarked on the apparent eagerness with which the masses followed obviously exacting and determined leadership. How then could such a take-over come about in Ghana?

As clearly and objectively as possible I shall attempt to give some answers to these questions. I shall lay bare the structure of Ghana and point out the inherent weaknesses in that structure, the dangers from within and without, the mistakes made and the lessons other developing countries can learn. The imperialists and neo-colonialists are stepping up their drive in Africa. They are determined to halt progressive and anti-colonialist movements. Confronted as they are with ever-increasing difficulties within NATO, they are trying to turn themselves into a police force to guarantee the safety of their interests. South Africa and Portugal are more defiant than ever, and now Southern Rhodesia is joining South Africa in an effort to keep the Black man in subjugation.

I was the Director of Television in Ghana. In view of the fact that my home and offices were in the most "sensitive area," the area which first had to be taken over and "subdued," that my work was twisted into a horrible caricature of itself, that I escaped with only what could be crammed into suitcases and that some of my closest associates and friends are in dungeons, in exile or dead; considering all this, my objectivity may at times be a bit strained.

But, the other evening over Radio Cairo came the strains of a familiar Negro spiritual:

If I had a Hammer—I'd beat out Freedom,
If I had a Bell—I'd ring out Danger,
If I had a Song—I'd sing of Justice and Brotherhood
All over this World.

Well, I have a Hammer and I have a Bell; and the Song is buried deep in my heart. So here goes:

The Internal Structure of Ghana

The area of Ghana is approximately that of Great Britain, but the population is only seven and a half million. It was from the coast of Guinea, where Ghana is situated, that most of the slaves were carried off to America. Beginning in the 16th century, for more than three hundred years, the lands bordering on the Gulf of Guinea were the cause of fighting between the Portuguese, Spaniards, Dutch, Danes, French and English. Gold and crude diamonds were discovered early. The profitable traffic in slaves increased the struggle for possession. But, by the beginning of the 20th century most of this land had been divided between Great Britain and France.

With the production of cocoa the Gold Coast became one of the more important of the British colonies. They deemed it worthwhile to make some improvements in the lot of the "natives." Mission schools, where the young were taught to fear God and the white man, were encouraged. Mission "boys" made the "best" servants. The sons of subdued Chiefs of once powerful hereditary dynasties and a selected few from among those who, for some reason, were "especially deserving" were given secondary or even university education—the brightest being sent to England. This small *elite* attained bourgeois status. They acquired bourgeois culture and values and regarded the "natives" in much the same light as did the whites. On a somewhat lower scale were those trained for the civil service which was exacting, efficient and completely regimented. Faithful civil servants were sure of a good job for life, with pay considerably higher than their fellows. (Of course, not approaching the salary paid white civil servants sent out from Europe.) Another group allowed some freedom of action by the colonial masters was the traders, who by means of controlled "privileges" extorted, cheated and bullied the mass of people without stint. Many of these original traders were women, forerunners of the *market women* of today. These *market women* are well organized and had been an ever-present problem in pre-*coup* Ghana. Skilled in cornering trade and forcing up retail prices, their aim in life was to get rich quick through "free enterprise." They are opposed to any form of economic control.

In colonial days Accra was a sprawling commercial and administrative town, with a number of imposing, white Government buildings, one wide tree-lined street where large, comfortable houses set back in gardens, a polo ground, race track and sports club—trappings which made for pleasant, easy colonial life. The ubiquitous mosquito had prevented Europeans from permanently settling on large tracts of land as they did in East Africa. They came to the Gold Coast primarily to take out the riches which they found there. All roads led to the sea. Most of the native *elite* lived in Kumasi or Cape Coast. Those who did live in Accra occupied neat cottages tucked away on winding roads along with upper civil servants. There was plenty of available space but the "natives" who did not occupy servants' quarters in the yards, were crowded together in corrugated, tin huts near the waterfront, without sanitation or water.

Kwame Nkrumah returned to the Gold Coast in 1947 after an absence of fifteen years. He was not of the bourgeoisie. He belonged to a small tribe of hardy fisherfolk and artisans. Fathers of the Mission School which he had attended helped him through secondary school. Then, he went off to America. He had no money, but he managed to work his way through Lincoln University in Pennsylvania. After taking the master's degree, he went to London, found more work and took courses at the London School of Economics. Then followed some travel in Europe. Nkrumah returned home filled with ideas, all of them fusing into one burning purpose—to free his country from British rule!

Meanwhile, the colonial masters felt quite safe from any political upheaval which might threaten their profits from the Gold Coast. They contemplated that in due time the reins of government would be handed over to the Gold Coast *elite,* whose social status and "superior intellectual qualifications" equipped them for the exercise of political power.

It was therefore a distinct shock when in the 1949–51 struggle for political power, the newly organized Convention People's Party, under the leadership of Kwame Nkrumah, won the election and took office under a constitution which gave the colony internal self-government. It was a shock from which certain of the bourgeoisie have never recovered.

Independence was celebrated March 6, 1957, when the name "Gold Coast" was discarded and the country took the name of an ancient West African kingdom—Ghana. The Republic of Ghana came into being July 1, 1960, and Kwame Nkrumah was inaugurated first President of the Republic.

With a strong Constitution uniting the country, the Convention People's Party (CPP) now moved forward to lay the foundations of a socialist economy, to curb exploitation by foreign capitalists and reduce dependence on foreign investments, to hasten industrialization and to expand and improve free public education at all levels. To clarify understanding about its socialist program, train activists and future officials, the Government established at Winneba an Institute of Ideological Studies. Here such subjects as Economics, History and Political Science were taught from a socialist viewpoint and research was undertaken into the application of Socialism to Ghanaian conditions. Teachers were invited and came from Socialist countries. These, together with the African scholars, made up an articulate socialist-oriented intelligentsia. It was made clear, however, that Socialism was an intellectual concept, a goal towards which the young must be directed, a way of life to be taught, not a dogma to be imposed on the people of Ghana.

23

Kwame Nkrumah: African Liberator, No. 3, 1972

SHIRLEY GRAHAM DU BOIS

Shirley Graham Du Bois was a children's book author, composer, and activist. Following Kwame Nkrumah's death, she wrote this appreciation of the accomplishments of Dr. Nkrumah for Freedomways.

Whatever Ghana is today, or will be tomorrow, is because of the vision, determination, courage and hard work of Kwame Nkrumah, who led the British Gold Coast Colony out of colonialism, took back the name of the ancient West African kingdom, and founded the Republic of Ghana. Now, at last, two months after his death, the body of this great African Liberator and Statesman is going home for burial. According to a communiqué issued June 15, President Sekou Touré, who has protected and honored Kwame Nkrumah in death as he had protected and cherished him in life, has consented to let the body leave Guinea where, surrounded with an honor guard, it lay in state. Thousands of white-robed mourners had filed past, after which the Guineans went on to console those faithful and loyal Ghanaians who had remained with their President throughout his long and painful exile.

Months before, President Touré had informed the present military regime of Ghana that Kwame Nkrumah was fatally ill and begged them to allow him to return home to die. *They refused.* When, however, he was dead, they sent a delegation to Guinea for the body. And President Touré would not let them take it because they would give no assurance that the Founder and late President of Ghana would be received and buried with all due honors. Indeed, during the last week in May, Colonel Acheampong, Chairman of the Council, stated on radio and television that "Dr. Nkrumah's" body could not be received for burial because compliance with President Touré's "conditions" would "negate the February, 1966 revolution" (the military *coup* which overthrew Nkrumah!) and this the "National Redemption Council" could not do because they believed in the February 1966 revolution!

No amount of delayed eulogies, excuses or tears will ever wipe away the shame of these refusals—a shame which will forever blot the name of Ghana and every Ghanaian! It is a greater shame than that of the 1966 *coup.* For that *coup* is known to have been planned and engineered by outside neo-colonialists and imperialists, who had decided that "Nkrumah Must Go!" These enemies of Africa managed to buy the help of a few stooges and ambitious powerseekers, but the people of Ghana had no part in overthrowing President Nkrumah. And the bitter years which have passed without him have opened their eyes to how they were deluded and tricked into accepting something they did not understand. His death shook them out of their lethargy, as nothing else would have done. There is no question about the wild and unrestrained grief which swept over the country. Always, deep in their hearts was the assurance that "Osagyefo" would come back, would lift the oppressive burdens from their shoulders, would "straighten things out" as he had done before. They took comfort from the fact that he was, indeed, only three hundred miles away among brothers who loved him. Now, suddenly they learned that this one, on whom they pinned their hopes for the future, had died in a far away land, died among strange faces, among strange men and strange customs. There had been no talking drums to announce his passing, no gong-gong to summon familiar faces to his side, no dirges recounting a litany of his deeds. "Osagyefo," "Kwame Atoapem," "Show Boy" lay cold and still in a lonely hospital far away. For the African the tragedy was complete!

Neither the military rulers of Ghana nor the watching neocolonialists expected the massive demonstrations of mourning and the clamoring demand to "bring Osagyefo home" which erupted all over the country. They did not expect that many African countries would declare days of national mourning for him, nor that many heads of state would want to attend his funeral—nor the messages of sorrow which poured in from nearly all important capitals of the world. "All this," wrote the *Legion Observer* "for a man who had lost office and been forced into exile six years ago."

But on May 4th *The Palaver,* an independent weekly in Accra wrote:

> The entire world suddenly awoke from its mental stupor to learn of the untimely death of one of Africa's greatest and more revered sons which sad event occurred last Wednesday in the Socialist Republic of Rumania.
>
> The whole world—East, West, North and South—became aware that one man who at one time or the other dominated the world political scene was no more. The earth stood still, so to speak, church bells tolled and many peoples, black and white, mourned the loss of a great man of Africa. . . .

None of the lies and slanders heaped upon President Nkrumah following the *coup* of February 1966 have blinded Africans to the fact that he was foremost in breaking the fetters of colonialism, in opening the eyes of Africans and erasing the crawling mentality which centuries of domination had stamped on their brains. It was he who projected the African Personality to the world—a personality of *strength, beauty* and *dignity.* Now though the broken heart is still—though the tired and tortured flesh withers away and is no more, the indomitable spirit of this great son of Africa will lead on! His words which he set down so carefully and painstakingly up to his last days, will lead the ultimately victorious Freedom Fighters as they go forth to battle. His words will sustain them in their struggle; his singleness of purpose, determination and untiring drive will continue to inspire Africans and the dispossessed children of Africa, wherever they may be. The world noted his words, spoken at midnight on March 5, 1957, when the British Colony, the "Gold Coast," was wiped off the map and Ghana came into being. On that night, as the new flag was raised for the first time, as Ghana's first national anthem was played and thousands of happy Ghanaians shouted for joy—Kwame Nkrumah silenced that rejoicing for a moment to say:

"The independence of Ghana is meaningless as long as any part of Africa is not liberated!"

This Leader had vision which pierced distant horizons, stretched his people to their utmost capacity and reached for the heights of man's achievements.

A short time after his death I was invited by African students—Ghanaians, Nigerians, Zimbabweans—attending universities in the northeast section of the United States—to speak at a Memorial at Yale University. They had secured from the United Nations a recording of the speech Kwame Nkrumah made before the United Nations Assembly in 1960. As his voice rang out in the auditorium of Yale University Law School it was as if this Black man stood before us. He had faced the United Nations not merely as representative from Ghana—but as spokesman for the continent of Africa. He laid before them the dire situation in the Congo where Patrice Lumumba was struggling to liberate his people from the awful slavery imposed upon them by Belgium; he talked of Namibia, the true name of South West Africa, which in spite of countless resolutions and demands made by the United Nations, was sinking deeper and deeper into the deadly coils of South Africa; he talked of Rhodesia, where a few thousand whites had seized domination over millions of Blacks— were driving them from their lands and taking over all the resources of this British colony, while Great Britain's Prime Minister, Harold Wilson, declared that Britain could not use "force" to safeguard the rights of the millions because Ian Smith and his cohorts were "kith and kin" of the British!

Kwame Nkrumah was the first African to appear on the rostrum of the United Nations and he warned that unless that body heed its Charter, unless those who come together to "safeguard the security and peace of humanity" exert their combined strength and prevent the continuing rape of Africa, the United Nations would sink into useless and hypocritical oblivion and the world would be engulfed in strife. Surely, as we look around at the world today, as we witness the avowed helplessness of the United Nations to do anything effective, we grasp the prophetic wisdom of Nkrumah's words.

And what would seem to be Nkrumah's reward for being the foremost architect of Africa's emancipation from foreign domination—to see his Government overthrown and to die a wanted man with a price on his head for any man who would bring him to Ghana dead or alive? To continue to be lied about by those enemies of Africa who had subverted his people and who, having, as they thought, rid themselves of Nkrumah, cast aside Ghana, and were only too glad to see that promising little country sink into a morass of ignominy? How could such tragic events transpire? How, indeed, could the February 1966 *coup* in Ghana have been staged?

Without attempting an analysis of colonialism—in which lie all the roots of African struggles today—I shall describe some of the remnants of colonialism as I saw them in Ghana. I was first in that country in December 1958, one year after its "independence"—having gone there to deliver my husband's address to the First All-African Peoples Conference, called by the then Prime Minister Nkrumah.

This was the first such gathering of peoples from all over Africa to be held on that continent. Dr. Du Bois had tried in vain to hold a Pan-African Congress in Africa, but the ruling colonial powers would not allow it. In opening the December Conference, Nkrumah designated it as the Sixth Pan-African Congress, but explained that because it included peoples of such diverse backgrounds, languages, cultures and customs it was more easily understood as a Conference of "All African Peoples." It is a fact that every African who since that time has emerged as a leader of his people was in Accra that week, including Patrice Lumumba, Julius Nyerere, Tom M'Boya, Kenneth Kaunda and masked Freedom Fighters from South Africa, Portuguese Angola and Mozambique.

The latter part of the week I was taken by an Afro-American professor to Ghana University, on the outskirts of Accra. Here I encountered open hostility to the Conference—and heard the accusation that it was just "a communist get-together"! I was amazed until I learned that most of the teachers in that University were from South Africa!

On July 1, 1960, Ghana became a Republic and Kwame Nkrumah was inaugurated the Republic's first President. My husband and I were in the country when, ten days later, all relations with South Africa were cut off—planes and ships going or coming from South Africa could not stop at Ghana and all South Africans in the country were given a certain number of days to sign an affidavit condemning apartheid or leave the country. That same week full diplomatic relations were established with the Peoples Republic of China and Ghanaian and Chinese Ambassadors were exchanged.

The first project into which I was drawn was the remaking of schoolbooks. British colonials had little interest in schools for "natives," but there were mission schools of various creeds. All of them charged a fee, depending on how poor or how affluent the Church happened to be—all copied the British style of uniform, which had to be bought. This meant, of course, that the masses of children were not in school at all, and except for children of civil servants, affluent chiefs or traders, who found favor in the eyes of the white rulers, few continued into what were called secondary schools. (The very few university students were sons of the "elite" being trained by the British to help them rule the Colony.)

Free education of every child in Ghana was Nkrumah's idea. And immediately construction of schools began all over the country. There was the problem of finding teachers; even before that was solved came the necessity of rewriting textbooks. Books being used in the schools had been sent out from Great Britain and, from first to last, were for creating loyal subjects of the British crown. These books sought to instill in every "native" the desire to be as good an "Englishman" as he could! Thus the missionaries taught little Africans to sing: "Wash me and I shall be whiter than snow"! (Snow never falls in Ghana.) All illustrations in the books were of white children, dressed for England and doing the things an English child would do. Thus, a smart little fellow in Accra might well recite the names of all the kings and queens of England beginning with King Arthur, could trace the course of the Thames and describe the landscape of Scotland, but he would know nothing about Ashanti kings, the kings of ancient Ghana or Mali, nor would he know the course of the Volta or Congo Rivers or the countries bordering on Ghana. The Black student in Ghana was taught to imitate the marching of red-coated British soldiers and to look forward to celebrating the Queen's birthday!

We set about changing all this. Two excellent Afro-American artists had arrived in the country. One was engaged to make drawings for our new schoolbooks; the other was soon teaching Ghanaians to see *themselves* and to draw themselves with truth and beauty. Construction of a publishing plant began; Ghanaians were sent to Germany—where books in Europe were first printed—to learn the skill of printing. When, early in 1964, Ghana's National Publishing House opened it was certainly the most modern, best equipped such plant on the continent of Africa and one of the finest to be seen anywhere.

Yes, Kwame Nkrumah spent money—the people's money—to build *for the people*. Nor were they impoverished during these efforts. Ghana is rich in natural resources. There were those who complained when they could no longer buy South African apples, pears and grapes. But an abundance of fruit hung from the trees in Ghana— and pineapples grew almost wild along the roadsides.

In May 1963, Nkrumah's *Africa Must Unite* was introduced at the First African Summit Conference which met in Addis Ababa, Ethiopia. This book surveyed the plentiful and widespread rich re- sources of the continent and emphasized what combining all would mean for strength and power. *Africa Must Unite* was seized upon with avid interest. It increased and inspired liberation movements throughout the continent and evoked consternation among colonial powers. That book, coupled with his later *Neo-Colonialism: The Last Stage of Imperialism*, decided western powers that *Nkrumah must go!* They recognized him as their implacable and most dangerous oppo- nent—incorruptible and magnetic. And so the *coup* in February 1966—one month after the Volta River Project had been inaugu- rated—the project designed to bring economic independence to Ghana. And it must be noted that total *economic independence* of any part of Africa rings the death knell for foreign control.

In nearly thirty years of turbulent but enviable public life, Kwame Nkrumah came to be regarded by friends and foes alike as the theo- retician and strategist of the African Revolution.

His public life—with its tribulations and triumphs, its successes and failures, its pageantry and color—when seen in historical perspective becomes a chronicle of the new Africa, continental in scale, socialist in content, slowly but surely rising out of the smoldering ruins of colonialism and the crumbling ramparts of neo-colonialism.

One may review his ideological approach to the African Revolution under three categories:

1. The struggle against colonialism in one country.
2. The promotion of continental revolution against imperialism.
3. The welding of many states into one society as the condition for securing full, development within the context of national independence.

The ten years, 1947–1957, from his return to the Gold Coast to the attainment of independence by the newly named Ghana, saw

Nkrumah immersed in leading a colonial revolution in his own country. His theory of colonial revolution is embodied in *Towards Colonial Freedom,* with valuable personal sidelights in *Ghana: The Autobiography of Kwame Nkrumah,* in *I Speak of Freedom* and in numerous newspaper articles and public speeches.

At this time he projected the slogan: "Seek ye first the political kingdom and everything shall be added unto it."

The cardinal principle of Nkrumah's theory of colonial revolution is reliance on the common people. Their best interests are secured only when the revolt against colonial oppression and exploitation is carried to its logical climax.

The attainment of political independence is not the end of the road. Economic independence must be attained. This requires complete national reconstruction. And the untying of all links that subordinate the economy of the liberated territory to that of the ousted rulers.

Nkrumah worked towards three goals: self-reliance, a socialist path of development, a continental approach to the problems of economic development, defense and diplomacy.

He saw Africa as part of the world and declared that the twentieth century is "a century of continuing revolution." Therefore the African revolution must seek external conditions favorable for its development and final victory. He urged the solidarity of the African peoples with the anti-imperialist forces in other parts of the world.

I visited President Nkrumah several times during his exile. I always found him cheerful and busy. He lived in a comfortable villa, on the waterfront, surrounded by loyal Ghanaians, cared for and honored by the Guinean people. He planned, worked, hoped and lived only to return to Ghana. He refused invitations from distant countries, refused lucrative offers to occupy chairs in various universities; he would consider nothing which would take him farther away from Ghana.

He wrote constantly: His *Challenge of the Congo* appeared the year after his exile. This was followed by *Dark Days in Ghana,* a frank discussion of what had happened in Ghana; then came his *Handbook for Freedom Fighters;* last year his *Class Struggle in Africa,* a brilliant Marxist analysis of the situation on the continent of Africa. Even when his health failed and his Brother Sekou Touré wanted to send him to Europe for the best possible medical care—he continued to write. Now, finished and soon to be published are his *The Revolutionary Path* and *Rhodesia and the White Minority Settlers.*

Kwame Nkrumah, Teacher, Pathbreaker, Leader—faithful and loving disciple of that other Great Teacher! When, in 1960, the newly inaugurated President of the Republic of Ghana invited Du Bois to join him in his tremendous efforts to make Ghana a mighty pilot light for all Africa, my husband willingly agreed. He was happy and proud to undertake the planning and constructing of an *Encyclopaedia Africana,* believing as he did that "this will be the crowning work of my life." And that year W.E.B. wrote and dedicated a poem to Kwame Nkrumah which he entitled "Ghana Calls." I offer here a few verses:

> I lifted up mine eyes to Ghana
> And swept the Hills with high Hosanna;
> Above the sun my sight took flight
> Till from that pinnacle of light
> I saw dropped down this earth of crimson green and gold,
> Roaring-with colour, drums and song,
>
> Happy with dreams and deeds worth more than doing.
> Around me velvet faces loomed
> Burnt by the kiss of everlasting suns;
> Under great stars of midnight glory
> Trees danced and foliage sang;
>
> . . .
>
> I lifted my last voice and cried
> I cried to heaven as I died:
> O turn me to the Golden Horde
> Summon all western nations
> Towards the Rising Sun.
>
> And Africa leads on.
> Pan Africa!

24

Socialism Is Not Racialism, No. 2, 1970

HON. JULIUS K. NYERERE
President, United Republic of Tanzania

The following article first appeared as an appendix to the original Arusha Declaration, which set forth principles for building socialism in Tanzania.

The Arusha Declaration and the actions relating to public ownership were all concerned with ensuring that we can build socialism in our country. The nationalization and the taking of controlling interest in many firms were a necessary part of our determination to organize our society in such a way that our efforts benefit all our people and that there is no exploitation of one man by another.

Yet these actions do not in themselves create socialism. They are necessary to it, but as the Arusha Declaration states, they could also be the basis for fascism—in other words, for the oppressive extreme of capitalism. For the words with which I began my pamphlet "Ujamaa" in 1962 remain valid; socialism is an attitude of mind. The basis of socialism is a belief in the oneness of man and the common historical destiny of mankind. Its basis, in other words, is human equality.

Acceptance of this principle is absolutely fundamental to socialism. The justification of socialism is Man—not the State, not the Flag. Socialism is not for the benefit of black men, nor brown men, nor white men, nor yellow men. The purpose of socialism is the service of man, regardless of color, size, shape, skill, ability, or anything else. And the economic institutions of socialism, such as those we are now creating in accordance with the Arusha Declaration, are intended to serve man in our society. Where the majority of the people in a particular society are Black, then most of those who benefit from socialism there will be Black. But it has nothing to do with their blackness, only with their humanity.

Some years ago I made the point that fascism and racialism can go together, but socialism and racialism are incompatible. The reason is easy to see. Fascism is the highest and most ruthless form of the exploitation of man by man; it is made possible by deliberate efforts to divide mankind and set one group of men against another group.

In Nazi Germany the majority were incited to join in hostile actions against the Jews—who were a minority religious and ethnic group living among them. "I hate Jews" became the basis of life for supporters of the Nazi Government.

But the man or woman who hates "Jews" or "Asians" or "Europeans" or even "West Europeans and Americans" is not a socialist. He is trying to divide mankind into groups and is judging men according to the skin color and shape they were given by God. Or he is dividing men according to national boundaries. In either case he is denying the equality and brotherhood of man.

Without an acceptance of human equality there can be no socialism. This is true however "socialist" the institutions may be. Thus it was that when Nazi Germany organized the Krupp group of industries no socialist could rejoice; for it simply meant that the fascist state was more highly organized than ever. Nor do socialists welcome the news that South Africa has established an oil trading and refining company in which the State owns a controlling interest. We know that this simply makes that fascist state more efficient in its oppression and more able to defend itself against attack.

We in Tanzania have to hold fast to this lesson, especially now as we advance on the socialist road. For it is true that because of our colonial history the vast majority of the capitalist organizations in this country are owned and run by Asians or by Western Europeans. Twenty years ago we could have said all the capitalists in this country were from those areas; we cannot say this now. For the truth is that capitalism and capitalist attitudes have nothing whatsoever to do with the race or national origin of those who believe in them or practice them. Indeed, nobody who was at Arusha needs any more proof that the temptations of capitalism ignore color boundaries. Even leaders of TANU [Tanzanian party of peasants and workers] were getting deeply involved in the practices of capitalism and landlordism. A few had started talking of "my company." And very many others would have done so if they could; they were capitalists by desire even when they could not be so in practice. Hence the resolution on leadership. Hence the difficulties we must expect in enforcing this resolution.

Socialism has nothing to do with race, nor with country of origin. In fact any intelligent man, whether he is a socialist or not, realizes that there are socialists in capitalist countries—and from capitalist countries. Very often such socialists come to work in newly independent and avowedly socialist countries like Tanzania because they are frustrated in their capitalist homeland. Neither is any intelligent man blind to the fact that there are frustrated capitalists in the communist countries—just as there will in time be frustrated capitalists in Tanzania. It may even be that some of those frustrated capitalists from Eastern countries come to work with us.

Neither is it sensible for a socialist to talk as if all capitalists are devils. It is one thing to dislike the capitalist system and to try and frustrate people's capitalist desires. But it would be as stupid for us to assume that capitalists have horns as it is for people in Western Europe to assume that we in Tanzania have become devils.

In fact the leaders in the capitalist countries have now begun to realize that communists are human beings like themselves—that they are not devils. One day they will realize that this includes the Chinese communists! It would be very absurd if we react to the stupidity they are growing out of and become equally stupid ourselves in the opposite direction! We have to recognize in our words and our actions that capitalists are human beings as much as socialists. They may be wrong; indeed by dedicating ourselves to socialism we are saying that they are. But our task is to make it impossible for capitalism to dominate us. Our task is not to persecute capitalists or make dignified life impossible for those who would be capitalists if they could. . . .

The Arusha Declaration talks of Men, and their beliefs. It talks of socialism and capitalism, of socialists and capitalists. It does not talk about racial groups or nationalities. On the contrary, it says that all those who stand for the interests of the workers and peasants, any-where in the world, are our friends. This means that we must judge the character and ability of each individual, not put each person into a pre-arranged category of race or national origin and judge him ac-cordingly. Certainly no one can be a socialist unless he first tries to do this.

For if the actions taken under the Arusha Declaration are to mean anything to our people, then we must accept this basic oneness of man. What matters now is that we should succeed in the work we have undertaken. The color or origin of the man who is working to that end does not matter in the very least. And each one of us must fight, in himself, the racialist habits of thought which were part of our inheritance from colonialism.

It is not an easy thing to overcome such habits. But we have always known that it is necessary, and that racialism is evil. We fought our independence campaign on that basis. And the equality of man is the first item in the TANU Creed. For in our constitution we say "TANU believes (a) That all human beings are equal; (b) That every individual has a right to dignity and respect."

If we are to succeed in building a socialist state in this country it is essential that every citizen, and especially every TANU leader, should live up to that doctrine. Let us always remember two things. We have dedicated ourselves to build a socialist society in Tanzania. And So-cialism and Racialism are incompatible.

25

Selected Speeches and Writings on Peace, No. 1, 1971

PAUL ROBESON

Paul Robeson delivered this speech, "Playing Catch-up," in October 1953. It was printed in the magazine Freedom, *which Robeson published and Louis Burnham edited, and reprinted in* Freedomways' *special issue on Paul Robeson.*

Playing Catch-Up

For 90 years since Emancipation our people have been playing "catch-up" in American life. We have been battling for equality in education, health, housing and jobs.

And now, today, 90 years later, despite all the croaking about the great progress we're making, any Negro who's not looking for a second-string job on Eisenhower's "team" will tell you we've still got a long way to go.

How are we going to get there?

Will shooting down Chinese help us get our freedom? Will dropping some bombs on Vietnamese patriots who want to be free of French domination help American Negroes reach a plane of equality with their white fellow-citizens? And, most important, will a war in support of Malan in South Africa, or the British exploiters in Kenya, or the French in Tunisia place Black Americans on the same footing with whites?

To ask the question is to answer it. No!

No one has yet explained to my satisfaction what business a Black lad from a Mississippi or Georgia sharecropping farm has in Asia shooting down the yellow or brown son of an impoverished rice-farmer.

Mr. Eisenhower or Senator McCarthy would have us believe that this is necessary to "save" the so-called "free world" from "communism." But the man who keeps that Negro sharecropper from earning more than a few hundred dollars a year is not a Communist—it's the landlord. And the man who prevents his son from attending school with white children is not a Communist—it's Governor Talmadge or Governor Byrnes of the U.S. delegation to the United Nations.

I believe, and I urge upon this convention the belief, that any Negro who carries his brains around with him and has not been bought and paid for must agree that it is time for 15 million colored Americans to disassociate themselves from a foreign policy which is based on brandishing the atom bomb, setting up hundreds of air bases all over the world, and threatening colored peoples with death and destruction unless they humbly recognize the inalienable right of Anglo-Saxon Americans to sit on the top of the world.

Negroes, as I said, are still playing "catch-up." And with the kind of war that the atom-happy U.S. diplomats are planning we won't be catching up—we'll just be "catching," and relinquishing any hope for liberation and freedom.

I say that, even though Eisenhower is meeting at this very moment with Churchill in Bermuda, we will not, and must not support the British overlords in Kenya—we will fight to free Kenyatta! I say, even though Laniel of France is right there with Eisenhower and Churchill, we must not approve the squandering of billions of American taxpayers' money on the dirty war in Indo-China—we must insist that the French rule in France and leave the Vietnamese to govern themselves. And I trust that this convention will record that it is against the interests of Negro workers, the entire Negro people and the nation as a whole to pursue one step further the suicidal, blundering, threatening, war-minded foreign policy which is the hallmark of the Administration. What Negroes need, and all American needs, is PEACE.

The following piece by Robeson was published in Freedom *in March 1954 and reprinted in* Freedomways' *special issue on Paul Robeson.*

Ho Chi Minh Is the
Toussaint l'Ouverture of Indo-China

As I write these lines, the eyes of the world are on a country inhabited by 23 million brown-skinned people—a population one and a half times the number of Negroes in the U.S. In size that country is equal to the combined area of Mississippi, South Carolina and Alabama. It's a fertile land, rich in minerals; but all the wealth is taken away by the foreign rulers, and the people are poor.

I'm talking about Vietnam, and it seems to me that we Negroes have a special reason for understanding what's going on over there. Only recently, during Negro History Week, we recalled the heroic exploits of Toussaint L'Ouverture who led the people of Haiti in a victorious rebellion against the French Empire.

Well, at the same time that the French were fighting to keep their hold on the Black slaves of Haiti, they were sending an army around to the other side of the world to impose colonial slavery on the people of Indo-China. And ever since then the Indo-Chinese have been struggling to be free from French domination.

"My children, France comes to make us slaves. God gave us liberty; France has no right to take it away. Burn the cities, destroy the harvests, tear up the roads with cannon, poison the wells, show the white man the hell he comes to make!"

Those fiery words, addressed to his people by Toussaint L'Ouverture when Napoleon sent Le Clerc with an army of 30,000 men to re-enslave Haiti, are echoed today by Ho Chi Minh, who is the Toussaint of Vietnam. Yes, and a French general called Le Clerc was also sent against Ho Chi Minh, but like the Blacks of Haiti, the plantation workers of Indo-China have proved unconquerable.

In 1946 France was forced to recognize the Republic of Vietnam, headed by Ho Chi Minh; but like the double-crossing Napoleon in the time of Toussaint, the French colonial masters returned with greater force to re-enslave the people who had liberated themselves. The common people of France have come to hate this struggle; they call it "the dirty war"; and their rulers have not dared to draft Frenchmen for military service there.

"Who are the Vietminh?" said a French officer to a reporter from the Associated Press. "Where are they? Who knows? They are everywhere." And the reporter wrote: "Ho Chi Minh's barefoot hordes infiltrate French-held territory at will in the guise of peasants, arms concealed under brown tunics. They have allies who hide them and feed them—allies who are not Communists but people who hate the French, hate the foreigner and want him to go."

Now, when France wants to call it quits, Eisenhower, Nixon and Dulles are insisting that Vietnam must be re-conquered and held in colonial chains. "The Vietnamese lack the ability to govern themselves," says Vice-President Nixon.

Vast quantities of U.S. bombers, tanks and guns have been sent against Ho Chi Minh and his freedom-fighters; and now we are told that soon it may be "advisable" to send American GI's into Indo-China in order that the tin, rubber and tungsten of Southeast Asia be kept by the "free world"—meaning White Imperialism.

The whole world cries out for peace; but Dulles insists that the war must go on and threatens Asians again with atomic and hydrogen bombs.

That's the picture, and I ask again: Shall Negro sharecroppers from Mississippi be sent to shoot down brown-skinned peasants in Vietnam—to serve the interests of those who oppose Negro liberation at home and colonial freedom abroad?

What are our Negro leaders saying about this? They are all too silent.

The true issues involved are well known, for only recently, *The Crisis*, official organ of the NAACP, published an article filled with factual proof that the Vietnamese are fighting against colonial oppression. The article shows that the charge of "Red Aggression" in Indo-China is a phony, and that the sympathies of our people belong with the side resisting imperialism.

Three years ago Mordecai Johnson, president of Howard University, said that "For over 100 years the French have been in Indo-China, dominating them politically, strangling them economically, and humiliating them in the land of their fathers. . . . And now it

Paul and Eslanda Robeson and Freedomways *staff.*
(Left to right) J. H. O'Dell, Eslanda Robeson, John H. Clarke,
Norma Rogers, and Esther Jackson at a salute to Paul Robeson
sponsored by Freedomways, *New York City, April 22, 1965.*

looks as though they can win, and as they are about to win their liberty, we rush up and say: 'What on earth are you all getting ready to do? . . . We are the free people of the world, we are your friends, we will send you leaders. . . .'

"And they look at us in amazement and they say: 'Brother, where have you been? Why, if we'd known you was a-comin' we'd have baked a cake.'"

Today, more than ever, is the time for plain speaking.

Peace can be won if we demand it. The imperialists can be halted in their tracks. And as we think about Ho Chi Minh, the modern-day Toussaint L'Ouverture leading his people to freedom, let us remember well the warning words of a Negro spokesman, Charles Baylor, who wrote in the *Richmond Planet* a half century ago:

"The American Negro cannot become the ally of imperialism without enslaving his own race."

26

The Giant Stirs,
No. 1, 1966

W.E.B. DU BOIS

Dr. Du Bois wrote this in February 1955 in The World and Africa, *a week before his eighty-seventh birthday. The editors chose to run it as an editorial entitled "The Giant Stirs."*

The Negro press discusses race relations in the United States, reports news of the Negro groups and personal items. Its chief demand for 150 years has been political, civil and social equality with white Americans.

Here they are advancing rapidly and today it is clear that they have a chance to trade wide breaks in the American color line for acquiescence in American and West European control of the world's colored peoples. This is shown by the pressure on them to keep silence on Africa and Asia and on white working-class movements, and in return to accept more power to vote; abolition of separation in education; dropping of "Jim Crow" units in our military forces and gradual disappearance of the Negro ghetto in work and housing. . . .

It is fair to admit that most American Negroes, even those of intelligence and courage, do not yet fully realize that they are being bribed to trade equal status in the United States for the slavery of the majority of men. When this is clear, especially to black youth, the race must be aroused to thought and action and will see that the price asked for their cooperation is far higher than need be paid, since race and color equality is bound to come in any event.

27

The Freedom Movement
and the War in Vietnam,
No. 4, 1965

ROBERT S. BROWNE

Robert S. Browne taught economics at Fairleigh Dickinson University at the time this article appeared. He had lived in Vietnam and Cambodia from 1955 to 1961 while working for the U.S. foreign aid program. In 1965 he returned to Vietnam to lecture at the Buddhist University in Saigon, to evaluate the current Vietnamese political situation, and to visit friends and (his wife's) relatives. This was the first article against the Vietnam War published by a Black journal.

During the several years which I lived in Vietnam, I enjoyed an intimacy with Vietnamese life which was probably unique for an American. Although I could never escape the obvious truth that I was a foreigner, the fact that I was a non-white, Vietnamese-speaking member of a Vietnamese family, frequently made me privy to conversations intended only for Vietnamese ears [Negro readers will readily understand what I mean] and provided me an unusual measure of insight into the depths of Vietnamese thinking and emotions. Unquestionably, it is this unique insight which led me as early as 1960 to become a constant and vigorous critic of the United States policy in Vietnam.

Although the stimulus for this disaffection with the American effort in Vietnam derived primarily from my awareness of what suffering we were inflicting upon the Vietnamese people by imposing upon them the hated dictatorship of President Diem and his family, my lifelong interest in international political affairs had made me extremely skeptical of the American official policy in Southeast Asia long before I ever went to live there. America's acquiescence in France's 1946 re-occupation of her former Indochinese empire had early alerted me to our government's unwillingness or incapacity to extend the idea of freedom to the non-white peoples of this part of the world, and after 1950 the open support by the United States of the French colonial war in Indochina had clearly placed America in opposition to the aspirations of the Vietnamese, Laotian and Cambodian peoples.

When, in 1954, the French finally decided to sue for peace in Vietnam, the United States took upon itself the responsibility of attempting to fill the so-called vacuum which America typically assumed would be created by the departure of the white colonizers. In large measure, it is the Vietnamese peoples' resistance to this paternalistic approach to them, with its implicit assumption that they are incapable of resolving their own problems, which lies at the base of the United States-Vietnam conflict. The myriad domestic problems of Vietnam have been completely overshadowed by America's insinuation of its presence into the Vietnam political scene, which has aggravated the existing factionalism amongst the Vietnamese and elevated their internal quarrel into an international *cause celebre,* with the resultant massive destruction which we see taking place today.

The belief that there was a "white man's burden" in Indochina which America was obliged to assume was clothed, not in the 19th century garment of protecting commercial or religious interests, but in the modern cloak of resisting the spread of international communism. Using the pretext that communism was the worst fate which could befall the Vietnamese people, but stubbornly refusing to submit this value judgment to a plebiscite amongst the Vietnamese people, Washington proceeded to assume major responsibility for directing Vietnamese affairs. That the Vietnamese were reluctant to accept either Washington's direction of their country or its assessment of what was best for their welfare, however, was strikingly illustrated by President Eisenhower's comment on the failure of the Vietnamese peasants to cooperate with the U.S. program. As late as 1960 *i.e.*, after 6 years of massive American influence in Vietnam, Eisenhower remarked that "our biggest problem is to convince the Vietnamese people that communism is their number one enemy." But in 1965, after yet an additional 5 years of United States interference on a ferocious scale, the Vietnamese people are even less ready than before to do Washington's bidding. Having brought only strife, suffering, and unimaginable destruction to their country, the U.S. has become the object of undisguised scorn for these people who only 10 short years ago had hardly heard of America. What they perhaps resent most is that there are now only two alternatives remaining available to them—communism, or a continuation of the wholesale slaughter of their people—the opportunity to neutralize their country having been lost to them by the United States' interference.

Dulles Policy Discredited

Not surprisingly, the political thinking which initially rationalized our Vietnam policy back in 1954–55 has been discredited by events as well as by most responsible persons in Washington itself. The basic plank of this policy, the Dulles proposal to contain Chinese communism by ringing China with a network of pro-American states "pending China's collapse from within," has proved to be both unworkable and falsely premised. A neutralized S.E. Asia, free of cold war pressures, for which Nehru, Sukarno, and Sihanouk pleaded at Bandung and subsequently, was dismissed as "immoral" by Secretary Dulles as he proceeded to pit Vietnam against Cambodia, Thailand against Indonesia, and within Vietnam, to pit a pro-American, largely capitalist and Christian faction against a nationalist, largely socialist and Buddhist one. The ultimate guarantee of continued western control of the region, however, was supposed to lie in a so-called mutual assistance organization in which five European nations joined with three Asian nations to determine the future of Southeast Asia. It was misleadingly called the Southeast Asia Treaty Organization.

As the unworkability of the policy became apparent, President Diem, the politician whom the U.S. had supported to assume the leadership of the South Vietnamese government, resorted to terror to impose his will upon the Vietnamese people. Not surprisingly, this provoked a counteraction which, being denied any legal means of protest, organized itself into a rebel movement and adopted, guerrilla tactics to establish its position. Alarmed at the speed and effectiveness with which this resistance movement began to grow, the United States decided in 1961 to commit itself to a major military stance to defend the government of President Diem in Vietnam. (Although President Johnson attributes this decision basically to President Eisenhower, Eisenhower denies the charge and claims that his administration's commitment to President Diem was economic and political, but not military.)

It was not possible for the Vietnamese guerrilla forces, dubbed "Viet Cong" by Diem, to match the build-up in sophisticated arms and trained men which the United States provided to the South Vietnam government. However, these U.S. arms increasingly served to supply the rebel forces as well, some of them being captured from the American and Vietnamese government troops and others reaching the rebels via Black market sales or as gifts from defecting government troops. These defections, as well as the increasing sympathy for the rebels arising as a protest against such American-backed outrages as the strategic hamlet programs, which summarily uprooted the villagers from their homes, and the wholesale burnings of villages, substantially swelled the ranks of the rebels. The politically severed northern half of Vietnam, under communist rule, also increasingly supplied small arms assistance to the southern rebel forces. Not unexpectedly, the rebels' growing dependence on the North to enable them to withstand the United States' build-up strengthened the degree of communist influence within their movement, a fact which may have surprised Washington but which surprised no one else.

Modern planes, the latest in United States weaponry, chemicals, and gas were turned against the rebels, and even more so against the innocent Vietnamese peasants from whom the rebels are indistinguishable. Four more years of warfare, however, failed to turn the tide in favor of the United States' government forces. In 1963, the myth of Diem's popular democracy had been exploded by a half dozen Buddhist monks who, in self-sacrificing protest, had dramatically cremated themselves in the streets of Vietnam, forcing the United States finally to admit Diem's unpopularity and to withdraw its support from him. This led to his rapid overthrow and assassination, to the undisguised, if unbecoming, glee of millions of Vietnamese people who declared three days of festivities in celebration.

In early 1965, the United States materially changed the character of the war by extending its aerial bombardment into North Vietnam, and then in the summer of 1965 President Johnson finally admitted the obvious: the Vietnamese were either unable or unwilling to win this war and the United States must do it for them. A major American military commitment was made, with some 125,000 men to be sent to Vietnam by year's end. A few days later the new United States Ambassador to Vietnam was reported by the *New York Times* to have stated that we wouldn't withdraw from Vietnam even if the Vietnamese government asked us to do so. South Vietnam's transformation into an undisguised American colony was thus complete, except that control of most of South Vietnam's territory was daily being bloodily disputed.

In South Vietnam itself, which I revisited in 1965 after a four-year absence, I found the people crying out for surcease from the sorrow which the ill-conceived American involvement in their affairs had brought them, but despairing because they saw no way to exert any influence over the events taking place in their country. The general feeling was that the Americans had gained so much control over Vietnamese affairs that any genuine expression of the people's wishes was absolutely impossible. With the exception of the small but influential northern refugee segment of the Catholic community, there seemed to be virtually no support for the American effort to impose a military solution to the Vietnamese quarrel. Catholics and Buddhists, students and workers, intellectuals and peasants were as one in their desire to bring a halt to the destruction of their country by the massive American military machine. The National Liberation Front, as the rebels are more properly called, had won wide respect for itself because of its ability to frustrate the efforts of the most powerful country in the world. The degree of communist influence in the NLF was a hotly debated question among the Vietnamese, but even among those who most loudly condemned the NLF for its communist orientation there was general admission that it was the only genuinely nationalist movement in the country. Many of those with whom I talked believed that a victory by the NLF would eventually lead to a communist government in South Vietnam, but this seemed generally to be preferable to the continued destruction of their country. Indeed, most every one felt that the National Liberation Front would ultimately be victorious *in any case* because the rebels had so wide and devoted a following whereas few people had any real respect for the succession of corrupt Saigon governments, whose basic allegiance to a foreign power [the United States] seemed to be quite well known. What particularly frustrated the people was the insistence by the Americans that the war continue to be fought out year after year, at such a high toll in Vietnamese life and property, when the ultimate outcome was already so plain to see.

Protest of U.S. Policy Increasing

As American military involvement in Vietnam has grown more massive and as aerial bombing has expanded into neighboring Laos, Cambodia, North Vietnam, and up to the very frontiers of China, a groundswell of protest and indignation has arisen from amongst the intellectual and religious segments of the American populace and from many foreign quarters previously not openly opposed to American policy. Reports of indiscriminate burnings and bombings of Vietnamese villages, often gleefully confirmed in morbid detail by sadistic American officers boasting with obvious satisfaction of the numbers of the "yellow bastards" which they have bagged, send waves of horror through the more sensitive segments of the American public.

The Vietnam war is gradually replacing civil rights as the top story of the mid-sixties, and because the protest against the United States policy in Vietnam has been primarily made on moral grounds, as was the demand for civil rights, there has been an inevitable coincidence of the two movements on various levels. This has been particularly noticeable on the organizational circuit, where many of the groups which have been most vocal in their support of civil rights are the same ones which are most outspoken against the worst aspects of United States involvement in Vietnam. Especially prone to this double involvement have been the northern-based student movements, the pacifist organizations, and the more militant religious institutions. Inevitably, this duality of interests led to growing pressure upon the major civil rights organizations to extend their scope sufficiently to encompass a position on the vital Vietnam question. Martin Luther King, as a Nobel Peace Prize winner and world symbol of non-violent resolution of conflicts, was particularly urged to take a public position on Vietnam. As the personification of America's moral conscience, his endorsement was viewed as especially significant for the moral protest against United States atrocities in Vietnam.

These pressures introduced a new and potentially revolutionary dimension into the civil rights movement, and perhaps into Negro thinking generally. Traditionally, the American Negro has been single-minded to a fault insofar as his social consciousness was concerned. He has bestirred himself solely about problems directly involving his welfare *as a Negro*. Issues involving him only as a citizen, but not as an ethnic group, were of little interest to him; and certainly foreign policy, one of the most sophisticated of public affairs, was generally beyond his sphere of interest. No wonder then that the effort to involve the civil rights movement in the Vietnam crisis met strong resistance. Roy Wilkins, the leader of the National Association for the Advancement of Colored People, adopted the curious position that foreign policy was not a proper sphere for public analysis and criticism. On the other hand, James Farmer of the Congress of Racial Equality was willing to offer his critical judgment of the Administration's foreign policy, but insisted on doing it as an individual, vigorously opposing his organization's taking a public stand on Vietnam. The Southern Christian Leadership Conference and the Student Non-Violent Coordinating Committee have openly supported efforts to seek a peaceful solution to America's involvement in the Vietnam conflict and perhaps the most durable tie between the civil rights and the peace movements is the growing tendency for the peace movement to adopt the non-violent techniques perfected by the latter two organizations. Following publication of a moving "open letter to Martin Luther King" from the Vietnamese Buddhists, a letter in which he was urged not to remain silent in this moment of great "suffering caused by this unnecessary war," Dr. King publicly added his great prestige to the burgeoning nationwide moral condemnation of the ungodly American activities in Vietnam.

The principal arguments against the civil rights movement's involvement in the Vietnam protest hinge on: (1) the risk of losing significant financial support from civil rights contributors who either support the United States policy in Vietnam or who for other reasons do not favor popular opposition to American foreign policy; (2) the risk of causing dissension among activists in the civil rights movement who may hold differing views on Vietnam; (3) the risk of the civil rights movement's being smeared as communist-oriented; and

(4) the risk of dissipating scarce energy and resources in a peripheral activity.

Of these four reasons, the first would appear to be the most serious. With the Negro still far, far short of achieving anything approaching first class citizenship status, the civil rights leaders could be held irresponsible if they permitted their organization to become financially impoverished except for the most compelling of reasons. Since the principal business of these organizations is to fight for civil rights, a direct linkage between the Vietnam protest and the success of the civil rights program would have to be demonstrated to warrant risking a significant cut-off of funds. Whether in fact any noticeable loss of contributors would indeed result is problematic at this stage and would probably depend on which organization one is thinking about. Undoubtedly, the NAACP would be the most vulnerable to this sort of retaliation, its more conservative approach to problems presumably being a reflection of generally more conservative sources of financial support.

The second objection, the risk of dissension among the civil rights workers themselves, is probably slight. Although the liberals who do oppose the Vietnamese war usually act from a strong position of moral indignation, the others appear relatively ambivalent or indifferent to the war and are unlikely to be antagonistic to those who do come out against it.

Red-baiting is a real risk, of course. It is, however, one which the civil rights organizations have been facing increasingly in any case. The more popularly based civil rights movements have advanced to the place where traditional middle class approval and respectability are no longer given priority over program achievements. Their organizations are perhaps sufficiently self-secure to ignore the hysteria of the red-baiters, although recognizing the threat which such attacks represent to their fund-raising capabilities. As with the first reason, the more conservatively based organizations are likely to be the more sensitive to this menace.

The extent to which scarce resources, other than leadership, would be transferred from the civil rights struggle to the Vietnam protest would appear to be largely under the control of the civil rights organizations themselves. A simple statement of support shifts no resources and while there is a growing tendency for some civil rights activists to devote a portion of their energy to the peace movement, this trend is likely to proceed independently of the organizational position which is adopted. Naturally, to the extent that the leaders choose to play a continuing role in the Vietnam protest, there will be a diluting of their principal function and it is to be hoped that they would refrain from overextending themselves in this way.

Growing Alliance of Civil Rights and Peace Movement

On the other hand, there are strong arguments favoring a civil rights alliance with the Vietnam protest, or with the peace movement generally. These also fall under four headings:

1. the recognition that the civil rights movement represents the moral conscience of America and therefore naturally belongs in the vanguard of the Vietnam protest, felt now to be the number one moral issue confronting American society.
2. the argument that the billions of dollars being diverted to the Vietnam war represent funds which might otherwise be available for giving substance to the programs necessary for raising the Negro to a level of real equality in American life.
3. the belief that the civil rights objectives are unachievable under the present organization of American society and therefore must necessarily be fought for as part of a larger effort to remake American society, including its foreign policy.
4. the view that the Vietnam war is intimately involved in American racist attitudes generally, and therefore falls naturally within the range of American Negroes' direct sphere of interest.

That the civil rights movement has reinvigorated and restored a strain of morality to an increasingly purposeless and alienated American society is generally conceded, and it is also probably safe to predict that as the American public becomes aware of the true nature of its government's role and activities in Vietnam, the Vietnam involvement may well become the leading moral issue in America. Comparison of United States atrocities in Vietnam with the Nazis' extermination of Jews in Germany are being made increasingly and by responsible moral leaders, so that an explosive potential is already developing. That the presence of a powerful moral strain in the two issues leads automatically to their joining forces is not axiomatic, however, although it is certainly highly desirable to have the perennially weak voices of morality being raised in unison and gaining strength from mutual reinforcement.

The argument that funds spent in Vietnam can be used for constructive projects at home is indisputable. The only matter for question here is whether the funds would, in fact, be used for the poverty program if they were not being used in Vietnam. Our Congress is notoriously more generous in voting funds for military purposes than for programs of social welfare.

The viewpoint that achievement of full civil rights for the Negro requires ultimately a thorough going revision in American society has a variety of rationalizations. Its mildest formulation is probably contained in the manifesto entitled, *The Triple Revolution,* a scholarly document prepared by a group of leading American intellectuals who envisioned a revamping of American society around three foci: peace, civil rights, and automation. Civil rights as well as international peace were viewed as inseparable from the economic ordering of our society, and the dynamic of automation was seen as both the challenge and the hope for the necessary reordering of our society so as to make peace and civil rights an achievable reality.

The more extreme approaches to the remaking of American society derive from the various Marxian interpretations of human existence which view the Negro's low status as a necessary facet of American capitalism and which places Vietnam in a comparable slot in the global capitalist arrangements to which the United States is partisan. The tendency of the economic position of the Negro in America to go backward despite the efforts currently being made in his behalf is duplicated by the growing relative impoverishment of most of the underdeveloped [colored] nations of the world. These parallel phenomena strongly reinforce the demand for dramatic new approaches to the organization of economic affairs domestically as well as internationally. Some form of socialist organization is most frequently advocated.

However, the complexity and controversiality of such proposals render them unpromising rallying cries for arranging an immediate marriage between the civil rights and the peace movements. In any case, the United States interference in Vietnam is not a particularly convincing case of the classical Marxist argument that the foreign policy of American capitalism is explainable solely in terms of seeking markets and sources of primary products to exploit for American benefit. It is not primarily the dollar which is sending 125,000 American troops to Vietnam: it is fear of a strong, independent China, and although the basis of this fear may be partly in the ultimate economic threat which a revitalized China portends, one suspects that America's racist obsession—in this case, with the "yellow peril"—plays the significant role in the anti-Chinese hysteria.

Is Racism Involved in Vietnam War?

We are thus brought to the final consideration: whether or not there is a racist aspect to the Vietnam war, and if so what implications this has for American Negroes. Speculation on this topic opens a Pandora's box of considerations and can predictably arouse the greatest interest among Negroes themselves for it confronts them with their most difficult contemporary dilemma, that of identity. The dual streams of thought historically running through American social development—the plural society versus the melting pot—are currently reflected within Afro-American society in the separatism of the Black Muslims and other Black nationalist groups versus the integrationist objectives of the Negro middle class. The emergence of Africa has raised the negritude concept—a mystic bond tying together all peoples of Negroid descent, transcending national boundaries. Amongst the much larger community of all colored peoples the common heritage of subjugation and exploitation which has been their lot until the post World War II era has created a vague sense of community which finds special nourishment in the problems of underdevelopment which they all share and in their common revulsion to any expression of white racial superiority and colonialism, of which they have all been victims. The so-called "wars of liberation" which the communists praise and the Americans condemn are well understood by the American Negro, who has faced similar struggles himself.

American Negroes inescapably feel a pull toward this mass of colored people, even as they attempt simultaneously to win acceptance into American society, for they know that America will forever be a white society, and they are instinctively skeptical that their full acceptance into it can ever be achieved. Fearing that a move to Africa may demand too great an adjustment of them, but doubtful about achieving a satisfactory role in American society, Negroes are already groping toward some new cosmopolitan political arrangements which would relieve them of their dilemma. During a series of visits to a number of Negro college campuses last year, I was interested to note how many of the students recoiled from the hypothetical prospect of taking up arms against Ghana, with whom United States relations were particularly strained at that time. (The rescue of the American flag from desecration at the hands of rioting Ghanaians by a Negro United States embassy employee, which had occurred shortly prior to my visit, was soundly criticized by many of the Negro students.)

Whether such sentiments will crystallize into a political position or not is impossible to predict, but the Vietnam conflict could certainly become a catalyst in that direction. Certainly, no one will deny the growing international implications of race. That the spectacle of white Americans bombing and burning Asians has an explosive potential has been frequently alluded to by the State Department itself, and the U.S. government has worked diligently to try to convince other Asian nations to send combat troops to Vietnam so as to minimize the stark racial appearance of the conflict. General De Gaulle has publicly warned of the racial polarization which he saw developing in the world, and China has made frequent reference to race in her competition with the USSR for influence with the non-white nations.

To see innocent, uprooted American youths being incited to maim and murder women and children in Vietnam last summer was indescribably depressing to me, but to see American Negroes forced to engage in such atrocities absolutely enraged me. I was further appalled by what seemed to be a disproportionately large number of Negro faces among the United States troops and I could only wonder if this were the Pentagon's way of attempting to deflect the accusations of whites killing non-whites—and at the same time a way of driving a wedge between American Negroes and the colored people of Asia[1] I have noted other racial manifestations which give one cause for reflection. On August 17, 1965, the *New York Herald Tribune* carried a front-page column which concerned itself with the views of Negro troops in Vietnam. The purpose of the column seemed to be to prove that the American G.I.'s in Saigon found the

---

[1]The following interesting item was reported last April in the liberal Parisian weekly *L'Express*, by veteran French reporter Georges Chaffard, who traveled extensively behind the lines, i.e., in Vietcong territory, in the Vietnamese war. Commenting on the abundant supplies of American weapons in the hands of the Vietcong, he quotes a French planter in the rebel territory: "These are weapons sold to the Vietcong by soldiers of the National Army or by some Negroes in the U.S. Army. . . . It's as simple as that."

The Negro GI's may be more astute politicians than their Pentagon bosses!

Vietnamese to be anti-Negro. (Similar charges were publicized by *The New York Times* three weeks later.) These allegations are completely at variance to my own lengthy experience in Vietnam where I encountered no racism whatsoever on the part of the Vietnamese but on the contrary found many of them sympathetic with the Negro struggle in America. Indeed, considering the prominence afforded these anti-Negro allegations one wonders why so little publicity was given to the fact that in May of 1964 the Saigon taxi drivers' union called for a one week boycott of all foreign passengers *except American Negroes.*

One does not wish to be overly suspicious in this matter. Yet, one of the most depressing aspects of contemporary American diplomacy is America's obsessive fear of the American Negro's intimacy with other colored nationals. I have written elsewhere of the attempts to convince the Negro that he has nothing in common with the African. Although the Asian is a virtual stranger to the American Negro, a base for friendship and understanding between them certainly exists. I personally recall how, on the occasion of my first encounter with the venerable Tri Quang, leader of the Vietnamese Buddhists, I was momentarily thunderstruck at his appearance for, with his hair clipped short in the traditional style of the Buddhist monk, he looked exactly like any Negro whom one might meet on 125th Street in Harlem. Just as I question how it can be in America's interest to continue its futile effort to dominate and rule South Vietnam, even so do I question whether it is in the best interest of the American Negro to accept with equanimity the role which he is perhaps being obliged to play in this racially charged struggle. As a minimum, some effort should be made by Negroes to determine whether Negroes are in fact being used in excessive numbers in Vietnam so as to deflect the growing Asian accusations that the Vietnamese war is a confrontation between whites and non-whites. If such practices are substantiated, they will indeed be grave ones.

Whether or not any organized Negro protest against the Vietnamese war should take the suggested form of a refusal to do military service deserves considerable thought. Such a call appeared last summer in Mississippi, and later a similar call was circulated by a group entitled Afro-Americans for Freedom. The Mississippi protest was based primarily on the inappropriateness of American Negroes going off to kill unknown Vietnamese with whom they had no quarrel at a time when they had real, visible enemies who were murdering their families and friends in Mississippi, Alabama and Georgia. The latter protest had a slightly different philosophical basis in that it urged American Negroes to refuse to fight any other colored peoples. It, too, cited the substandard treatment of Negroes in America, but it was unclear if this were being offered as the rationale of the protest or if the ideological foundation lay more in the negritude concept mentioned earlier.

Verbalized objection by Negroes to military service is by no means new to the American scene. Although the position historically taken by the majority of Negro spokesmen has been a demand for full and nondiscriminatory participation for Negroes in America's military establishment, there has long been open expression of the contrary opinion as well. The advent of the Vietnam conflict, however, finds the American Negro for the first time in a position where his decision on this matter could be of serious national, and even international significance. It is only with the 1960's that the Negro finds himself with adequate sophistication and self-involvement, with adequate organization and leadership—Black, grass roots leadership—so that mass collective action could be even remotely possible.

Should Negro Americans
Refuse Military Service?

Whether or not the time has come to utilize Negro power in this way promises to become a major topic of controversy. When I first read of the Mississippi statement urging Negroes not to fight in Vietnam I greeted it as a worthy first step toward bringing the beleaguered Vietnamese people the peace and self-determination which they so desperately want. A moment's reflection, however, caused me to realize that the implications of the proposed military service boycott were much broader in scope than a simple moral objection to the wanton murder which we are committing in Vietnam. Although such a boycott, if it caught hold amongst both whites and Negroes, might well offer some relief to the Vietnamese peoples, it holds equally the potential for creating of America a true force for peace at this critical moment for human survival. It could become the first step in promoting a genuine human community surpassing the narrow boundaries of the nation-state, which is basically a European concept in any case. By the same token, however, so drastic a step poses a severe risk to the entire Negro struggle to win acceptance into the "Great Society" of President Johnson and obviously should not be taken without sober thought.

James Baldwin has bemoaned the fact that the Negro is working so hard to gain acceptance into a society which is basically sick and in decline, an observation with which many will agree. But certainly our glorious struggle is for something greater, something more substantial than merely to win for Negroes an opportunity to imitate their white compatriots—to immerse themselves in a color television or to kill themselves in an overpowered automobile. Hopefully, our vision of a better world relies as much on the spiritual values as on the material ones. Is it not conceivable, then, that the Negro people, who understand the white man's hypocrisy better than any one else and who are already applying an enema to the rot which has for so long contaminated America's domestic social organization, may spark an international purification as well?

Whether we are indeed ready to undertake this ambitious task or not, there should be no disagreement regarding the urgency of insuring that, as non-whites, we are not being inadvertently manipulated into an untenable position within the global framework. We must amass all of our wits so as to steer a careful course between the Scylla of American racism and the Charybdis of foreign intrigue. We intend to be tools of neither. Rather, Afro-Americans can perform no greater service to their country and to humanity than to use their unique position to encourage international racial amity and to prevent international racial conflict. They can do mankind no greater disservice than to allow themselves to be used as tools in precipitating such a catastrophe.

28

A Time to Break Silence, No. 2, 1967

MARTIN LUTHER KING JR.

In this speech delivered April 4, 1967, at Riverside Church in New York City and reprinted in Freedomways, *Dr. King came out publicly against the Vietnam War for the first time. The following are excerpts.*

I come to this magnificent house of worship tonight because my conscience leaves me no other choice. . . . The recent statements of your executive committee [Clergy and Laity Concerned About Vietnam] are the sentiments of my own heart. . . . "A time comes when silence is betrayal." That time has come for us in relation to Vietnam. . . .

I have seven major reasons for bringing Vietnam into the field of my moral vision. There is at the outset a very obvious connection between the war in Vietnam and the struggle I, and others, have been waging in America. A few years ago there was a shining moment in that struggle. . . .

Then came the build-up in Vietnam, and I watched the program [the War on Poverty] broken and eviscerated as if it were some idle political plaything of a society gone mad on war, and I knew that America would never invest the necessary funds or energies in rehabilitation of its poor so long as adventures like Vietnam continued to draw men and skills and money like some demonic destructive suction tube. So I was increasingly compelled to see the war as an enemy of the poor and to attack it as such.

Perhaps the more tragic recognition of reality took place when it became clear to me that the war was doing far more than devastating the hopes of the poor at home. It was sending their sons and their brothers and their husbands to fight and to die in extraordinarily high proportions relative to the rest of the population. We were taking the Black young men who had been crippled by our society and sending them 8,000 miles away to guarantee liberties in Southeast Asia which they had not found in Southwest Georgia and East Harlem. So we have been repeatedly faced with the cruel irony of watching Negro and white boys on TV screens as they kill and die together for a nation that has been unable to seat them together in the same schools. So we watch them in brutal solidarity burning the huts of a poor village, but we realize that they would never live on the same block in Detroit. I could not be silent in the face of such cruel manipulation of the poor.

My third reason moves to an even deeper level of awareness, for it grows out of my experience in the ghettos of the north over the last three years—especially the last three summers. As I have walked among the desperate, rejected and angry young men I have told them that Molotov cocktails and rifles would not solve their problems. I have tried to offer them my deepest compassion while maintaining my conviction that social change comes most meaningfully through non-violent action. But they asked—and rightly so—what about Vietnam? They asked if our own nation wasn't using massive doses of violence to solve its problems, to bring about the changes it wanted. Their questions hit home, and I knew that I could never again raise my voice against the violence of the oppressed in the ghettos without having first spoken clearly to the greatest purveyor of violence in the world today—my own government. For the sake of those boys, for the sake of this government, for the sake of the hundreds of thousands trembling under our violence, I cannot be silent. . . .

Strange Liberators

And as I ponder the madness of Vietnam and search within myself for ways to understand and respond with compassion, my mind goes

constantly to the people of that peninsula. I speak now not of the soldiers of each side, not of the junta in Saigon, but simply of the people who have been living under the curse of war for almost three continuous decades now. I think of them too because it is clear to me
that there will be no meaningful solution there until some attempt is
made to know them and hear their broken cries.

They must see Americans as strange liberators. The Vietnamese
people proclaimed their own independence in 1945 after a combined
French and Japanese occupation, and before the communist revolution in China. They were led by Ho Chi Minh. Even though they
quoted the American Declaration of Independence in their own document of freedom, we refused to recognize them. Instead, we decided to support France in its re-conquest of her former colony.

Our government felt then that the Vietnamese people were not
"ready" for independence, and we again fell victim to the deadly
western arrogance that has poisoned the international atmosphere
for so long. With that tragic decision we rejected a revolutionary
government seeking self-determination, and a government that had
been established not by China (for whom the Vietnamese have no
great love) but by clearly indigenous forces that included some communists. For the peasants this new government meant real land reform, one of the most important needs in their lives.

For nine years following 1945 we denied the people of Vietnam
the right of independence. For nine years we vigorously supported
the French in their abortive effort to re-colonize Vietnam.

Before the end of the war we were meeting 80 per cent of the
French war costs. Even before the French were defeated at Dien Bien
Phu, they began to despair of the reckless action, but we did not. We
encouraged them with our huge financial and military supplies to
continue the war even after they had lost the will. Soon we would be
paying almost the full costs of this tragic attempt at re-colonization.

After the French were defeated it looked as if independence and
land reform would come again through the Geneva agreements. But
instead there came the United States, determined that Ho should
not unify the temporarily divided nation, and the peasants watched
again as we supported one of the most vicious modern dictators—
our chosen man, Premier Diem. The peasants watched and cringed
as Diem ruthlessly routed out all opposition, supported their extor-
tionist landlords and refused even to discuss re-unification with the
North. The peasants watched as all this was presided over by U.S. influence and then by increasing numbers of U.S. troops who came to

help quell the insurgency that Diem's methods had aroused. When Diem was overthrown they may have been happy, but the long line of military dictatorships seemed to offer no real change—especially in terms of their need for land and peace.

The only change came from America as we increased our troop commitments in support of governments which were singularly corrupt, inept and without popular support. All the while the people read our leaflets and received regular promises of peace and democracy—and land reform. Now they languish under our bombs and consider us—not their fellow Vietnamese—the real enemy. They move sadly and apathetically as we herd them off the land of their fathers into concentration camps where minimal social needs are rarely met. They know they must move or be destroyed by our bombs. So they go—primarily women and children and the aged.

They watch as we poison their water, as we kill a million acres of their crops. They must weep as the bulldozers roar through their areas preparing to destroy the precious trees. They wander into the hospitals, with at least 20 casualties from American firepower for one "Vietcong"-inflicted injury. So far we may have killed a million of them—mostly children. They wander into the towns and see thousands of the children, homeless, without clothes, running in packs on the streets like animals. They see the children degraded by our soldiers as they beg for food. They see the children selling their sisters to our soldiers, soliciting for their mothers.

What do the peasants think as we ally ourselves with the landlords and as we refuse to put any action into our many words concerning land reform? What do they think as we test out our latest weapons on them, just as the Germans tested out new medicine and new tortures in the concentration camps of Europe? Where are the roots of the independent Vietnam we claim to be building? Is it among these voiceless ones?

We have destroyed their two most cherished institutions: the family and the village. We have destroyed their land and their crops. We have cooperated in the crushing of the nation's only non-communist revolutionary political force—the unified Buddhist Church. We have supported the enemies of the peasants of Saigon. We have corrupted their women and children and killed their men. What liberators!

Now there is little left to build on—save bitterness. Soon the only solid physical foundations remaining will be found at our military bases and in the concrete of the concentration camps we call fortified hamlets. The peasants may well wonder if we plan to build our new Vietnam on such grounds as these? Could we blame them for such thoughts? We must speak for them and raise the questions they cannot raise. These too are our brothers.

Perhaps the more difficult but no less necessary task is to speak for those who have been designated as our enemies. What of the National Liberation Front—that strangely anonymous group we call VC (Viet Cong) or Communists? What must they think of us in America when they realize that we permitted the repression and cruelty of Diem which helped to bring them into being as a resistance group in the South? What do they think of our condoning the violence which led to their own taking up of arms? How can they believe in our integrity when now we speak of "aggression from the North" as if there were nothing more essential to the war? How can they trust us when now we charge them with violence after the murderous reign of Diem and charge them with violence while we pour every new weapon of death into their land? Surely we must understand their feelings even if we do not condone their actions. Surely we must see that the men we supported pressed them to their violence. Surely we must see that our own computerized plans of destruction simply dwarf their greatest acts.

How do they judge us when our officials know that their membership is less than 25 per cent communist and yet insist on giving them the blanket name? What must they be thinking when they know that we are aware of their control of major sections of Vietnam and yet we appear ready to allow national elections in which this highly organized political parallel government will have no part? They ask how we can speak of free elections when the Saigon press is censored and controlled by the military junta. And they are surely right to wonder what kind of new government we plan to help form without them— the only party in real touch with the peasants. They question our political goals and they deny the reality of a peace settlement from which they will be excluded. Their questions are frighteningly relevant. Is our nation planning to build on political myth again and then shore it up with the power of new violence?

Here is the true meaning and value of compassion and non-violence when it helps us to see the enemy's point of view, to hear his questions, to know his assessment of ourselves. For from his view we may indeed see the basic weaknesses of our own condition, and if we are mature, we may learn and grow and profit from the wisdom of the brothers who are called the opposition.

So, too, with Hanoi. In the North, where our bombs now pummel the land, and our mines endanger the waterways, we are met by a deep but understandable mistrust. To speak for them is to explain this lack of confidence in western words, and especially their distrust of American intentions now. In Hanoi are the men who led the nation to independence against the Japanese and the French, the men who sought membership in the French commonwealth and were betrayed by the weakness of Paris and the wilfulness of the colonial armies. It was they who led a second struggle against French domination at tremendous costs, and then were persuaded to give up the land they controlled between the 13th and 17th parallel as a temporary measure at Geneva. After 1954 they watched us conspire with Diem to prevent elections which would have surely brought Ho Chi Minh to power over a United Vietnam, and they realized they had been betrayed again.

When we ask why they do not leap to negotiate, these things must be remembered. Also it must be clear that the leaders of Hanoi considered the presence of American troops in support of the Diem regime to have been the initial military breach of the Geneva Agreements concerning foreign troops, and they remind us that they did not begin to send in any large number of supplies or men until American forces had moved into the tens of thousands.

Hanoi remembers how our leaders refused to tell us the truth about the earlier North Vietnamese overtures for peace, how the President claimed that none existed when they had clearly been made. Ho Chi Minh has watched as America has spoken of peace and built up its forces, and now he has surely heard of the increasing international rumors of American plans for an invasion of the North. He knows the bombing and shelling and mining we are doing are part of traditional pre-invasion strategy. Perhaps only his sense of humor and of irony can save him when he hears the most powerful nation of the world speaking of aggression as it drops thousands of bombs on a poor weak nation more than 8,000 miles away from its shores.

At this point I should make it clear that while I have tried in these last few minutes to give a voice to the voiceless on Vietnam and to understand the arguments of those who are called enemy, I am as deeply concerned about our own troops there as anything else. For it occurs to me that what we are submitting them to in Vietnam is not simply the brutalizing process that goes on in any war where armies face each other and seek to destroy. We are adding cynicism to the process of death, for they must know after a short period there that none of the things we claim to be fighting for are really involved. Before long they must know that their government has sent them into a struggle among Vietnamese, and the more sophisticated surely realize that we are on the side of the wealthy and the secure while we create a hell for the poor.

Somehow this madness must cease. We must stop now. I speak as a child of God and brother to the suffering poor of Vietnam. I speak for those whose land is being laid waste, whose homes are being destroyed, whose culture is being subverted. I speak for the poor of America who are paying the double price of smashed hopes at home and death and corruption in Vietnam. I speak as a citizen of the world, for the world as it stands aghast at the path we have taken. I speak as an American to the leaders of my own nation. The great initiative in this war is ours. The initiative to stop it must be ours. . . .

In 1957 a sensitive American official overseas said that it seemed to him that our nation was on the wrong side of a world revolution. During the past 10 years we have seen emerge a pattern of suppression which now has justified the presence of U.S. military "advisors" in Venezuela. This need to maintain social stability for our investments accounts for the counter-revolutionary action of American forces in Guatemala. It tells why American helicopters are being used against guerrillas in Colombia and why American napalm and green beret forces have already been active against rebels in Peru. It is with such activity in mind that the words of the late John F. Kennedy come back to haunt us. Five years ago he said, "Those who make peaceful revolution impossible will make violent revolution inevitable."

Increasingly, by choice or by accident, this is the role our nation has taken—the role of those who make peaceful revolution impossible by refusing to give up the privileges and the pleasures that come from the immense profits of overseas investment.

I am convinced that if we are to get on the right side of the world revolution, we as a nation must undergo a radical revolution of values. We must rapidly begin the shift from a "thing-oriented" society to a "person-oriented" society. When machines and computers, profit motives and property rights are considered more important than people, the giant triplets of racism, materialism, and militarism are incapable of being conquered.

A true revolution of values will soon cause us to question the fairness and justice of many of our past and present policies. On the one hand we are called to play the Good Samaritan on life's roadside; but that will be only an initial act. One day we must come to see that the whole Jericho Road must be transformed so that men and women will not be constantly beaten and robbed as they make their journey on Life's highway. True compassion is more than flinging a coin to a beggar; it is not haphazard and superficial. It comes to see that an edifice which produces beggars needs re-structuring. A true revolution of values will soon look uneasily on the glaring contrast of poverty and wealth. With righteous indignation, it will look across the seas and see individual capitalists of the West investing huge sums of money in Asia, Africa and South America, only to take the profits out with no concern for the social betterment of the countries, and say: "This is not just." It will look at our alliance with the landed gentry of Latin America and say: "This is not just." The Western arrogance of feeling that it has everything to teach others and nothing to learn from them is not just. A true revolution of values will lay hands on the world order and say of war: "This way of settling differences is not just." This business of burning human beings with napalm, of filling our nation's homes with orphans and widows, of injecting poisonous drugs of hate into the veins of peoples normally humane, of sending men home from dark and bloody battlefields physically handicapped and psychologically deranged, cannot be reconciled with wisdom, justice and love. A nation that continues year after year to spend more money on military defense than on programs of social uplift is approaching spiritual death. . . .

The People Are Important

These are revolutionary times. All over the globe men are revolting against old systems of exploitation and oppression and out of the wombs of a frail world new systems of justice and equality are being born. The shirtless and barefoot people of the land are rising up as never before. "The people who sat in darkness have seen a great light." We in the West must support these revolutions. It is a sad fact that, because of comfort, complacency, a morbid fear of Communism, and our proneness to adjust to injustice, the Western nations that initiated so much of the revolutionary spirit of the modern world have now become the arch anti-revolutionaries. This has driven many to feel that only Marxism has the revolutionary spirit. Therefore, Communism is a judgment against our failure to make democracy real and follow through on the revolutions that we initiated. Our only hope today lies in our ability to recapture the revolutionary spirit and go out into a sometimes hostile world declaring eternal hostility to poverty, racism, and militarism. With this powerful commitment we shall boldly challenge the status quo and unjust mores and thereby speed the day when "every valley shall be exalted, and every mountain and hill shall be made low, and the crooked shall be made straight and the rough places plain."

A genuine revolution of values means in the final analysis that our loyalties must become ecumenical rather than sectional. Every nation must now develop an overriding loyalty to mankind as a whole in order to preserve the best in their individual societies. . . .

29

Muhammad Ali: The Measure of a Man, No. 2, 1967

EDITORIAL

Muhammad Ali (formerly Cassius Clay) held the title of world heavyweight champion in boxing. In protest against the war in Vietnam, he refused to be drafted into the United States military. In retaliation, the World Boxing Association took away his title and would not permit him to box professionally.

In recent months, with increasing frequency, it has been necessary to use the Editorial pages of FREEDOMWAYS to call attention to attacks upon particular individuals by the Government as well as other agencies of power. This has been necessary because these instances symbolize and mirror the larger pattern of what is happening in America today.

Consequently, our last Editorial (Winter '67) dealt with the unseating of Congressman Adam Clayton Powell, More recently, the withdrawal of the world heavyweight boxing title from its rightful holder, Mr. Muhammad Ali, by the World Boxing Association and various state Athletic Commissions is the latest case in point.

This arrogant, presumptuous act by the moguls of the boxing business was effected in a matter of hours after Muhammad Ali refused induction into the Army at Houston, Texas. Mr. Ali is also threatened with indictment by the Federal Government because of his anti-draft stand. This attack upon Mr. Ali occurs at a time when voices are heard in the U.S. Congress demanding that dissent be crushed and the First Amendment ignored. The huge anti-Vietnam War demonstrations in New York and San Francisco this spring have obviously placed the question of stopping the war in Vietnam on the agenda of our time and can no longer be ignored.

Mr. Ali's case raises questions of great import for the entire country, and most especially for the 22,000,000 Americans of African descent. This is quite aside from any consideration of the blatant immorality of the particular war against the Vietnamese people which Muhammad Ali is protesting together with millions of other Americans. It is also aside from considering his constitutionally guaranteed right to practice his religious beliefs as a matter of conscience.

While we are not claiming any special privilege for Negro Americans, what we are challenging is the moral right of this nation, *based upon its record,* to insist that any Black man must put on the military uniform, at any time, and go thousands of miles away from these shores to risk his life for a society which has historically been his oppressor.

Muhammad Ali, as Cassius Clay, fought for "his country" and won at the 1960 Olympics in Rome, only to return to his home town, Louisville, Kentucky, and be refused service at a lunch counter because he is a Black man. Where was the Federal Government then, to uphold his human rights? And where is the Federal Government today as civil rights workers in Louisville face screaming mobs, throwing rocks and bottles at them as they peacefully march to end housing discrimination? We are reminded that the State of Kentucky established its fame and wealth in the American Republic by breeding race horses and Negroes (both for sale, of course).

Stripping Muhammad Ali of the heavyweight title, which he earned the hard way, happens to be considered good business by the money-grabbing jackals who control the boxing syndicates. By stealing the heavyweight crown from the champion, they hope they can stimulate competition and a new era of prosperity at the box office. Such are the ethics of "our glorious free enterprise system."

"I won't wear the uniform," declared the world heavyweight champion. Of all the rhetoric used to express opposition to the Vietnam war, these words may prove to be the most eloquent as a statement of personal commitment. They are words which should echo among the youth in every ghetto across this land. In taking his stand as a matter of conscience, the world heavyweight champion may be giving up a small fortune, but he has undoubtedly gained the respect and admiration of a very large part of humanity. That, after all, is the measure of a Man.

The Editors

30

The GI Movement vs. the War: A Symposium, No. 4, 1970

RALPH DAVID ABERNATHY, HOWARD LEVY, and J. H. O'DELL

The radio program Martin Luther King Speaks, *William S. Stein, director, broadcast this symposium. At the time, Howard Levy was an organizer of the GI movement against the war, Reverend Ralph David Abernathy was a leader of the Southern Christian Leadership Conference (SCLC), and J. H. O'Dell was a* Freedomways *editor.*

. . .

Levy: Actually the GI movement started about 1967 or early 1968. Up until that time, anti-war people felt that by definition the GI was the enemy and he was the enemy because he wore a uniform of the Army and he therefore couldn't be for peace, they said. And then in 1968, actually January of 1968, the first anti-war coffee house opened up and it opened up in Columbia, South Carolina, which has the distinction of being the home of the Fighting Gamecocks of the

University of South Carolina and also the Home of Fort Jackson, a very large basic training base. The name of the coffee house was the UFO and they called [it] the UFO because it opened up across the street from the USO and it was an overnight success. . . .

It was really just a pun on the USO which a lot of the GI's felt wasn't serving their interest at all; it [USO] was nothing more than a propaganda front for the Army while they served them a little bit of coffee and donuts on the side. So the coffee house opened up and it was an immediate overnight success. In the beginning, a thousand, fifteen hundred GI's would come through the coffee house a week and they'd listen to music. They listened to people talk about the war in Vietnam, mostly people who opposed the war in Vietnam. Shortly after the coffee house opened up, a group of the GI's had a "pray-in" at Fort Jackson. They tried to pray for peace, and they were ordered to leave. They were told that you could not pray for peace on an Army post! You're allowed to pray for war, but praying for peace was carrying freedom of religion a bit far, and they [GI's] put out a newspaper. They called the newspaper, *Shore Times*. So things started happening and because of the success of that first coffee house, the people who set it up opened up two more coffee houses. They opened up one in Tacoma, Washington, called the "Shelter Half. . . ."

A lot of guys opposed the war in Vietnam, but there was no way that they could express that opposition, because all the peace groups were so hostile to them and almost hated them. And he felt that opening up a coffee house would provide one way to allow the GI's to express their real feelings about the war in Vietnam. . . .

Abernathy: So many Black men are in the Army at this particular time simply because they could not find jobs after graduating from high school. Neither could they pay the costly and high tuition fees to enter college and this was the best "job" available to them. But they don't believe in war anymore. Many are trying to provide for their aging mothers or to send their sisters through college and they get caught up in the vicious system. Countless numbers, far out of proportion to the Black population, are dying and fighting upon the front lines and now once they're thrown into it, they see this drastic and unjust system and they wish not to be a part of it.

Levy: No question about it. I think the other thing that you're going to find is that not only are the GI's against the war, but the Black

GI's are also very, very much concerned with *racism* in the Army. It's really an open secret. You know the Black youth is kind of in a bind because as you suggest he often can't get a job in his home town, he has to get a job to support his family and his loved ones and he gets into the Army as the only alternative in some instances. Then when he gets into the Army, he finds out that he's the one who's given the combat duty, he's the one that is in the front lines charging up "Hamburg Hill." He also finds that he's the one that gets the worst jobs in the Army, he becomes the cook, and he scrubs the floors and he mows the lawns. Those are the kinds of jobs that he gets and all of the promises that the Recruiting Sergeant made about how he's going to advance his education and how he's going to learn electronics and aviation and all the rest of it, is for the majority of Black GI's untrue. Now it's untrue also for the majority of white GI's, but it's even more untrue for the majority of Black GI's. So they get themselves in the Army and they find out that the Sergeant, the Platoon Sergeant and the First Lieutenant and the Major and the Colonel are often white Southerners, who are openly and overtly racist and they find not only that, but they find that many of the white soldiers are racist. So they go into a place like Saigon, for example, and they find that the bars are segregated, the poolrooms are segregated. So that even in a war zone, I mean everybody's buddy-buddy when they're in the middle of a fire fight, out there in the middle of Vietnam, but then when they come back into Saigon or Hong Kong or Tokyo for their rest and relaxation, they're right back in the same segregated society that they left maybe in Alabama or Mississippi or Georgia.

Abernathy: Well, you know that's almost unbelievable. I know that so often when the Black soldier's killed in Vietnam and his body's shipped back to these United States he could not be buried in the cemetery of his choice in certain sections of the United States. But you mean in Saigon the pool rooms and places of amusement might be segregated also?

Levy: This is what I understand. . . . Another form of opposition is to hold rallies. Now, within the last six or eight months, there've been a lot of rallies held, maybe 10 or 20 rallies near GI posts. . . . May 16th was significant because May 16th is the traditional day that the Army calls Armed Forces Day. Now, this year GI's planned counter-

demonstrations! You know May 16th is usually when the Army pa-
rades its men through the town with a lot of pomp and circumstance
and the artillery is paraded through the town and the planes fly over-
head and it's a very glorified day for the Army. This May 16th the
GI's planned counter-demonstrations which they called Peoples
Armed Forces Day, and the result of that was that the Army was
forced to cancel, for the first time in the history of this country,
Armed Forces Day on 25 major military bases. And the reason why
they cancelled Armed Forces Day was because by cancelling it, they
then were able to restrict the GI's to post and by restricting them
to post they prevented the GI's from going to the GI counter-
demonstrations. They knew that if they allowed the GI's to go to the
counter-demonstrations they would turn out in massive numbers.
Now, it's true, you know, that a thousand GI's out of a base of
maybe twenty or twenty-five thousand is still not a majority of the
GI's but it has to be appreciated that those fellows are taking a
tremendous risk every time they go to a demonstration, every time
they publish a newspaper and we've had innumerable guys court-
martialed for merely *reading* the newspapers. It's a summary court-
martial; and they usually get a month or two or three in the
stockade. . . .

Abernathy: . . . We come to a new stage in the movement today and
that is the right for a people's government. This is nothing new. It
was written by Thomas Jefferson and the Founding Fathers of this
nation almost two centuries ago when they spoke of no taxation
without representation. Ours is a Government "of the people, by the
people and for the people" and whenever the government becomes
so corrupt then it is the right of the people to change that government. We are going to stay on that case until this corruption of the
government is really changed and we can experience Freedom,
Equality, and Justice for all mankind and that great Negro spiritual
will become the anthem in the hearts of all men, "Ain't Gonna Study
War No More." So I applaud my brothers in the GI movement,
"Keep it up. . . ."

31

Three African Freedom Movements, No. 1, 1962

OUR SPECIAL CORRESPONDENT

Freedomways' *"special correspondent" made this report on the African National Congress (ANC) and two other liberation movements thirty years before the end of apartheid and the victory of the ANC.*

The purpose of this article is to briefly survey the history, aims and leaders of three African freedom movements in the Union of South Africa and the Territory of South West Africa and their international coordinating committee, The South Africa United Front. No attempt is made to systematically analyze the place of these organizations in the wider social, economic and political context of the Union; nor to survey all the African, Asian, Coloured and European organizations engaged in the struggle for human rights; nor, finally, is any attempt made to preview the future of the white man in South Africa.

Introduction

In the Union of South Africa ten million Africans and two million Asians and Coloureds are governed without their consent or participation by three million whites. From 1652 to the present the South African economy has been dependent upon the use of African labor. Since Black labor is the key to white prosperity all South African political regimes have been predicated on keeping the African as an impoverished toiler and have decreed that all relationships between white and Black shall be that of master and servant.

To implement these economic motives and maintain white supremacy each successive regime has imposed severe taxes on the African and stripped him of his land, controlled his work and travel by "passes," and in 1948 the Malan government created a legalized system of white supremacy called apartheid to ensure that the African people remain a cheap, docile, impoverished labor supply. This well-organized framework of exploitation has been buttressed by the racist attitudes of Church (Dutch Reformed) and State which suggest that the Black man has no soul and that it was God's will that the heathen savage should be brought under the civilizing forces of white christianity.

In the last 60 years the Union of South Africa has undergone a period of rapid industrialization and urbanization. While white South Africa has prospered there has been a heavy toll of Black labor. For example, since 1900 more than 36,000 Africans have been killed in the gold mines and the rate is now more than 1,400 killed in mine accidents per year. Africans toil underground for thirty cents a day and when they are killed through the negligence of mine authorities, as in Coalbrook where 431 men lost their lives, their widows get a lump sum of $500 paid at the rate of $10 a month.

In the process of industrial change the African worker has recognized that his labor has been exploited to create a politico-economic system which keeps him impoverished, denies him citizenship and deprives him of his basic human rights. By withholding his labor through sit-down strikes and work stoppages the African has forged a weapon against the daily symbols of white oppression: the taxes, the pass laws, the forced removals from one reserve to another and all the other paraphernalia of apartheid. His march toward freedom and self-determination has been met with blistering vehemence by the government. White South Africans have slaughtered hundreds of Africans in the Massacres at Cato Manor, Windhoek, Pondoland, Sharpeville and Langa; and thousands of Black men are incarcerated without due process in prisons and concentration camps. All militant African political organizations are banned and their leaders are either in jail, under house arrest or in exile. Meanwhile whites are arming themselves with fighter planes, Sten guns and Saracen tanks supplied by Great Britain, France, Belgium and the Rhodesias.

But the will of the African people is undaunted and the struggle for freedom and independence continues. Within South Africa there are three organizations which are vehicles for African political expression: The African National Congress, The Pan-Africanist Congress and The South West African National Union. Outside South Africa they are a united front engaged in enlisting the support of world opinion and resources to bring about the total liberation and independence of the African people.

The African National Congress (ANC)

The African National Congress (ANC) is the oldest continuing protest and freedom organization in the Union of South Africa. In the 48 years of its existence—from its founding in 1912 to its banning in 1960—the ANC has carried the message of unity and freedom to all corners of southern Africa. Today, forced into the underground by the Union government it continues its operations with the whole-hearted support of the African masses, African exiles and friends in the major capitals of the world.

From the Great Zulu wars to the present struggle Africans have always resisted white tyranny. During the period 1882–1909 the first parliamentary-type organizations came into existence. The Native Education Association protested the pass laws, the Native Electoral Association organized the African vote and Native Congresses were formed in Natal and Transvaal. In 1909 a Native Convention met to discuss the Act of Union by which the British Colonies of Natal and the Cape and the northern republics of Transvaal and the Free State were welded into a self-governing Union with no provision for African participation or franchise.

Under these historic circumstances the African National Congress was founded January 8th at Bloemfontein. It was the first national convention that brought together chiefs, headmen, teachers, ministers, leaders of organizations and delegates from all parts of the Union and the Protectorates. Leading personalities at this convention were Prof. D. D. Jabavu; John L. Dube, leader of the Natal Native Congress and the first ANC president; and Sol T. Plattje an active leader in the African Coloured Peoples Organization in the Cape.

The initial aims of the ANC were racial unity and mutual aid, the abolition of the pass laws and the extension of full democratic rights to the African. These aims were to be implemented by deputations, boycotts and work stoppages as indicated in a brief chronicle of their early activities: In 1913, in their first major battle, the ANC protested and sent deputations to Great Britain concerning the Land Act which stripped Africans of their rights to own land outside the reserves; in 1919 they supported the wage demands of Johannesburg municipal workers and as a result many of their leaders were arrested; in 1935 they participated in the All-African Convention which opposed the removal of African voters from the common roll in the Cape and the establishment of a "whites only" national Parliament with a separate Council for Native Representation.

The African National Congress was throughout this period a Black man's organization pledged to the attainment of African freedom not only in South Africa but throughout all the African continent. Through their slogan *Mayibuye iAfrika* (Let Africa Return), their anthem *Nkosi Sikilele iAfrika* (God Bless Africa), their flag with the vivid colors Black for the people, Green for the verdant land and Gold for her mineral riches, the concept of a free united Africa spread to all parts of Africa. And, at the early Pan African Congresses called by the eminent American scholar of African descent, Dr. W.E.B. Du Bois, ANC leaders impressed their ideas upon delegates from every corner of the African world.

During the period 1938–1948 a number of significant events set the stage for a new phase of militant action by the African National Congress. First, Africans participated in the war against fascism, albeit as unarmed clean-up squads, and this was understood by them to be a step forward to their eventual attainment of full citizenship. This hope never materialized and many young Africans became convinced that they must liberate themselves from a politico-economic system at home that was far worse than the fascism of Nazi Germany. Secondly, African leaders were encouraged by the Allied political documents, especially the Atlantic Charter which affirmed "the right of all people to choose the form of government under which they may live," and they modeled a new set of African demands based on the principle of human rights. Finally, it was during the war years that Pan Africanism came of age and challenged the whole system of racialism and colonialism. Henceforth, it was said, Africans and persons of African descent would create their own destiny under their own banner, Pan Africanism, in cooperation with their own selected allies.

In South Africa the ANC moved swiftly toward a more militant position. In 1943 the ANC Youth League was formed under the leadership of Oliver Tambo, Joe Matthews, A. M. Lembede and Nelson Mandela and others. They called upon the Congress and all Africans to pursue a more vigorous forthright and open opposition to racial injustice. Slowly, the ANC, aided by the Pact of 1946 with the South African Indian Congress gathered the bulk of the non-white population behind a passive resistance campaign and a national strike and broadened the struggie against the Union government's policies. In 1948 however the Malan regime came into power with the support of all segments of the white community and codified the earlier racial statutes and practices into a legalized system of white supremacy and exploitation called apartheid. And, in 1950 the government under the guise of the Suppression of Communism Act outlawed all organized African and non-white opposition to their racist policies.

The wartime and post-war eras were therefore critical periods for the ANC and its leaders, Rev. Z. R. Mahabane, Prof. Z. K. Matthews, Dr. A. B. Xuma and Dr. J. Moroka. As a result of these crises, however, the ANC did emerge with a greater awareness of the resoluteness with which the government intended to pursue their policies of apartheid and a greater awareness of the need for unity among all South Africans engaged in the struggle for human rights and African freedom.

The Defiance of Unjust Laws Campaign was the first significant test of the new strength and confidence of the ANC. In this passive resistance campaign 10,000 Africans, Asians, Coloureds and whites defied the apartheid laws and voluntarily went to jail. One of the outstanding supporters of this campaign was Chief Albert John Luthuli, a man whose life history parallels that of the ANC.

Chief Luthuli is a tall robust man who has been a minister, teacher and leader among the Abasemakholmeni Zulu people for most of his

63 years. He spent thirty years of his life in patient moderate attempts to bring about change in the government's policies. In 1952 he was summoned before a government tribunal for his support of the Defiance campaign and told either to resign from the ANC or be deprived of his chieftaincy. He refused to do either and replied:

> Who will deny that thirty years of my life have been spent knocking in vain, patiently, moderately and modestly at a closed and barred door? What have been the fruits of moderation? The past thirty years have seen the greatest number of laws restricting our rights and progress until today we have reached a stage where we have almost no rights at all. It is with this background and with a full sense of responsibility that, under the auspices of the ANC I have joined my people in the new spirit that moves them today, the spirit that revolts openly and boldly against injustice and expresses itself in a determined and non-violent manner. What the future has in store for me I do not know. It might be ridicule, imprisonment, concentration camp, flogging, banishment and even death. I only pray to the Almighty to strengthen my resolve so that none of these grim possibilities may deter me from striving, for the sake of the good name of our beloved country, the Union of South Africa, to make it a true democracy and a true union, in form and spirit, of all the communities in the land.

For these words Chief Luthuli was deposed by the government, but he was immediately elected as president of the ANC and has since been a leading figure in the defiance of apartheid laws and the movement for African freedom. In many ways he is today the spiritual leader of the African people as well as the president of their major political movement.

On Congress Freedom Day, June 26, 1955, a Congress of the People was held in Transvaal and delegates from all races and regions adopted a Freedom Charter which began:

> We, the people of South Africa, declare for all our country and the world to know that South Africa belongs to all who live in it, black and white, and that no government can justly claim authority unless it is based on the will of all the people.

The Charter also demanded that African rights be secured in regard to universal suffrage, equality before the law, the right to work, freedom of movement, security, education and peace. In addition, they called for an end to restriction on land ownership, a redivision of the land, and the "transfer of the mineral wealth, the banks and monopoly industry, to the ownership of the people as a whole."

Through this Congress the ANC entered into an alliance with white and Coloured as well as Asian democratic organizations dedicated to the achievement of a non-racial South Africa based on equal rights for all. This Congress Alliance led to renewed activity against apartheid laws. In December 1956 they supported the Alexandra bus boycott and one month later 156 ANC and Alliance members and supporters were arrested and charged with high treason, a crime punishable by death. However, the roots of the ANC program were so strongly entrenched among the masses that on June 26, 1957, literally from their prison cells, they called a massive one-day stay-away-from-work boycott which stopped the wheels of industry in all major urban areas.

During 1958–1960 the toll of Africans killed by the police had mounted rapidly: 3 at Cato Manor June 17, 1959; eleven at Windhoek December 10, 1959; and on March 21, 1960 at Sharpeville eighty Africans were shot in the back by the police. That same week in Johannesburg to give evidence at the treason trial Chief Luthuli publicly burned his pass and called for a National Day of Mourning.

The immediate consequence of the Sharpeville shootings was the declaration of a State of Emergency and the publication of the Emergency Regulations which prohibited all gatherings and processions and empowered the police to arrest anyone in the interests of public safety without charge and for any specified time. Under these acts 20,000 people were arrested and detained. At the same time the ANC, the Alliance organizations and the Pan-Africanist Congress which had initiated the Sharpeville protests against the pass laws, were banned and Chief Luthuli and other leaders were arrested. In this manner the government stripped the Africans of their legislative political organizations through which they had been able to express their opposition to the government's policies.

Since 1960 the African National Congress has carried on its fight against apartheid from the underground with the full support of the African masses. It has become increasingly clear to the ANC leadership, however, that the real struggle is for the establishment of a democratic non-racial state. On the eve of the birth of the Republic of South Africa May 31, 1961 (as declared by the nation's white vot-

ers), 1,400 delegates from one hundred and forty-five African people's organizations solemnly met at Pietermaritzburg and called for a
new non-racial constitution:

> We declare that no constitutional form of government decided without
> the participation of the African people, who form an absolute majority
> of the population, can enjoy moral validity or merit support either
> within South Africa or beyond its borders.
>
> We demand that a national convention of elected representatives of
> all adult men and women on an equal basis, irrespective of race, color
> or creed or other limitations, be called by the Union Government not
> later than May 31, 1961, and that the Convention shall have sovereign
> powers to determine, in any way the representatives decide, a new non-
> racial democratic constitution for South Africa.

Furthermore, the manifesto declared, should the government ignore this demand all Africans must be ready to organize in town and
country to oppose oppression and to win freedom. It was the full intention of the assembled African delegates that a government refusal
to accede to their demands would mean the struggle was now clearly
out in the open—it would be a struggle between African democracy
and white fascism—to the end.

To answer this challenge the government called out the entire
Army and turned South Africa into an armed totalitarian state where
"white men stalk black men in the dead of night and mothers prepare
breakfast with loaded 45's."

This is the situation inside South Africa today.

Outside South Africa the African National Congress has joined in
a United Front with the Pan Africanist Congress, The South West
African National Union and the South African Indian Congress to
mobilize international opposition to South African racism and to win
support for the complete independence of the African people. . . .

32

The African–American Manifesto on Southern Africa, No. 4, 1976

This ten-point manifesto was adopted at a conference convened by the Congressional Black Caucus, September 24–25, 1976, in Washington, D.C., Representatives attended from the NAACP, PUSH, AFRICARE, Black Economic Research Council, National Council of Negro Women, and members of the Congressional Black Caucus. It initiated campaigns in the United States to end apartheid and to free Nelson Mandela.

There comes a moment in the affairs of humankind when honor requires unequivocal affirmation of a people's right to freedom with dignity and peace with justice.

This is such a moment. We express solidarity with Africans protesting racism and oppression in the streets of Soweto, Port Elizabeth, Capetown, Johannesburg and elsewhere. The intransigence of white settlers in Zimbabwe and Namibia and the bloody repression of Blacks in South Africa have created explosive environments which threaten world peace and raise the spectre of an internationalized, anti-colonial war which could have an ominous impact on race relations in America and abroad.

Inaction in face of such a threat is betrayal of our future—betrayal of humanity, betrayal of the long line of Black men and women who have given their lives in the struggle for freedom.

Conscious of our duty to speak, and recognizing our responsibilities to humanity and to the revolutionary ideals of our forebears, we, the descendants of Africa, meeting in Washington, D.C., on this 200th anniversary of the first modern war for independence, proclaim our unswerving commitment to immediate self-determination and majority rule in Southern Africa.

We do this because we are African-Americans, and because we know that the destiny of Blacks in America and Blacks in Africa is inextricably intertwined, since racism and other forms of oppression respect no territories or boundaries.

We do this because we are African-Americans and because we have a mandate from our revolutionary predecessors: from Crispus Attucks to W.E.B. Du Bois, from Dinizulu to Amilcar Cabral, from Martin Luther King to Malcolm X, from Nkrumah to Lumumba, from Nat Turner to Whitney Young, from Sojourner Truth to Mary McLeod Bethune, to proclaim the truth of the Revolution of 1776, which is also the truth of the Revolution of 1976 in Southern Africa.

In this spirit and with this understanding, we contend that it is mandatory for all Americans, and especially Americans of African descent, to understand the root causes of strife in Zimbabwe, Namibia and South Africa. These root causes are:

Despotism and racism that serve to polarize the white government and the African majority;

The continuing violence by the Europeans to sustain institutions of racism and exploitation;

Economic exploitation.

The history of our common struggle and recognition that our cause is just have brought us this day to proclaim and adopt the following 10 points:

1. We believe the present government of South Africa is the main barrier against majority rule in Southern Africa because of its continued illegal occupation of Namibia, its refusal to implement economic sanctions against Rhodesia and its unwillingness to share political and economic power with Blacks within its own borders. Specifically, if present negotiations fail or are unacceptable to African liberation leaders and the

African people of Zimbabwe, Namibia and South Africa, the
President of the United States should:

Support a finding in the Security Council that South Africa's continued illegal occupation of Namibia is an act of aggression and a
   threat to the peace, calling for action under Chapter 7 of the
   United Nations Charter.
Provide assistance, both humanitarian and military, to the liberation
   movements through the Organization of African Unity.
Impose a mandatory arms embargo against South Africa and a stop-
   page of shipments of equipment to be used by the military, including all technology and nuclear material.

2. We totally support the liberation of Southern Africa from
   white minority rule by means of armed struggle, where necessary, and affirm the right of the African liberation movements to seek necessary assistance from whatever sources
   available to achieve self-determination and majority rule. We
   firmly reject the notion that such assistance implies external
   domination within Cold War context. However, we are unal-
   terably opposed to external intervention from whatever quarter designed to thwart the inevitable extension of African freedom to the southern tip of Africa.
3. Negotiations can achieve a genuine peace only when they
   occur between the contending forces. High level diplomatic
   involvement by the U.S. and other powerful, concerned states
   can be of positive assistance, but they can be considered "successful" only when they achieve the full liberation of the suppressed people. In light of this principle we look to the representatives of the Front Line States and the organized fighting
   forces of the suppressed populations for the standard by which
   to judge the success of good will negotiations involving third
   parties. Transitional arrangements to majority rule must include an opportunity for the organized fighting forces to participate in the drafting of constitutional arrangements and the
   free public discussion and voting which is required for their
   ratification. *Therefore, we support the five Front Line Presidents*
   in their call on the United States to support the Freedom
   Fighters if Prime Minister Vorster and Mr. Smith obfuscate the
   fundamental changes which the struggle in Zimbabwe is on

the verge of accomplishing. Similarly, *we oppose United States support for any settlement in Zimbabwe and Namibia that compromises the freedom of Blacks in South Africa.*

And in this connection, we urge the Administration to call upon South Africa to release its political prisoners and to begin negotiating with them and other Black leaders toward the establishment of a real democracy which guarantees majority rule and human rights for all.

The people of Zimbabwe, Namibia and South Africa, and the independent African states acting in their behalf, have tried for more than half a century through petitions, representations, negotiations, peaceful demonstrations, appearances before the United Nations and through appeals to international tribunals to achieve self-determination through majority rule. It is a matter of fact and history that these peaceful efforts have never received the full support of western powers. Multinational corporations and industrialized nations, headed by the United States and including Great Britain, France, Germany, Israel and Japan, which collectively account for over 60 percent of all trade with South Africa, reinforced the white minority ruled regimes through expanded investments, violation of economic sanctions and arms embargoes, and by sales of military related equipment and nuclear technology to South Africa.

4. *We strongly condemn the Pretoria Government* for crimes against humanity through its wanton killing of hundreds of African youthful demonstrators and its wholesale detention without legal redress of Africans and their allies. We urge that the U.S. provide special political refugee status, similar to that accorded to the Cubans, to Africans forced to emigrate from Zimbabwe, Namibia and South Africa because of political repression.

5. *We, in support of the Organization of African Unity, oppose any U.S. Government recognition of the "Transkei"* and United States corporate investment in that "Bantustan" whose independence will deny Africans their birthright to full economic and political participation in the entire Republic of South Africa.

6. We reject any U.S. policy that stresses "Minority Rights" rather than "Human Rights" in Southern Africa, since mi-

nority rights in context implies the preservation of European privilege. Therefore, we question any large-scale financial subsidy of "Minority Rights" for Rhodesian whites, which would serve to reward the villains at the expense of the victims. Moreover, we denounce those pronouncements by Administration officials that repeatedly speak of the need for "moderate leadership," of "responsible government" and any policy which interferes with the right of the people to decide for themselves their system of government. Neither the United States nor any other power has the right to impose any government on the people of Namibia, Zimbabwe or South Africa. Self-government is the most inalienable of all rights.

7. We believe that independence in Namibia—including Walvis Bay, the principal port presently considered part of South Africa—must be achieved according to the guidelines set forth in Security Council Resolution 385 of January 30, 1976, which demands that South Africa withdraw and end its illegal administration of Namibia, and transfer power to the people of Namibia with the assistance of the United Nations; that is, release all political prisoners, hold free elections under United Nations supervision and control and "abolish all racially discriminatory and politically repressive laws and practices, particularly bantustans and homelands."

   SWAPO (South West African Peoples' Organization) must have a principal role in any negotiations. The Turnhalle Conference should have no standing whatsoever since it excluded SWAPO participation and is the creation of South Africa.

8. *We urge proper recognition of the expanded potential of the United Nations as a fully representative body.* The people and government of the United States must accept the changing perspective of U.S. interests among the family of nations and work within the United Nations and its affiliated institutions to deal with the emerging North-South issues which are the principal sources of tension and potential conflict in global affairs. Majority ruled African nations now constitute nearly one-third of United Nations membership, and consequently, are a pivotal group in that body.

   We urge the U.S. to join the Council on Namibia, contribute to the U.N. Trust Fund, and we condemn the use of

the veto by our government in the Security Council to protect South Africa.

9. *We urge our government to recognize the People's Republic of
Angola and support its admission to the United Nations.* The
PRA has joined the other Front Line States in efforts to ob-
tain an appropriate settlement in Southern Africa. U.S. align-
ment on the same losing side with South Africa during the
Angolan conflict demonstrated the bankruptcy of the government's Africa policy. This error should not be perpetuated. A
normalization of relations with the Angolan Government will
facilitate any U.S. involvement in bringing about a just peace
in the region.

10. We condemn the role played by the United States and other
foreign corporations and banks, which by their presence and
activities collectively have participated in the oppression of
Blacks and have undergirded the repressive white minority
governments of Southern Africa. No longer must Mr. Vorster
be able to exact U.S. political support as ransom for America's
hostage private corporations. Multinational corporations
must recognize that the South African economy is not sound,
and that the investment climate there is no longer favorable.
The government should institute a program of tax disincen-
tives to U.S. corporations operating in South Africa, Zimbabwe and Namibia. And should those corporations remain
unprepared to use their leverage to bring about concrete steps
towards economic and political justice in South Africa, and to
operate there, in Namibia and in Zimbabwe on the basis of
fair and non-discriminatory employment practices, humane
working conditions and just compensation for the exploitation of African resources, they should withdraw.

Our Commitment

We challenge the Judeo-Christian community, the labor movement,
the media and the political, business, and civic leadership in this
country to see that our government upholds its values and its historical commitment to self-determination, freedom and justice, and to
understand that the appeasement of South African can only invite an
escalated war that will exacerbate racial tensions in the United States.

Finally, in turn, we commit ourselves to mobilizing Black Americans and others of good will to formulate and support a progressive U.S. policy toward Africa. And we state our opposition to those Blacks who work directly or indirectly to support white minority regimes in Southern Africa.

The policies we have recommended are not only morally just, they are in America's best interests. Africa's economic and strategic importance to the United States in an increasingly interdependent world must be fully recognized.

33

South Africa and the USA, No. 4, 1976

EDITORIAL

. . . U.S. corporate investments in South Africa have increased several times over in the last 15 years. Loans are made by the U.S. Government to South Africa through the International Monetary Fund; and full opportunity is provided for South Africa to sell gold and other products in the U.S. market. These are the economic relations and support systems which help provide the fascist apartheid regime with stability.

Auto workers should organize a major petition drive demanding that Ford and General Motors shut down their operations in South Africa. This could be made an issue at the bargaining table in this year's contract negotiations. Most countries in the United Nations have already broken diplomatic relations with South Africa; the United States has not. On the contrary, current U.S. policy in the U.N. continues to be one of blocking all efforts at forcing economic and military sanctions against the Pretoria regime.

Sustained picket lines around the headquarters of Chase National Bank and Bank of America in every city, educating their depositors that their money is being used to underwrite apartheid in South

Africa, demanding that these banks stop making loans to South Africa and close their South African offices—these are the kinds of actions needed. If they have done nothing else, recent events in South Africa and the ruthlessness with which the apartheid government has responded to the people's democratic demands have buried the myth that U.S. corporations should remain in South Africa as an influence toward ending apartheid. That myth has been propagated by liberals and conservatives alike as a rationale for increasing U.S. corporate investment in South Africa since the Sharpesville murders in 1960. U.S. corporations are in South Africa for one reason only—the super-profits they get from the cheap labor and miserable conditions of the African workers which the fascist apartheid system makes possible. And the United States Government maintains economic, political, and diplomatic relations with the Nazilike government of South Africa for the same reason: it is good for General Motors, Exxon, IBM, and Kissinger's boss, the Rockefeller brothers.

No wonder Prime Minister Vorster can arrogantly announce a policy of "no concessions" to the just demands of the African majority and continue to occupy Namibia illegally and militarily in defiance of the United Nations. This policy of die-hard racism and colonialism has the official support of the United States even while lip service is being given to "majority rule" in Africa. The continuing fundamental reality is that the U.S. State Department supports the Afrikaaner Nationalist regime in South Africa because that regime is a faithful protector of American corporate interests and the "Free World" alliance.

The people of South Africa supported by the civilized international community, which opposes fascism and crass exploitation, will overcome this tyranny. Our challenge here in the United States is to resolutely join in that support effort.

34

Northern Ireland Through Black Eyes, No. 1, 1982

JEAN CAREY BOND

Jean Carey Bond, an editor of Freedomways, *traveled to Northern Ireland with a seven-person delegation to meet with Catholic civil rights activists and representatives of social and political organizations. The New York H-Block/Armagh Committee sponsored the trip. Independent producer St. Clair Bourne shot a film of the delegation's visit,* The Black and the Green, *for public television.*

The large Black man in the embroidered dashiki and crocheted skull cap strikes a chord on his well-traveled guitar and invites the youthful audience to join him and his companions in singing one last song—"We Shall Overcome." The man does not have to lead the song for the youngsters know it well, every note, every word. They sing passionately and with less solemnity than we used to sing this anthem in the days of lunch-counter sit-ins and Freedom Rides and Bull Connor's dogs.

The time is December 1981, and the place is a community center in Belfast, Northern Ireland. The 200 or so singers, whose voices almost drown out the powerful baritone of the Black man on stage, are

Irish. From whence spring their feelings of camaraderie with us, a delegation of mostly Black Americans who rarely encounter such kindred spirits in a group of white folks?

Part of the answer lies in a play called "Plastic Bullets," put together and performed by the young people that night at the community center. It tells about the children and adults who have been mortally wounded in the streets by so-called "non-lethal" weapons, weapons rejected by Northern Ireland's British occupiers for use in their own country, but considered apt for controlling the predominantly Catholic, anti-colonialist communities of Belfast and other Northern Irish cities. The dramatic scenes, music, recitations and slides recall some of the theater the U.S. civil rights era produced. Watching the play, one wondered if the plastic bullet is not a fitting contemporary symbol of Britain's centuries-old oppression of the "inferior" Irish people, and of the double indemnity visited upon Northern Ireland's minority Catholic population.

The answer is written, too, in the physique of West Belfast, by all appearances deserving of its title, Catholic ghetto. Low-slung, ancient-looking brick dwellings dominate the area's streets, grim in their uniformity, familiar in their aspect of poverty. Occasionally, the old stone gives way to concrete or that low-budget brick so common to the public housing projects of Harlem and the South Bronx. Shops are sparse and seem to be mostly of the "mom-and-pop" variety, with an occasional fast-food franchise thrown in (vinegar on your chips, luv?). The streetlights are few and dim; buses pass only once in a blue moon and are jammed. Vintage black taxis pass frequently on planned routes, picking up passengers until they're full. They are owned and operated by a community cooperative as an alternative form of public transportation because the authorities have a habit of terminating service whenever the people decide to protest their condition boisterously in the streets. Other, more deadly vehicles are also evident: Armored Saracen tanks manned by British soldiers, who look like Darth Vader come to life in their helmets with wrap-around visors.

Garrisons of the resident police force, the Royal Ulster Constabulary (RUC), heavily season the landscape, encircled by barbed-wire fences. One of these is the infamous Castleraegh, referred to by the locals as the neighborhood torture center.

We had been to Long Kesh that morning (known officially as the Maze Prison). Unable to enter the prison, we had stood in the visi-

tors' parking lot, bearing witness you might say, while sentries
watched us from their guard towers. As our van traversed the few
miles back to town, we looked at the passing scene and were silent
for the most part. Our driver saw the roadblock before we did. He
said the prison sentries had alerted RUC headquarters about us.
They knew we were coming. Don't tell them who you're staying
with, he said—no names. They stopped us, with automatic rifles
drawn, and ordered us out of the van. The young officer in charge
was arrogant and abusive to the point of parody. He strutted, he
glowered, he threatened like cops do throughout the world who believe that the uniform and gun provided them by the state mandate
any and all forms of intimidation. After examining our passports, he
searched the van for about fifteen minutes—even reading a diary that
he found in the glove compartment. When he opened the hood to
look at the engine, he cocked his rifle. After grilling our driver for a
few minutes in a nearby armored truck, he told us to drive on.

The wall murals adorning West Belfast also reply and are as eloquent as the area's prison-like character is profane. "Blessed are those
who hunger for justice," reads one mural, referring to the hunger
strike that claimed the life of Bobby Sands and nine of his fellows last
fall. Another: "You can kill the revolutionary but never the revolution"; and another: "Victory to the IRA." The colors are vibrant, the
lettering precise. They were painted with great care by teenagers.

We hear another piece of the answer in our hosts' descriptions of
the stereotypes directed at them by many Britishers and Protestant
Irish, and we are overcome by a feeling of déjà vu. "Catholics are lazy
and dirty." "All they know how to do is breed children." "Irish culture is backward and of no consequence," etc., ad nauseam. How
does this discrimination work, we ask, when all of you are white:
How does one tell a Catholic from a Protestant or a "Brit"? If you
live in Twinbrook, we are told—that's Twinbrook Estates, where
Bobby Sands' family lives—you are marked. When you apply for a
job, they look at your address and at the name of the school you attended, and they know. You don't get the job.

The overriding reason for the warm reception accorded our delegation is the credit assigned by the Catholic people of Northern Ireland to the 1960s civil rights movement in the U.S. for inspiring the
current phase of their struggle to end Britain's colonial domination
and the 50 years of sectarian discrimination and repression which
have accompanied it.

. . . Tony was as warm and attentive a host as anyone could be, and he took good care of Kathy and me throughout the delegation's visit to Belfast. At the apartment in Twinbrook Estates that his friend had vacated to accommodate us, he slept on the living room floor under two overcoats. Only a few months prior to our coming, he had been released from Long Kesh where he had served four years "on the blanket." Tony laughs a lot, especially at his own jokes. But his eyes fragment the laughter into slivers. The first time I noticed was at the nightclub—a nationalist hangout—where we had gone to hear a popular group sing Irish freedom songs. He stares, rarely blinking. He stares, not into space but through time. Tony is still in Long Kesh, perhaps for life. . . .

The process that pervaded the Northern Ireland scene during the years 1976 to 1981 was dramatic and heart-rending, its best known component being the five-month strike in 1981 whereby ten very young men, through sheer force of will, hungered themselves to death. . . .

Visiting Belfast as we did, in the recent aftermath of the hunger strike, our delegation was struck by the community's unflagging, though anguished, solidarity with and respect for all of the prisoners in Long Kesh and Armagh, and by their belief that the ultimate sacrifice of Bobby Sands and nine others had not been a misguided and futile "tactic." Rather they see it as an eloquent statement of faith and commitment to justice made by courageous young men on behalf of a desperate people. . . .

Ballymurphy, a Catholic section in Belfast visited by our delegation, is considered one of the most depressed urban areas in Western Europe. . . . Ballymurphy looks and feels like apartheid. The housing development called Devis Flats is the kind of place that must have looked shoddy even when it was new. Surveillance towers stand within it, permitting the British soldiers stationed in them to oversee activity on the exterior walkways that encircle the low-rise dwellings. Five people, we were told, have been shot on the walkways by the soldiers. Arriving at Devis at 2:30 A.M., we slept in the tiny apartment of Tony's friend. Upon awakening later in the morning, we met the little boy of the house, ten years old. "Our section is the only part of Devis the Brits can's see from the towers," he told us, as he grappled with Rubic's Cube and his dog at the same time. When he left the room, Tony told us that the dog was a new one. The soldiers had thrown his other dog down a stairwell, killing him. . . .

The historic and current experiences of the Irish people we talked with are key to their perceptions about the nature of their struggle. Theirs is a "Third World" struggle, they told us, a fight against British colonialism in particular and imperialism in general—a fight for self-determination. Their allies, they said, are the Black people of South Africa, the Palestinians, Afro-Americans.

A just struggle, by whatever name, continues in Ireland. The IRA, with its political arm Sinn Fein, is central to it but there are other forces as well. For example, there is the Irish Republican Socialist Party, co-founded by the internationally known Bernadette Devlin McAliskey. In the wake of the hunger strike, the prisoners in the north are still subject to the authorities' whims—a concession granted here, a privilege withheld there. Nationalists are still drawing inordinately long prison sentences for actions that, if committed by supporters of the status quo, are likely to go unpunished. (Bobby Sands was serving fourteen years for having been in a van with three people in which a single revolver was found.) While observing the Irish struggle from afar, we would do well to heed the words of a member of our delegation, James Dunn: Amid U.S. media distortions of what is going on in Northern Ireland, we must not allow ourselves to forget who the criminals really are.

PART FOUR

Moving North

ESTHER COOPER JACKSON
CONSTANCE POHL

In the late 1960s, some civil rights activists shifted their focus from desegregation in the South to problems of discrimination around the country. The subjects of the articles included in this section reflect some of this change.

Women's equality deserves special mention, for the women who sustained *Freedomways* were pioneers in that area of human rights. Black women were the heart of the collective that produced *Freedomways* for 25 years. Shirley Graham Du Bois, Augusta Strong, Jean Carey Bond, and Ruby Dee were present at the birth of the journal, and later women like Alice Walker and Angela Davis joined them as contributing editors. The magazine introduced readers to new Black women poets, such as Audre Lorde, Nikki Giovanni, Alice Walker, and June Jordan, as well as more established writers, like Gwendolyn Brooks. Jean Carey Bond edited the special issue devoted to the playwright Lorraine Hansberry. (Many of these works appear in Part 6, Culture and the Cause of Black Freedom.)

Augusta Strong wrote about Black women in freedom's struggles, an excerpt of which is included in this section. In another of her articles, "Southern Youth's Proud Heritage" (see Part 1), Strong tells of the role of women in the Southern Negro Youth Congress.

The women contributors to *Freedomways* spoke in clear, strong voices about Black women's issues. As early as 1965—before the surge of the women's liberation movement—Sarah Wright denounced the caricatures of women in contemporary literature. (Her speech is found in Part 6 of this volume.) Angela Davis took on the serious problem of rape and racism, and Dorothy Burnham viewed gender and race prejudice from the sober, if passionate, vantage of the scientist.

Freedomways also addressed the issues in education, the criminal justice system, Black power, and labor unions. A sampling of such articles is included here.

35

Anti-Semitism and Black Power, No. 1, 1967

OSSIE DAVIS

Ossie Davis sent this letter to the Readers' Forum of Freedomways. *Several years earlier Davis had delivered the eulogy at Malcolm X's funeral. He authored the Broadway play* Purlie Victorious *and was a founding member of* Freedomways.

In February of 1966, *Liberator,* a magazine on whose advisory board I sat, published an article, "Semitism in the Black Ghetto" by Eddie Ellis, which I felt went beyond the bounds of Black nationalism. I felt it was racist and said so to the Editor, a man whom I still respect, Dan Watts. But "Semitism in the Black Ghetto" blows it for me, but good, and but definitely. This is where I get off!

If Mr. Ellis has proof of the wild and unsupported contentions that he made (how dare he charge that W.E.B. Du Bois was "used" by "Zionists" to attack Marcus Garvey?) where is that proof? Jews are active in civil rights; Jews do have policy-making positions in civil rights organizations; Jewish philanthropies were, and still are, influential in Negro affairs. But is this due to their "evil cunning"—or to our weaknesses! Mr. Ellis says all these activities are part of a Zionist plan to make Negroes scapegoats instead of themselves. But where the hell is the proof? Mr. Ellis doesn't even offer us a "Protocols of Zion"!

We could argue for years about what Jews have done *to* and *for* Negroes in this country; and whether what has been done has resulted in good or bad for the Negro people. But who in his right mind can argue that that which was done and is being done by Jews in particular, whether good or bad, is part of a gigantic plot to dupe and take advantage of Negroes; a deliberate, agreed-upon "Zionist," "Jewish Community," "Semitic" plot against Negroes?

Where is that proof!

I am not sentimental about Jews, Negroes, or anybody else. And I am not grateful. People should fight for freedom because they believe in freedom. I know Jews who do, and I know Jews who don't; I know Negroes who do, and I know Negroes who don't. A man should fight for what he believes in—and the fact that he fights is his reward. I owe him nothing.

Harlem is a deprived and exploited community, but are Jews the only ones who profit from this exploitation? No! Are Jews the ones who profit *most* by this exploitation? I strongly doubt it. (Mr. Ellis would have done us all a favor if he had conducted a survey to determine who, in fact, really owns Harlem.)

Whatever Jews are guilty of exploiting Harlem, are not guilty because they are Jews, but because—along with many Catholics, Protestants, Negro and white—they are exploiters. In a war against all exploiters whomsoever, I am an ally. But Mr. Ellis seems to be calling for a *war* against Jews. If that is the case, I am an enemy.

You see, I consider myself a Black Nationalist, and proud to be one but not a Black racist. And I consider the difference between them too fundamental for compromise.

Black Nationalism is as legitimate and honorable a vehicle of the Black man's anguish as Irish nationalism was to the Irish, and Zionism to the Jews. But *Black racism* is no different from any other racism. I think few people will doubt my love and respect for our late Brother Malcolm X. I call your attention to an article in the *New York Times* by M. S. Handler, quoting a letter he had received abroad from Malcolm. In this letter Brother Malcolm specifically renounced racism and pledged himself to spend the rest of his life making up for the *racism* he had formerly preached. That Malcolm at last became wise enough to see racism as a vicious, destructive crime against the human spirit with most frightening implications; that he sharply set it apart from nationalism; that, above all, he set out to undo the harm he himself had done in formerly advocating Black racism—is the measure of his personal integrity and his greatness as a man and as a leader.

The beauty of Brother Malcolm was that he was intelligent enough to grow away from past errors, and to stretch out his hands towards *truth* even if they shot him down for it. Malcolm X was a Black Nationalist in the true sense of the word. Can we who love him be less?

New Rochelle, New York

Following is an excerpt from a letter by James Baldwin concerning the same magazine, Liberator, *and published in* Freedomways. *Baldwin wrote* Blues for Mr. Charlie *and* The Fire Next Time.

. . . The specific reason for this rather long letter is the series of articles concerning the Jew in Harlem (in *Liberator* magazine). I think it is most distinctly unhelpful, and I think it is immoral, to blame Harlem on the Jew. For a man of Editor Dan Watts' experience, it is incredibly naive. Why, when we should be storming capitols, do they suggest to the people they hope to serve that we take refuge in the most ancient and barbaric of the European myths? Do they want us to become better? Or do they want us, after all, carefully manipulating the color, Black, merely to become white?

James Baldwin
Bebek, Istanbul, Turkey

36

Address to Labor: Who Built This Land? No. 1, 1971

PAUL ROBESON

Paul Robeson delivered this speech to the National Labor Conference for Negro Rights in 1950.

. . . Who have been the guarantors of our historic democratic tradition of freedom and equality? Whose labor and whose life has produced the great cities, the industrial machine, the basic culture and the creature comforts of which our "Voice of America" spokesmen so proudly boast?

It is well to remember that the America which we know has risen out of the toil of the many millions who have come here seeking freedom from all parts of the world:

The Irish and Scotch indentured servants who cleared the forests, built the colonial homesteads and were part of the productive backbone of our early days.

The millions of German immigrants of the mid-nineteenth century; the millions more from Eastern Europe whose sweat and sacrifice in the steel mills, the coal mines and the factories made possible the industrial revolution of the Eighties and Nineties; the brave Jewish people from all parts of Europe and the world who have so largely enriched our lives on this new continent; the workers from Mexico and from the East—Japan and the Philippines—whose labor has helped make the West and Southwest a rich and fruitful land.

And, through it all, from the earliest days—before Columbus—the Negro people, upon whose unpaid toil as slaves the basic wealth of this nation was built!

These are the forces that have made America great and preserved our democratic heritage.

They have arisen at each moment of crisis to play the decisive role in our national affairs.

The Strength of the Negro People

In the Civil War, hundreds of thousands of Negro soldiers who took arms in the Union cause won, not only their own freedom—the freedom of the Negro people—but, by smashing the institution of slave labor, provided the basis for the development of trade unions of free working men in America.

And so, even today, as this National Labor Conference for Negro Rights charts the course ahead for the whole Negro people and their sincere allies, it sounds a warning to American bigotry and reaction. For if fifteen million Negroes, led by their staunchest sons and daughters of labor, and joined by the white working class, say that there shall be no more Jim Crow in America, then there shall be no more Jim Crow!

If fifteen million Negroes in one voice demand an end to the jailing of the leaders of American progressive thought and culture and the leaders of the American working class, then their voice will be strong enough to empty the prisons of the victims of America's cold war.

If fifteen million Negroes are for peace, then there will be peace!

And behind these fifteen million are 180 million of our African brothers and sisters, 60 million of our kindred in the West Indies and Latin America—for whom, as for us, war and the Point Four program would mean a new imperialist slavery. . . .

Africa in World Affairs

What special meaning does this challenge of the colonial world have for American Negro workers and their allies?

We must not forget that each year 4,000 tons of uranium ore are extracted from the Belgian Congo—the main source of United States supply. And that Africa also provides more than half the world's gold and chrome, 80 per cent of its cobalt, 90 per cent of its palm kernels, one-fifth of its manganese and tin, one-third of its sisal fiber and 60 per cent of its cocoa—not to mention untold riches yet unexplored.

And with this wealth, Africa produces also an immeasurable portion of the world's human misery and degradation.

But the African peoples are moving rapidly to change their miserable conditions. And 180 million natives on that great continent are an important part of the colonial tidal wave that is washing upon the shores of history and breaking through the ramparts of imperialist rule everywhere.

The Congo skilled worker extracting copper and tin from the rich mines of the land of his fathers may one day be faced with the same materials in the shape of guns provided his Belgian rulers by the Truman Administration under the Marshall Plan—but he is determined that the days of his virtual slave labor are numbered, and that the place for the Belgians to rule is in *Belgium* and *not in the Congo*.

And 25 million Nigerians—farmers, cattle raisers, miners, growers of half the world's cocoa—are determined that the land of *our* fathers (for the vast majority of American Negro slaves were brought here from Africa's West Coast)—shall belong to their fathers' sons and not to the free-booters and British imperialists supported by American dollars.

And twelve South African workers now lie dead shot in a peaceful demonstration by Malan's fascist-like police, as silent testimony to the fact that, for all their pass laws, for all their native compounds, for all their Hitler-inspired registration of natives and non-whites, the little clique that rules South Africa are baying at the moon. For it is later than they think in the procession of history, and that rich land must one day soon return to the natives on whose backs the proud skyscrapers of the Johannesburg rich were built.

Tompkins Park rally for jobs, Brooklyn, New York, summer 1963.

How are we to explain this new vigor of the African independence movements? What is it that shakes a continent from Morocco to the Cape and causes the old rulers to tremble?

The core of the African nationalist movements, the heart of the resistance to continued oppression, the guiding intelligence of the in-

dependence aspirations of the Africans is invariably the organizations
of the workers of the continent. Trade unions have arisen all over
Africa and, as everywhere in modern times, they are the backbone of
the people's struggle.

And what is true of Africa is even more strikingly true in the West
Indies, in Cuba, Brazil and the rest of Latin America where 60 million Negroes are building strong trade unions and demanding a new
day.

The Tasks of Labor

Your tasks, then, are clear. The Negro trade unionists must increasingly exert their influence in every aspect of the life of the Negro
community. No church, no fraternal, civic or social organization in
our communities must be permitted to continue without the benefit
of the knowledge and experience which you have gained through
your struggles in the great American labor movement. You are called
upon to provide the spirit, the determination, the organizational
skill, the firm steel of unyielding militancy to the age-old strivings of
the Negro people for equality and freedom.

On the shoulders of the Negro trade unionists there is the tremendous responsibility to rally the power of the whole trade-union
movement, white and Black, to the battle for the liberation of our
people, the future of our women and children. Anyone who fails in
this does the Negro people a great disservice.

And to the white trade unionists present—a special challenge.
You must fight in the ranks of labor for the full equality of your
Negro brothers; for their right to work at any job; to receive equal
pay for equal work; for an end to Jim Crow unions; for real fair employment practices within the unions as well as in all other phases of
the national life; for the elimination of the rot of white supremacy
notions which the employers use to poison the minds of the white
workers in order to pit them against their staunchest allies, the
Negro people—in short, for the unbreakable unity of the working
people, Black and white, without which there can be no free trade
unions, no real prosperity, no constitutional rights, no peace for
anybody, whatever the color of his skin. To accept Negro leadership
of men and women and youth; to accept the fact that the Negro
workers have become a part of the vanguard of the whole American

working class. To fail the Negro people is to fail the whole American people.

I know that you who have come from all parts of the nation will meet this challenge. I have watched and participated in your militant struggles everywhere I have been these past years. Here in Chicago with the Packinghouse Workers; with auto workers of Detroit; the seamen and longshoremen of the West Coast; the tobacco workers of North Carolina; the miners of Pittsburgh and West Virginia; and the steel workers of Illinois, Indiana, Ohio, Michigan and Minnesota; the furriers, clerks and office workers of New York, Philadelphia and numerous other big cities and small towns throughout the land.

I have met you at the train stations and airports, extending the firm hand of friendship. You have packed the meetings which followed Peekskill to overflowing, thus giving the answer to the bigots and the warmakers. I know you well enough to know that, once the affairs of my people are in the hands of our working men and women, our day of freedom is not far off. I am proud as an artist to be one who comes from hearty Negro working people—and I know that you can call on me at any time—South, North, East or West—all my energy is at your call.

So—as you move forward, you do so in the best traditions of American democracy and in league with the hundreds of millions throughout the world whose problems are much the same as yours.

These are peoples of all faith, all lands, all colors, and all political beliefs—united by the common thirst for freedom, security and peace.

Our American press and commentators and politicians would discourage these basic human aspirations because Communists adhere to them as well as others. Now I have seen the liberty-loving, peace-seeking partisans in many parts of the world. And though many of them are not, it is also true that many *are* Communists. They represent a new way of life in the world, a new way that has won the allegiance of almost half the world's population. In the last war they were the first to die in nation after nation. They were the heart of the underground anti-fascist movements and city after city in Europe displays monuments to their heroism. They need no apologies.

Mr. Truman calls upon us to save the so-called Western democracies from the "menace" of Communism.

But ask the Negro ministers in Birmingham whose homes were bombed by the Ku Klux Klan what is the greatest menace in their lives! Ask the Trenton Six and the Martinsville Seven! Ask Willie McGee, languishing in a Mississippi prison and doomed to die within the next month unless our angry voices save him. Ask Haywood Patterson, somewhere in America, a fugitive from Alabama barbarism for a crime he, nor any one of the Scottsboro boys, never committed. Ask the growing numbers of Negro unemployed in Chicago and Detroit. Ask the fearsome lines of relief clients in Harlem. Ask the weeping mother whose son is the latest victim of police brutality. Ask Maceo Snipes and Isaiah Nixon, killed by mobs in Georgia because they tried to exercise the constitutional right to vote. Ask any Negro worker receiving unequal pay for equal work, denied promotion despite his skill and because of his skin, still the last hired and the first fired. Ask fifteen million American Negroes, if you please, "What is the greatest menace in your life?" and they will answer in a thunderous voice, "Jim-Crow Justice! Mob Rule! Segregation! Job Discrimination!"—in short white supremacy and all its vile works.

37

Three Challenges to Organized Labor, No. 4, 1972

JESSE L. JACKSON

The basis for this article was Reverend Jackson's keynote address delivered to a Meatpackers Union Convention in Florida, August 9, 1972.

. . . A hundred years ago in 1872 the forces of Labor and the Black Community were at that time mobilizing, regrouping, and developing to deal with the special problems which had arisen out of the Civil War. At that time the new born "National Labor Union" under William Sylvis and Isaac Meyers was beginning to pull together the forces that would fight for the eight-hour day and the dignity of the working people. And central to their responsibility at that time was the struggle to keep alive the Reconstruction effort which Afro-Americans were leading; an effort to reconstruct southern government, abolish the remnants of slavery, build a public school system, free to all children, and establish the right of women to serve on juries and receive their own pay checks for their work.

That year, 1872, was a high watermark in the number of Black and poor elected to office in the South. The history of this last hundred years has become generally well-known to us for we have been forced to examine it in more and more detail in order to better understand the many facets of the battles we were in during the last decade and a half.

The beginning of that common bond of struggle between these two worlds of the working people in America went through victories and success, strains and disruptions but the bond remained. It was revitalized and strengthened in the years of the great Depression and President Roosevelt's "New Deal." Mass production workers in the coal mines, on the ships and in tobacco plants and packinghouses gave new energy to the struggle for progress in our country in that great mass movement known as the CIO.

It is most significant for us that the CIO in organizing the unorganized not only struck a major blow for the working men and women of our country to enjoy a greater share of the abundant wealth they were creating, but Black and white workers in that period also made a special contribution in their assault upon certain practices of racial discrimination in the field of employment and accommodations. "An injury to one is an injury to all" became their battle cry and to the extent that they applied that slogan was precisely to the extent that they forced the economic royalists of big business to yield to certain demands.

These bitter battles bore fruit and some of the sharpest struggles of that period were led by the members of this Union.

One recalls with pride the significant Packinghouse Workers' strike of 1948, one of the longest and bloodiest strikes in the history of that industry, in which every provocation by the employers was defeated and the strike won even while several of our members suffered martyrdom.

The main feature of the years following World War Two was one in which these years were marked by a major effort on the part of those who had fought Labor over the years to break up the fraternal bond of struggle that had developed between organized Labor and the Black Community. A segregationist federal government headed by Harry Truman became the main vehicle for carrying out this assault upon the "New Deal" coalition and the main weapon in this assault was the hysteria of "McCarthyism."

Many elected Union leaders were tricked, bribed or otherwise corrupted into becoming servants of the Truman administration and the

Democratic Party in carrying out this policy designed to split the Labor Movement. Union brothers were turned against Union brothers as wild charges of "subversion" and "treason" were leveled against those rank and filers and Union heads who were critical of or opposed certain aspects of American foreign policy at that time. Just as the same thing happened as many of us began to oppose the Vietnam War of recent years.

The nation witnessed the tragedy of Organized Labor becoming a house divided against itself, and the fighting capacities, particularly of the CIO, became straitjacketed under the Taft-Hartley Law. The alliance that had been so steadily growing between Organized Labor and the Black Community, a fraternal effort based upon mutual self-interest, was thrown into confusion and temporary disarray by this assault.

These were the beginnings of the moral and political crisis which has reached such great depths today. Given the strain which the Truman-McCarthy period placed upon the "New Deal" coalition, the Black Community took the initiative to lead the progressive forces of the nation in resistance to this situation, for we had emerged from World War Two with the determination that, like other "Third World" peoples, our time of freedom had come.

So drawing upon the strengths that we had built up over the years in the form of the Black Church on the one hand and the growing number of Black trade unionists on the other, our Movement took the initiative to see that the "Human Rights" thrust kept on building. The strength and determination of the Black Community in the face of this period of chaos and hysteria were symbolized in the leadership of Paul Robeson in the continuing struggle for Human Rights. And I am sure it's a source of great pride to this Union that one of the most militant and solid bases of support for Paul Robeson and our Movement during that period was the Packinghouse Workers in Chicago.

The birth of the National Negro Labor Council which mobilized the sisters and brothers in such places as Cincinnati, Cleveland, and Detroit was a very significant development in the struggle cementing the unity of our people which was an urgent task in those difficult days. The spiritual and moral strength of our Movement developed and extended into the South where in Birmingham, Alabama, for example, the Black and white workers in the Mine, Mill and Smelter Workers Union fought pitched battles with the Ku Klux Klan and saved the life of the Union and its right to exist.

Finally, the dawn broke at Montgomery in 1955 as the Black Church gave us the giant leadership symbol of Martin Luther King, Jr. In mass direct action we had found a form of struggle for turning out the Black Community and mobilizing it as the spearhead of the Human Rights Movement. The South now became our main battlefield; a new chapter in our history as working people was opened up as we picketed, marched and boycotted in the struggle to end public segregation. The successful struggle for Civil Rights brought us, en masse, into the political arena seeking Civil Power—a radical reformation in the political life of the nation through the ballot. . . .

The Unfinished Business of the Human Rights Movement

We have reviewed briefly this history of our common struggle in order to better understand where we are now, and the *central role* we must play *together* to resolve the present national crisis. It is in this context that I have *three challenges* to put to you today.

The first challenge is to use the power we have to put economic rights the number one point on the human rights agenda of the nation. We have the right to go to almost any school in America, but we can't pay the tuition. We have the right to move into almost any neighborhood in America, but we can't pay the house note. We have the right to buy almost any car in America and we do buy them, *for about two months,* but we can't keep up the notes. So now we find ourselves in an era where we have the right to swim in a pool where there is no water; the right to go on a vacation without the money to take that vacation. . . .

The second challenge is going to be work now; it can't be done with just a resolution. It is our job to win back the blue collar workers who shifted from the coalition in 1968, thinking that "Law and Order" was the same as a job or an income. . . .

My closing challenge is urban voter registration. . . . The '65 Voting Rights Bill assumed that disenfranchisement was a southern problem, as opposed to a national problem. Daley's machine, just like Bilbo's machine and just like Long's machine in Louisiana, is not built upon how many voters he delivers. It's built upon how many *can't* vote. We find ourselves seven million unregistered Black voters. But I want you to know, and the whole world to know, every time our movement has made progress, it has been because we have kept pressure and a good clean relationship even with our peers. You will show me an Abraham Lincoln that did something for Black folk; I'll show a Frederick Douglass helping to write his speeches. You'll show me a Franklin D. Roosevelt, making progress with Black people, I'll show an A. Philip Randolph, threatening to march on Washington. You'll show me a John Kennedy, coming out a decent man, I'll show you a Martin Luther King, the prophet putting the pressure on him to make him do it. It is our job. . . .

38

Education and Black
Self-Image, No. 4, 1968

ALVIN F. POUSSAINT

Dr. Poussaint, a professor of psychiatry now at Harvard University Medical School, was a pioneer in the study of racism's effect on the individual's sense of self.

Many of the civil rights gains in recent decades have done a great deal to modify the negative self-concept of the Black man. The civil rights movement and the rise of militant Black nationalism have brought a new sense of dignity and respect to those Blacks most excluded from society by poverty and oppression in the rural south and northern ghetto. One factor that may have been important in helping to improve the self-image of the masses of Negroes was that Black men were leading the struggle, and not white men. This fact in itself probably made Negroes, through the process of identification, take pride in their group and feel less helpless knowing that they could bring about positive change in their environment. The feeling that one can have "control" over social forces is crucial to one's feelings of ego-strength and self-esteem. Thus, the movement brought to the Negro a new sense of power in a country dominated by a resistant white majority.[1]

The self-esteem of Black Americans was also enhanced as they were able to identify with the emergence of independent African nations who had Black heads of state, and other officials of government. Negroes everywhere could feel, too, that they had nations that had a sovereignty in what used to appear as a white-controlled world. If African nations could throw off colonialism, why could not Blacks be free from oppression in America?

This present Black drive for self-determination has begun to permeate much of the struggle for Black liberation in the United States and has spread to the very issue of the self-image and education of Negro children.

The pattern of teaching white supremacy has been part of the educational process in both "integrated" and segregated schools throughout the United States.[2]

The curricula of most American schools knowingly or unknowingly teach white racism. History is presented almost entirely according to the white man's mythology and Black history is either disparaged or ignored. Indians are continually ridiculed and made to appear as savage and ignorant. Even though the red man was murdered and his land stolen by white settlers, he is still pictured as "the bad guy" who savagely abused the good-intentioned, Christian white man. White revolutionary leaders such as George Washington, Paul Revere, are portrayed as grand and glorious heroes. On the other hand, Black slave revolutionaries such as Nat Turner are depicted as ignorant, misguided and perhaps deranged ingrates. In effect, white history has frequently encouraged the Black man to contentedly accept his state of oppression in America.

Textbooks and other teaching materials have usually presented the model of the white middle-class to be emulated and aspired to by Blacks. The styles of life and language in books meant to teach spelling, reading and history were white models that were often divorced from the realities of life of the Black child. How could he feel that he was a worthwhile human being if he was not white, and liv-

---

[1]Poussaint, A. F., "The Negro American: His Self-Image and Integration," *Journal of National Medical Association,* Vol. 6, pp. 419–423, Nov. 1966.

[2]Kvaraceus, W. C., et al., *Negro Self-Concept: Implications for School and Citizenship,* McGraw-Hill, Inc., New York, 1965.

ing in a clean suburban house like Dick and Jane? Negro models and
heroes are seldom presented for the Black youngster to emulate. In
fact, if he took the textbooks seriously, he might feel that Black people don't even exist: a complete negation of the Black man's sense of
self.

Many school activities that center around religious worship es-
pouse a white God, a white Virgin Mary, and a white Santa Claus.
Goodness and purity are said to be "white" and badness and sin are
said to be "black." The Black child has to fight, feeling a sense of
doom from the very start. Cultural material that is taught normally
focuses on European-Christian traditions and little is presented about
Asian or African life, history or culture. Even in colleges where so-
called "Contemporary Civilization" is taught, information about
Black cultures and African history is omitted. How is a Black student
to feel a comfort in being Black if blackness is constantly negated and
only whiteness legitimized?

But the schools are only one way in which children are "educated."
In America, the mass media—movies, TV, radio, newspapers, play a
major role in shaping the attitudes and feelings of all people. Television, for instance, is watched many hours a day by most youngsters
throughout the United States. What appears on the TV tube may
thus become crucial to Black children's self-concept. Yet the Caucasian media frequently make Black synonymous with evil itself and
condition Negroes to shuffle to the tune of "white is right." Black
people have revered characteristics which are Caucasian—pale skins,
straight hair, aquiline features—and disdain their own curly hair,
broad noses and full lips. Advertisers are usually selling "whiteness"
along with their soap, beer, deodorants, and automobiles. Sexual and
status symbols used to attract viewers reflect white beauty and cultural standards. As a result, many Black men and women learn to despise themselves and each other solely because they are Black.

If the media continue, on the whole, to depict Negroes negatively
and to foster white supremacy then this will far outweigh the effects
of even the best school for Black children. Therefore, Black energy
must also be spent in trying to undo racism in the media. Negroes
need to demand more participation and power in the news, movies,
TV, etc. The chance to present news, history, drama, etc., from the
Black perspective is crucial if the imprint of white bigotry is to be
blocked from young Black minds.

Only with strong assertive action by Blacks to restructure racist educational processes in America will young Blacks today be able to

Students reading Freedomways *at Junior High 271 in Brooklyn, New York, 1968. (From cover of* Freeedomways, *vol. 8, no. 4). Photo by Builder Levy.*

build a positive self-image that will lead Afro-Americans to greater growth, power and achievement.

A short time ago in the South, I asked a young 16-year-old Negro girl about her plans for attending the newly integrated local high school. She replied, "First of all, that ain't no 'integrated school'; that's a 'white school' and I ain't going no place where I have to be 'accepted' by any old white southern racists." I asked, didn't she believe in integration, and she snapped, "Not that *kind* of integration! If the white folks want to integrate, they can come to *my* school."

This young lady expresses the growing disenchantment of Black youth with the social and psychological consequences of American-style "integration." This disenchantment, at least in part, arises from the fact that integration has been marked by white resistance and tokenism. In addition, integration has taken place almost entirely on "white terms." Black people often find themselves in the demeaning and uncomfortable position of asking and demanding that the white man let them into his schools, restaurants, theaters, etc., even though they know that the white man does not want them. In the South and in the North, many Afro-Americans resent the indignity of being in the eternal position of "begging for acceptance" into the white man's institutions. Many Black youth are today unwilling (no matter how impractical it sometimes may seem) to sacrifice their psychological integrity in order to move more easily in a white world.

Even the recent civil rights laws did not effectively change the pattern of white relationships with Negroes. It became apparent that integration, especially in schools, was not to be integration in a real sense at all, but merely token placement of Negro children—that is, "one-way integration." Since integration is only a one-way street that Negroes travel to a white institution, then an implied inferiority of the Black man is inherent in the situation, because it is *he who must* seek out whites to better his position. This implies that only he can benefit and learn; that he has nothing to offer whites; that whites have nothing to learn from him or from his presence.

Since the number of Negroes at any white school is usually token, particular hardships are created for these individuals. They immediately find themselves surrounded by students who are generally the products of white (racist) homes. In this setting, since all people want to belong, many Blacks must become experts at "being liked and accepted."

Many Negro students who seek complete assimilation thus become preoccupied with "proving" to white people that they are "just like all other human beings," and worthy of being assimilated. At the same time they are expressing their willingness to give up most elements of their Black identity. This in itself means that to them they are giving up something of little value.

In seeking acceptance among whites many Blacks expend a great deal of internal energy trying to prove that they are "all right." Sometimes they must even show that they are special and highly superior Negroes. Black youth resent this type of psychological pressure from whites. Sidney Poitier in his current movies plays this role of the all-perfect, noble Negro. These roles have inspired many humorous remarks among Negro people. For instance, in his new movie about an interracial romance, "Guess Who's Coming to Dinner?" Black youth have quipped, "Is it a bird? Is it a plane? No! It's *Superspade!*"

Therefore, in such integrated situations, if the self-esteem of students grows, it may not be so much from feelings of comfort and satisfaction in being Black as it is more likely from their own conditioned beliefs that "white is right." Here a student has succeeded in a white world; thus he is either a successful pioneer or a martyr. His existence has been legitimized by virtue of the fact that he lived and succeeded among whites, the only true standard of excellence.

This severe pressure on Black students in such schools is greatly eased if they represent a good percentage of the student body. In this way they can gain much psychological support through their own organizations and social clubs. More recently they have shown in our high schools and colleges that they can organize effectively to bring about change in "integrated" schools that addresses itself more to Black needs and experience.

Even with so-called "integration" the Negro community is still left with "all-Black" schools that are generally controlled by a white establishment infected with various degrees of racism. Are children remaining in the "all-Black" school going to be made to feel a sense of negative self-esteem because they were not "integrated" and associating with white children? Are they to be forced to feel inferior because some misled educators state that only "integrated" schools can be "quality" schools? Are Black children in the inner city supposed to rot as they await "integration" that may not be delivered by America in their lifetime? Are these children to be doomed to a negative self-concept partly brought about by the white-controlled educational process?

The new directions of the civil rights movement and the rise of Black nationalism seek to answer these questions.

The Black Muslims, who have not espoused integration as a goal but rather Black nationalism and separatism, appear nonetheless to enhance the self-image of Negro adults and children by teaching Black pride.[3] Negro children in their schools become proud of being Black by learning of the many contributions of Blacks to the achievements of the world and America.

Presently, this drive to have power in shaping the basic education of Black children has expressed itself in the movement for community control of Black schools. Community control is an attempt to provide Black children with a quality education by modifying curricula to meet the special needs of Black children. White-controlled educational programs in Black schools in the ghetto have already dismally failed to meet the needs of Black students and the community.

Community control therefore serves the hope of shaking the whole educational bureaucracy out of its sometimes racist and indifferent attitudes toward the education of Negro children. It also attempts to prevent the alienation and failure of Black youth in schools controlled by negligent whites. Coleman found in his recent study that Negroes have a much lower sense of control over their environment that do whites. He also found that of three attitudes measured (another was self-concept), sense of control over environment showed the strongest relationship to achievement.[4] Community control is not "separatism" or "institutionalizing inferiority" as some have charged.

It, therefore, appears that educational programs that stress Black achievement, Black participation and power-sharing in the schools are crucially important for Black youth. A sense of "fate-control" that removes the overbearing feelings of helplessness is necessary in Black people's search for a positive identity.

Thus, new approaches to the education of Black youth and community control of schools become inextricably linked in the Black man's drive to foster a positive self-image in his children. Yet, the structural changes needed in our educational institutions are often vigorously resisted by an entrenched white, bureaucratic power structure. However as the upheavals in our cities suggest, the day has come when Black Americans will no longer idly stand by and see their children become sacrificial victims of an archaic and racist school system.

---

[3]Lincoln, C. E., *The Black Muslims in America,* Beacon Press, Boston, 1961. Haley, A., *The Autobiography of Malcolm X,* Grove Press, New York, 1964.

[4]Coleman, J. S., et al., *Equality of Educational Opportunity,* U.S. Office of Education, Government Printing Office, Washington, D.C., 1966, p. 289.

39

School Desegregation:
Seeking New Victories
Among the Ashes,
No. 1, 1977

DERRICK A. BELL

This appeared as a letter to the Readers' Forum. Derrick A. Bell Jr. is a lawyer, activist, teacher, and author of numerous books. He is now on the faculty of New York University Law School.

> *The harvest is passed. The summer is ended, and we are not saved. Is there no balm in Gilead? Is there no physician there?*
>
> *—Jeremiah, 8:20, 22*

Jeremiah's words of sorrow for the loss of Jerusalem seem a particularly appropriate epitaph for contemporary efforts to ensure decent schooling for urban Black children via the vehicle of integration. The civil rights campaigners push on courageously, but the campaign has come to a halt. In frustration and rage, the disciples of total integration turn on those latter-day prophets who counseled caution and were ignored. Now those who warned that integration and education might not be synonymous have impressive facts to support their fears.

No miraculous vision was required to warn that the dream of no more Black schools, no more white schools, just schools would not be realized through reliance on the social reformers' trilogy of litigation, legislation, and lots of luck. I do not rejoice in the likely realization of my predictions. For, in Biblical times and today, a foreseen defeat for one's cause is no less a defeat. The bitter demographic and political facts of the 1970's confound the hopes of all who in the 1950's and the 1960's worked to improve the schooling of minority children, not just those who were committed to integration.

Consider the fact that roughly half of the nation's non-white children live in the 20 largest school districts and attend schools that average 60% non-white. That non-white percentage is growing because there has been a massive violation of the Joe Louis principle. You may recall Joe Louis once responded to an opponent who threatened to tire the "Brown Bomber" with his footwork: "He can run, but he can't hide." Today, we see that folk with whom we had hoped to integrate not only can run but also, with the help of several Supreme Court decisions that enable suburban areas to exclude low-income housing projects, they have been permitted to hide. Support for public schools falters as middle class people—Black and white—desert the large public school system for private schools and for the suburbs.

Even when school desegregation is achieved, studies show little or no academic improvement for minority children. There is controversy on this point, but it is now clear that attendance at desegregated schools will not automatically increase achievement test scores for Black children.

With public opposition to school desegregation growing and integrated academic performance continuing to disappoint, no celestial vision was required to foresee the decline in judicial support that has become more evident with virtually every school decision the Supreme Court hands down. In 1974, the *Milliken v. Bradley* Court's decision put strictures on metropolitan relief so severe they virtually erased the possibility that majority Black urban districts, like Detroit with a 75% Black population, might be integrated with majority white suburbs. In 1975, in the *Pasadena City Board v. Spangler* case, limits were also imposed on efforts to redesegregate schools that were once desegregated and, because of population movements, have become segregated again. More recently in the Austin, Texas, case, the Court set stringent limits on what conduct by school board action would justify desegregation orders at all. In addition, the Court has agreed to review large scale busing orders in the Dayton, Ohio, case, and has vacated and remanded metropolitan relief lower courts had granted in Indianapolis, Indiana. The chances that the lower court decisions in those two cases will eventually be approved is not great.

For all of these reasons, I have concluded that we are witnessing the close of an era of much hope and no little accomplishment. . . .

Where then is the new Jerusalem? The answer, I suggest, is quite like the basic message of the prophets. It is not there; it is we. We witnessed today not the first failing of a major racial integration movement in our public schools; the first one failed in 1800 when the Black parents in Boston—some of the first public schools opened—despaired of being able to send their children to the public schools with whites; not because Black children were not admitted, but because they were treated so badly that they decided to withdraw them and seek a separate school. Another major failure occurred in the mid-1800s, after schools in Massachusetts and elsewhere in the North had been desegregated. By the end of the Reconstruction Era, systems across the country started to resegregate their schools. The effort to make the "separate but equal" doctrine function fairly for Black schools seldom was successful. Thus Blacks have tried both separate as well as integrated schools.

This teaches us, it seems to me, that we must rely on and work for (as W.E.B. Du Bois told us 40 years ago) neither separate schools nor integrated schools—we must work for education. We of the middle class must teach and assist the poor to use those techniques of prodding and pressure and persistence that we find essential to getting a decent education for our children. When the best route to that goal is through the process of racial balance and busing, we should not hesitate to take it. Where the most feasible route points toward making non-white schools effective, we should not shun that direction. And we shouldn't shun it because some fear that it is a return to separate but equal. It certainly need not be if we avoid the self-fulfilling prophecy regarding Black schools that W.E.B. Du Bois has warned us about. He said that all too often Black people worked to integrate a particular school; and if they failed in that effort, they lost all interest in that school, took no part in its work, expressed no concern, no participation, and before too long their fears were realized—it became a poor quality Black school.

We can be committed without being doctrinaire. We can be infinitely flexible in tactics but rigid in our determination to lessen restrictions on educational opportunity based on race and color. Our task must be less to overcome racism than to prevent racism from overcoming us. It is in that spirit that we can face future challenges with the courage Jeremiah showed even though the harvest has passed, the summer has ended, and we are not saved.

40

The Bakke Case and Affirmative Action: Some Implications for the Future, No. 1, 1978

HAYWOOD BURNS

Haywood Burns was dean of the law school of the City University of New York. On a visit to South Africa he died tragically in an auto accident at age 55 on April 2, 1996.

. . . The attempts to compare the experience of racial minorities in this country to the hardships of white immigrants and their progeny and to say to racial minorities, "They made it. Why can't you?" is to completely misapprehend the two situations. Discrimination and prejudice against various white groups in this country, as bad as they have been, are of a completely different order and character than those experienced by racial minorities. Discrimination and prejudice are not the same as legally and judicially sanctioned caste oppression.

The chance for upward mobility for whites has been there by reason of their whiteness. Even if it involved changing the name, the accent, style of dress, getting more education, the ladder was there for them. The person of color, however, had no such option. Not being able to change his or her color, the stigma—race—remained. Whites in this country were never subjected to an inferior legal status. An individual employer might have added to his Help Wanted ad "Irish need not apply," but there was never a law that Irish (or Jewish, or Italian, or Polish) persons could not be citizens, get an education, sit on juries, vote. The legal and social order has victimized racial minorities as a group. Though, of course, there are obvious and important differences, women too have been victimized as a group. There can be no fair-minded objection to providing group redress. The only intelligent societal response to these historic wrongs and group injuries is affirmative action to redress their results. Blindness to the racist and sexist past will only perpetuate that racism and that sexism.

While it is entirely appropriate to be concerned about any injury that may accrue to "innocent" parties by reason of affirmative action programs, it is unclear who, if anyone, that might include. Surely every white person, however free of direct implication in victimizing non-whites, is still a daily beneficiary of white dominance—past and present. Given the social history of deprivation and the social need for pluralistic opportunity, no white has an automatic, superior claim to educational and employment access predicated upon a higher standing on so-called objective tests. In the present historical context this should be clear when we consider (1) what we know about the questionable validity of such indicators, (2) other qualities and potentials which are not subject to testing or quantification, and (3) other societal values which we are or should be seeking to advance.

In non-racial areas, Americans are well familiar with the concept and practice of affirmative action. It has often been used to aid groups who have been held out of the mainstream for a time to assist them in gaining full and free participation in American life. Returning veterans, political refugees, the handicapped have all been the beneficiaries of various kinds of affirmative action. The principle should be no different when it comes to racial minorities and women.

In pressing the affirmative action case now and in [the] future there are a number of logical pitfalls and examples of specious reasoning and semantical by-play which must be identified and properly analyzed. One example is the attempt to call affirmative action "reverse discrimination." Not only is it ludicrous to suggest that minorities are now going to turn the tables and do to whites what has been done to minorities all along, but there is, in the language of equal protection law, a perfectly "rational basis for distinguishing" affirmative action programs of today from white racist discrimination of the past. One has only to look at their nature, content, and intent. Sometimes the argument is phrased in terms of a direct attack upon the concept of "preferential" or "special" attention. Those who argue that such a policy is wrong seldom are raising this argument in connection with the long-practiced and widely accepted special or preferential treatment afforded children of alumni or big contributors, but rather advance it in connection with programs that are designed to aid minorities. It is another way of arguing the "reverse discrimination" question. The premise from which this argument starts is that special treatment is wrong. Where it fails in its logic is in its refusal to distinguish between different types of special attention. It is as if to say that the person who removes a knife from your back is like the person who put it in there, since both require special attention.

One of the greatest sources of difficulty arising out of the Bakke case and the affirmative action debate is the issue of quotas. As often posed, the question of "quota" in affirmative action is a false issue. The need for some kind of numerical measure of progress seems self-evident. The confusion arises from the failure to distinguish between the reprehensible quotas of old which were designed to *limit* access and establish a *ceiling* on minority group entry, and those of today which are designed to *open* access and establish a *floor.*

Often in the past when the nation's highest court has been asked to resolve the most critical issues of racial justice of the day, its response has flown in the teeth of minorities seeking full recognition of their humanity and their just due. It was true in *Dred Scott* (Black people have no rights white people are bound to respect), it was true in *Plessy* (separate but equal is the law of the land). The current Supreme Court may steer a similar course on the affirmative action issue. Be that as it may, however the present Court decides to treat the Bakke issues and the cases that follow in its wake, the forces who struggle for justice must continue to wage that struggle, for the issues at stake transcend the confines of the legal process. Beyond any judicial fiat, affirmative action is a simple moral and political imperative with its justifications deeply rooted in history. Whatever the cur-

rent national climate, and however it is reflected in court rulings—
even if it is in another *Plessy*—the struggle must continue in order
that there be another *Brown* and, more important, another and more
equitable social ordering after a new *Brown*. For as important as affirmative action programs are, the long-range answers to the issues of
access lie less in constructing affirmative action programs than in
constructing a just society in which there will be educational and employment opportunity for all.

41

Negro Women in Freedom's Battles, No. 4, 1967

AUGUSTA STRONG

Augusta Strong was a veteran of the Southern Negro Youth Congress and a founding member of Freedomways.

> *Where is tomorrow born? How does the future start? On a winter working day. In a Negro woman's heart. . . .*

The day was December 1, 1955, when Rosa Parks, a working woman, took a seat on a bus in Montgomery and refused the driver's request to move to the back and give her seat to a white passenger. . . .

No one could have realized they were sharing in a momentous event. The handful in the bus were privileged to witness the opening of a new epoch which would see the revolutionary awakening of the long-oppressed Blacks of the United States. Mrs. Parks was taken off the bus and jailed. By that night a committee of women were protesting the arrest, calling upon local leaders for action. Three days later, the idea of a boycott of buses had taken hold, and a new young clergyman, Martin Luther King, Jr, was elected president of the association formed to organize to achieve their goals, which at that time were very modest.

Ten months later, a United States Supreme Court ruling struck down segregated travel on all municipal facilities, and the seemingly timeless facade of segregation in the South had received another in a series of mortal wounds. The Rosa Parks incident was over, but a new era of struggle had begun—a struggle that was to extend from the South to all parts of the nation.

It is an interesting circumstance that a woman and a women's committee gave the impulse to this new revolution of our day. Whatever impelled her—whether tiredness, frustration, suppressed anger, over-long humiliation—at that moment she became, as many other courageous women have, a center from which spread widening circles of social consciousness and resistance to oppression. Despite the image that has been kept alive in the public mind of the Negro woman as a patient matriarch or carefree harlot, there are countless stories, far more dramatic, of their role as inspirers, instigators, collaborators, and as leaders in the cause of freedom. . . .

Pre–Civil War Period

The first recorded petition made by an individual Negro to a legislature is the appeal of a woman, dated 1661, in Dutch, addressed to the government of New Netherlands, seeking freedom from slavery for the adopted son of Reytory Angola who ". . . with the fruit of her hands' bitter toil, she reared him as her own child, and up to the present supported him, taking all motherly solicitude and care for him, without the aid of anyone in the world." The petition happily was granted.

One of the more curious outrages of slavery was that sometimes the road to freedom meant buying one's self. Usually it was the male who took on additional work, if permitted by his master, which over the years earned him a sum to purchase liberty. In other instances, those who most ardently believed in freedom had to purchase slaves in order to free them. There is preserved the petition of Jemima Hunt, "free woman of color," in 1810 who contracted to pay ten pounds a year for ten years to a Virginia slave-owner to secure the freedom of her husband, Stephen, father of the children whom she supported through her daily labors. Many women who had escaped from slavery sent money to a third party to purchase a son, daughter, sister or brother. Other free Negro women in the North formed organizations for the purpose of raising funds to buy and liberate slaves; a few women devoted their lives and most of their earnings to this work.

From the beginning of the organized anti-slavery movement, Negro women were active participants and leaders. While the movement was interracial, such centers as Boston and Philadelphia and other areas also had all-Negro Ladies' Anti-Slavery Societies. They were represented in national and international gatherings, became accustomed to facing hostile mobs, circulating petitions, and effectively agitating against slavery.

Women were among the leaders of the New England Freedom Association, founded in 1845 by Negroes to assist fugitive slaves. Though their purpose was illegal, they boldly published their aims: ". . . to extend a helping hand to all who may bid adieu to whips and chains, and by the welcome light of the North Star, reach a haven where they can be protected from the mansteuler. An article of the Constitution enjoins us not to pay one farthing to any slaveholder for the property they may claim in a human being. . . . Our mission is to succor those who claim property in themselves, and thereby acknowledge an independence of slavery."

One of those who became famous and was widely regarded as a heroine for her daring exploits was Ellen Craft who with her husband, William, in 1849 made her way out of Georgia by a ruse. Since her color did not betray her identity, Ellen was able to travel disguised as a Southern gentlemen. Using money they had saved (through William's working nights and Saturdays after his master was served) they traveled the public conveyances and stayed at first-class hotels. Ellen carried her arm in a sling to account for the fact that she did not sign the register at hotels, for neither of them could read or write. Posing as her valet, her husband was able to remain constantly at her side during the risky experiments. After their escape the Crafts traveled widely for the Anti-Slavery Society for a number of years, talking to audiences in the United States and in Europe.

While the abolition of slavery remained the principal concern of the freedom movements of the pre–Civil War era, there was also continuous action around other issues. National and state conventions were called during the 1830's and 1840's which sought equal education, the right to vote and to serve on juries, the right to enroll in the militia, to bear arms in the Navy, to be eligible for settling on public lands, and the repeal of oppressive "black laws." At these gatherings, women were always present as delegates, and occasionally as leaders.

One of these conventions, representing Garrison's view of the Constitution as "a covenant with the devil and an agreement with hell," meeting in Cleveland in 1854 with a Negro woman, Mary E. Bibb as vice-president, proclaims in surprisingly contemporary terms: That no oppressed people have ever obtained their rights by voluntary acts of generosity on the part of their oppressors. . . . That if we desire liberty, it can only be obtained at the price which others have paid for it. . . . That we are willing to pay that price, *let the cost be what it may.*"

The Ladies' Anti-Slavery Society of Delaware, Ohio, in an address to a State convention of men in 1856, with eloquent rhetoric urges united action for freedom: "It was a Spartan mother's farewell to son. 'Bring home your shield or be brought upon it' . . . and we pledge ourselves to exert our influence unceasingly in the cause of Liberty and Humanity." The militancy of their words was echoed by other groups of women throughout the nation who followed eagerly the gallant attempt of John Brown and his 17 followers to seize the Harper's Ferry arsenal and free the slaves of the surrounding area. When Brown and his men were condemned to death a tremendous wave of indignation and sympathy found expression in Negro communities—meetings, demonstrations and resolutions paid tribute to the idealistic leader and letters of solidarity poured in.

A typical one, adopted at a meeting of The Colored Women of Brooklyn, was addressed to the martyr, while he was under sentence, to be executed a week later:

"We a portion of the American people . . . offer you our sincere and heartfelt sympathies in the cause you have so nobly espoused . . . We consider you a model of true patriotism, and one whom our enemy will yet regard as the greatest it has produced. . . . We shall ever hold you dear in our remembrance, and shall infuse the same feelings in our posterity."

From Frances Ellen Watkins Harper, poet and an indefatigable traveler and lecturer for the Abolitionist cause, came a pledge to never desist from the cause of freedom. Writing to John Brown in prison a few days before his death, she wrote:

"Although the hands of slavery throw a barrier between you and me, and it may not be my privilege to see you in your prison house, Virginia has no bolts or bars through which I dread to send you my sympathy. . . . You have rocked the bloody Bastille; and I hope that from your sad fate great good may arise to the cause of freedom. Already from your prison has come a shout of triumph against the giant sin of our country.

"I have written your dear wife, and sent her a few dollars, and I pledge myself to you that I will continue to assist her. Send my sympathy to your fellow prisoners. . . . If any of them, like you, have a wife or children that I can help, let them send me word. Yours in the cause of freedom."

Frances Harper, born of free parents, in Maryland in 1825, was then one of the best-known woman poets of her day. A striking woman of handsome features and commanding voice, she was an experienced and indefatigable speaker for the Abolitionist cause.

Orphaned early in life, she attended a School for Colored Children run by an uncle and aunt, but went to work at 13, and was largely self-educated. She left Maryland to teach school in Ohio and in the North where she came into contact with the Underground Railroad. She was engaged as a permanent lecturer for the anti-slavery movement, traveled and spoke, attaining wide popularity both as lecturer and poet. Fellow anti-slavery workers spoke of her as a "good and glorious" speaker. Her poems, moral and didactic, in the fashion of her day, are eloquent in their denunciation of slavery and in honor of those who have given their lives for freedom. She was still a woman in the prime of life when the Emancipation Proclamation was signed, and she greeted it with these enthusiastic words:

> It shall flash through the coming ages,
> It shall light the distant years;
> And eyes now dim with sorrow
> Shall be brighter through their tears.

Her last poems were published in 1900, when she was seventy-five years old, and she remained a figure in the freedom movement until her death in 1911.

John Brown's conviction that the slaves themselves must be armed and rise against the system had a following among the anti-slavery workers. One of them, Charles Remond, advocated an appeal for insurrection before the 1858 Massachusetts State Convention of Negroes. He proudly proclaimed himself a traitor to a government which condoned slavery, and declared that he would rather stand over the graves of his mother and sister than to feel that they might be violated at the whim of a slaveholder.

The sister of whom he spoke was as fiery an Abolitionist as her brother, a familiar figure on lecture platforms of the Anti-Slavery Society, for whom she lectured in the North and abroad in England, Ireland and Scotland where she was received with friendship and sympathy. During the Civil War she came to England, like other Abolitionist leaders, to win the support of the British for the liberation struggle of the slaves. Though British textile mills were closed and workers unemployed because of the disruption of cotton farming in the South, she spoke against British support of the Confederacy: "Let no diplomacy of statesmen, no intimidation of slaveholders, no scarcity of cotton, no fear of slave insurrections, prevent the people of Great Britain from maintaining their position as the friend of the oppressed Negro, which they deservedly occupied previous to the disastrous civil war."

Sarah Remond numbered among her antecedents a grandfather who fought in the American Revolution, a father who was an immigrant from the West Indies. She was born of free parentage in Salem, Massachusetts, was well educated and well read. She continued her education after the end of the Civil War, obtaining a medical degree in Florence, Italy, at the age of fifty-six, and working there as a practicing physician until her death. . . .

42

Racism and Contemporary Literature on Rape, No. I, 1976

ANGELA Y. DAVIS

Following is a critical review of Against Our Will: Men, Women and Rape *by Susan Brownmiller, based on two radio programs broadcast by KPFA, Berkeley, California, on January 15, 1976, and January 22, 1976.*

Sexual assaults against women occur far more frequently than anyone would dare to imagine. Rape, in fact, is one of the most common crimes committed in the United States today. Yet, until very recently rape was seen as that unspeakable act—perpetrated by psychopaths—which sometimes brutally erupted in the headlines of local dailies, or when relatives or friends were involved, it was shrouded in secrecy and talked about in whispers.

A tightly woven web of myths blurred the real and traumatic penetration of sexual violence into the lives of untold numbers of women. One thread of the web assumed the rapist to be a psychologically diseased creature, if not an oversexed, bestial Black man.

Another thread assumed the female victim to be a woman who secretly desired to be aggressively and violently taken, an outright prostitute or else an intrinsically "immoral" Black woman.

Today, at last, the process of unweaving and destroying this web has been initiated on a large scale. Within the women's movement and on its fringes, a flood of literature is beginning to pour forth on the subject of rape. For instance: *Rape: The First Source-book for Women* by New York Radical Feminists; *Rape, How to Avoid It and What To Do About It If You Can't* by June and Joseph Csida; Jean MacKeller's *Rape, the Bait and the Trap;* Diana Russell's *The Politics of Rape* and Susan Brownmiller's *Against Our Will: Men, Women and Rape.*

These books, along with many brochures and articles, have attempted, each in its own way, to set the record straight about the gravity of rape, the history and present incidence of the crime, the men who are its perpetrators and the women who are its victims. The solutions which have been proposed range from self-defense classes and rape crisis centers to a complete overhaul of the existing rape laws.

My own interest in the literature on rape was prompted by the Joanne Little case. In researching an article on the case, I was struck by the consistent evasion—by all but a few authors—of the special way in which Black men have been and continue to be framed up on fraudulent rape charges. Moreover, there also appeared to be little more than a passing sensitivity to the systematically ruthless ways in which Black women have been subjected to sexual violence by white men.

My continued reading of anti-rape literature has more than confirmed my original suspicions that much of it has acquired a decidedly racist edge. The most recent book on the subject—Susan Brownmiller's *Against Our Will*—is, in my opinion, the most conspicuously and outrageously racist of them all.

I was first introduced to her book when someone asked my opinion on a passage in which she describes the background of the lynching of Emmett Till, the fourteen-year-old Black boy who had allegedly whistled at a white woman in Mississippi. This is the passage I was asked to read:

Till's action was more than a kid's brash prank. . . . Emmett Till was going to show his Black buddies that he, and by inference, they, could get a white woman and Carolyn Bryant was the nearest convenient object. In concrete terms, the accessibility of all white women was on review. . . . And what of the wolf whistle, Till's "gesture of adolescent bravado?" . . . The whistle was not a small tweet of hubba-hubba or melodious approval for a well-turned ankle. . . . It was a deliberate insult just short of physical assault, a last reminder to Carolyn Bryant that this Black boy, Till, had in mind to possess her. [247]

Wading through the entire book, which, granted, is a meticulously researched, though misleading history of rape, I saw the idea burst forth, time after time, that Black men are the most likely candidates for rape.

This tendency to single out Black men as the rapists in our society is a dangerously unfortunate feature of an increasing number of studies on women and rape. Diana Russell's *Politics of Rape* contains descriptions of twenty-two cases of rape, among which are twelve women who have been raped by Black or Chicano men. Of the ninety-five interviews conducted in preparation for the book, only twenty-six percent involved Black men. Why the discrepancy between the total number of interviews and the ones published?

To isolate and criticize this element of racism which mars much of the anti-rape literature today is not, of course, to attack the anti-rape movement in general. On the contrary, such a critique is urgently needed in order to guarantee that this movement does not unwittingly provide fuel for the current offensive against Blacks, Puerto Ricans, Chicanos, Native Americans and Asians, as well as the working class as a whole.

Susan Brownmiller's book—the most thorough and most systematic study of rape to date—deserves special attention. In the first pages, she makes it abundantly clear that she perceives history itself as a fierce, unrelenting battle between the sexes.

Man's discovery that his genitalia could serve as a weapon to generate fear must rank as one of the most important discoveries of prehistoric times, along with the use of fire and the first crude stone axe. [14–15]

The contours and substance of history are determined, not by class struggle, but by the struggle between the sexes. Rape, or the threat of rape, is the prime weapon which has been used by men, since time immemorial, to subjugate women and keep them in an inferior position.

Rape emerges, then, not as a crime tied to the social forces of a given society, but rather as an immutable, inevitable biological fact, based in the anatomy of the male. How, therefore, does Brownmiller define rape? It is quite simply "a conscious process of intimidation by which *all* men keep *all* women in a state of fear." [15] . . .

In exploring the contemporary problem of rape, Brownmiller attempts to convince us once more that Black men are more inclined than their white counterparts to become rapists. In Chapter Six— "The Police Blotter Rapist"—we are informed that the "typical American rapist" is the typical American criminal; i.e., a working-class man or a "ghetto inhabitant."

> There is no getting around the fact that most of those who engage in antisocial, criminal violence (murder, assault, rape and robbery) come from the lower socio-economic classes; and that because of their historic oppression the majority of Black people are contained within the lower socio-economic classes and contribute to crimes of violence in numbers disproportionate to their population ratio. [181]

She hastens to add that

> We are not talking about Jean Valjean, who stole a loaf of bread in *Les Miserables,* but about physical aggression as "a demonstration of masculinity and toughness." [181]

Black men, she contends, are more likely to aggressively express their "masculinity," and this penchant is more likely to express itself through rape.

> Corporate executive dining rooms and climbs up Mount Everest are not usually accessible to those who form the subculture of violence. Access to a female body—through force—is within their ken. [194]

Brownmiller leans heavily on F.B.I. and police figures to confirm her thesis. But who would believe the F.B.I. and the police about anything these days? She thus breaks the news to us that Black men constitute almost half—forty-seven percent—of all reported rapists.

In a later chapter, however, she fleetingly alludes to the untold numbers of unreported rapes committed by so-called men of authority: therapists and doctors committing sexual assaults upon their female patients; producers coercing starlets; professors attacking students; bosses raping secretaries with impunity because these women are afraid to lose their jobs. Characteristically, she omits all the Black women domestic workers who have been raped by the "man of the house."

While she does admit that these are the cases that never make it to court, she quite conveniently does not pursue this side of the rape question. Thus she does not concretely discuss the resulting distortion of official rape statistics. . . .

Since her battle is one to be fought by women alone against the men who are the enemy—it is quite consistent that she would demand harsher prison terms for convicted rapists. It is equally consistent that she would demand the total integration of police forces and armed forces. (She wants these bodies to be composed of fifty percent women!!) Does she, however, not realize that as long as the judicial system remains as much of an instrument of racism and class subjugation as it is today, the punishments, regardless of guilt or innocence, will disproportionately fall on Blacks and other nationally oppressed groups as well as poor and working-class white people?

Since 1930, as Brownmiller knows, eighty-nine percent of all executions for rape have been performed on Black men. Black men in the South were eighteen times more likely to be executed on a conviction of raping a white woman than for raping a Black woman. Outside the South, rape convictions are also disproportionately heaped on Black and working-class men. Yet Diana Russell can make the astounding claim that courts outside the South are actually more lenient to Black men charged with rape because they fear being accused of racism. . . .

References

Brownmiller, Susan, *Against Our Will: Men, Women and Rape*. New York: Simon and Schuster, 1975.

Russell, Diana, *The Politics of Rape, The Victim's Perspective*. New York: Stein and Day, 1975.

"The Racist Use of Rape and the Rape Charge: A Statement to the Women's Movement from a Group of Socialist Women." Socialist Women's Caucus of Louisville, P.O. Box 11416, Louisville, Kentucky 40211.

43

Biology and Gender: False Theories About Women and Blacks, No. 1, 1977

DOROTHY BURNHAM

A scientist, Dorothy Burnham was a student activist in Brooklyn and in 1940 joined the staff of the Southern Negro Youth Congress.

Recently there has appeared in the popular press and in the scientific journals a number of books and articles which set out to demonstrate that the gender of women is defined by human biology. Some of the most exciting research in modern biology has been that which was concerned with the molecules which determine heredity. And it is no wonder that James Watson was lyrical in his account of the joint effort which resulted in the publication of the structure of DNA. When persuading his sister to type the manuscript, he told her that she was participating in perhaps the most famous event in biology since Darwin's books.[1]

---

[1]Watson, James, *The Double Helix* (New York: Atheneum, 1968), p. 221.

This elegant model of the gene is a product of the language, the instruments and the sophisticated technology of the mid-twentieth century. It appears to me to be somewhat irrational that the advanced ideas of genetics should be used by some scientists to support the antediluvian ideologies of racism and sexism.

The employment of prevailing authority to define the role of women in society is not, of course, new. For in determining that position, the establishment of the family structure and other aspects of the political and economic life of the culture depended. Whether the boundaries of women's "place in society" were erected with the bricks of theology or the cement of genetic determinism, the intention is that the barriers shall remain strong and sturdy.

Eliza Gamble[2] writing a half century ago pointed out that it did not seem strange that theology should be used to validate man as an infinitely superior being but that she did expect with the dawn of a scientific age that the prejudiced doctrines would disappear. Ms. Gamble would no doubt be extremely surprised to read the recent headlines regarding the right of women to serve in all professions including the priesthood and find that the theologians are still trying to hold up the sky.

Through generations, both the literature of mythology and the literature of science have been in good measure addicted to trying to prove the superiority of the male. Natural scientists have described the obvious physical differences between men and women and have moved on from that point to concoct great theories about differences in intelligence, emotional make-up and behavior. The scientists in an attempt to appear neutral declare that they are only investigating whether women are less objective, more nervous and less emotionally stable than men are. By these means, responsibility is disavowed when the gratuitous representation of women is translated to mean women cannot handle decision-making positions.

Carroll and Charles Rosenberg[3] cite 19th century physicians who wrote of the delicacy of the female nervous system as opposed to that of the human male. "Few if any questioned the assumption that in males the intellectual propensities of the brain dominated, while the

---

2 Gamble, Eliza Burt, *The Sexes in Science and History* (New York: G. P. Putnam. 1916), p. vii.

3 Rosenberg, C.S., and C. Rosenberg. "The Female Animal: Medical and Biological Views of Woman and Her Role in Nineteenth-Century America," *Journal of American History* (Sept. 1973), pp. 332–336.

female's nervous system and emotions prevailed over her conscious and emotional faculties." Physicians warned that the intellectual life if opened up to women might well deprive the species of good health. Some of the scientists of that period apparently believed that the brain and the reproductive organs drew on the same sources for nourishment and, therefore, to feed one would be to deprive the other. And since the chief function of women was reproduction the choice was clear—*forego education and intellectual pursuits*. During this period, one of the factions among those who opposed the vote for women emphasized the genteel, gentle nature of women, claiming that her biology suited her more for the parlor and the kitchen than for political life. They spoke emotionally of the necessity of protecting women from the trauma of real life outside the home. This argument of course neglected mention of the majority of poor and working-class women whose labors kept them out of the parlors—if indeed they had parlors to go to. . . .

Women were denied the right to vote on the basis of a different biology but working-class women and Black women were forced to work 8, 10, 12 hour days in industry or in the fields and in addition bore the load of housekeeping and child rearing.

Of course similar biological theories were advanced to account for the obvious superiority of whites over Afro-Americans. The exploitation of slave labor and Blacks after slavery was also defended on scientific grounds. Blacks had smaller brains with less capacity. Blacks were inherently happy-go-lucky. Black women were born without morals. These were not areas in which the scientists had difficulty getting an ear. As soon as the theories were proposed, the mass media spread the ideas abroad.

Some of the old biological biases against women and Blacks and non-Aryans have disappeared only to be replaced with less primitive and more up-to-date trappings. Steven Goldberg titled his book *The Inevitability of Patriarchy: Why the Biological Difference Between Men and Women Always Produces Male Domination*. . . .

The thesis of Goldberg and others is that the male hormones function to produce aggressive behavior in males, which leads to dominance and the rewards of leadership and superiority. I would like to note here that it has been my experience that, in most instances, Blacks and women are unrewarded for aggressive behavior and may very well be punished for exhibiting this characteristic. . . .

The conception of the biologically based inferiority of women, selected nations or races had led to such grave consequences as the oppression of women, the institution of slavery, the Fascist holocaust.
Those in power have not ever hesitated to use whatever weapons
come to hand to maintain and extend their power. And ideas are
popular weapons, particularly if people can be persuaded to adopt
ideas which are against their own interests. Exploitation of divided
peoples is a classic means of subjugation.

Those of us who have made a conscious effort to displant culturally implanted misconceptions about our fellow human beings know
how difficult is that exercise. Especially when everything in the culture deliberately or insidiously acts to reinforce the misconceptions.
Scientists who are a part of our environment, then, not only are contributors to the pollution of ideas but are indeed the receivers as well.
Cohen,[4] in speaking of the social functions of science remarks: "They
link science with society in such a way that science amplifies the social signals, which stimulates it and even exaggerates the worst of
them." If we examine the attitude of science and scientists towards
women we find that we come out badly. For not only have the scientists helped to justify the subordinate position of women in the society, but the scientific establishment itself for the most part has not
encouraged women scientists to become contributors or leaders. The
contribution of Rosalind Franklin to the theory and the development
of the DNA model was an integral and essential part of the work. Yet
she went largely unrecognized. And the Nobel Prize for Medicine
and Physiology was awarded to Crick, Watson and Wilkins in 1962
for their research and accomplishments. Watson himself acknowledged the overlooking of Franklin in the epilogue to his book *The
Double Helix*[5] saying, ". . . and we both came to appreciate greatly
her personal honesty and generosity, realizing years too late the
struggles that the intelligent woman faces to be accepted by a scientific world which often regards women as mere diversions from serious thinking."

Many other women have suffered similar treatment from the scientific community but indeed the majority of women never reach the

---

[4]Cohen, Robert, "Ethics and Science," *Science, Technology and Freedom* edited by Willis
Truitt and T. W. Solomons (Boston: Houghton Mifflin, 1974), p. 141.
[5]Watson, James, *The Double Helix*, p. 226.

point of considering a scientific career because they are conditioned from grade school up to avoid mathematics and science. And because the hurdles are even greater for minority peoples, the Black woman's opportunities in science are infinitesimally small.

If I sound more like a Black feminist than a biologist, the reason is—that's what I was first. I truly believe racism and sexism interact and reinforce each other and the effect of both is not arithmetical but geometrical on the subject.

I am well aware of the issues raised by the scientific community in regard to freedom of inquiry and freedom of speech. I do not, however, believe that anyone in America today would be given research money, facilities or publication privileges to prove a thesis relating to some supposed inferior qualities of white Anglo-Saxon males. . . .

44

Bangs and Whimpers: Black Youth and the Courts, No. 3, 1975

BRUCE McM. WRIGHT

Judge Bruce McM. Wright wrote this piece from his perspective as a Black judge on the New York City Bench.

Less cruel than Newgate, more antiseptic than Bedlam and not quite as dank as the Bastille, the country's prisons for juveniles and youthful offenders are nevertheless an accurate reflection of a harsh and unremitting temper and mood now rampant in adult America. Bearing such English county names as Spofford and Callagy Hall, the dungeons for puberty in New York City recall the cruelties of the sixties when Southern sheriffs herded Black children into makeshift corrals.

Victims of incest, sometimes by the age of five; called criminals for truancy as they flee teachers who do not teach; pictured as riotous, fun-loving and violently destructive in Black exploitation films such as *Cooley High;* the butt of such benign neglect (as Patrick Moynihan might put it) as murder at the hands of white police officers; targets of a lusting adult census to expose them to the same inhumane tortures and penalties as men of full age; reviled and viciously caricatured by such "educational" programs as the nationally seen *Sesame Street*, where the "Roosevelt Franklin Elementary School" is a chaos of "darky" accents and racist stereotypes; abused and stoned in centers of culture and learning such as Boston; goaded to suicide while held in durance vile, because as children of the streets, they happen not to have $1,500 handy for bail; treated in a custodial manner in schools which habitually abuse them with brutal corporal punishment; and suffering from the instant image-making of a bad press and the living room libel of garish television coverage, the Black youth of America are as condemned, isolated and alienated as a leper colony. . . .

Grave Discrepancies

There is something gravely out of joint about our criminal justice system, generally. But the specifics of the wrongs visited against minority youth are gloomy and depressing. Late in 1973, respectable judges and investigators placed a middle-class accent on the often heard lament in Black ghettos that the criminal justice system is more criminal than just. A panel of Family Court Judges who hear the criminal charges against those under sixteen described the system as a "failure." The *New York Times* devoted a front-page story to the release of the judges' report.[1] Some of the revelations in the report constitute indictments of both the police and the system in their harsh relationship with young Blacks.

After noting that 65% of those brought before the court on delinquency charges were Black, 21.5% Puerto Rican and only 11% white, the report stated: "the police are more diligent in apprehending Black children than white children." As a glaring example of a discriminatory approach, the report said that the charge most frequently leveled against white males in stolen car cases was "unauthorized use of a vehicle," while "virtually all Black males were charged with grand larceny [auto]."

---

[1]The Family Court Judges' report was published by the Judicial Conference of the State of New York in October, 1973. It was reviewed in the *New York Times,* October, 29, 1973.

Revealing was the pervasive effect of employment discrimination against Blacks and their absence of opportunity to amass those fortunes which permit contributions to charity and self-help. Thirteen percent of the Black children and ten percent of the Puerto Rican were confined in public facilities such as state training schools (reform schools). Only two percent of the whites were so placed, but even then, only in a facility run by the Department of Social Services. Indeed, only one white child among those who came before the court was placed in a state training school. . . .

That we may have passed beyond the threshold of that 1984 police society predicted by Orwell is a strong and allowable inference from the [State Commission of Investigation] report. Citing a lack of system-wide planning and resource allocation, the Commission deplored the fact that the Police Department receives "a disproportionate share of the funds available," while non-police agencies are "seriously underfunded." All of this tends to contribute to the general arrogance of the police, as they swagger through Black neighborhoods.

How else to account for the shooting deaths of Claude Reese, Jr., at the age of fourteen and Clifford Glover at the age of ten? Even the staid *New York Times,* not noted for liberal fanaticism, published an editorial on the shooting of young Reese by a white police officer which is notable for its cynical regard of the flimsy excuses advanced by white police officers whenever they shoot a young Black. The stories, the *Times* said, all have "a profoundly depressing familiarity."

A white police officer responds to a call involving a Black or Puerto Rican youth, a shot is fired and the youngster dies. Later, though the stories are confusing, the police officer is said to have thought he saw a lethal weapon—a gun or a knife—in the dead youth's hand. It turns out that the weapon cannot be found or is substantially more innocent than the officer thought it was when he discharged his gun.

. . . .episodes like the shooting of the Reese child . . . still occur with such appalling frequency that the training and screening of police officers must be deemed deficient. (*New York Times* editorial, September 19, 1974.)

A little over a year before young Reese was shot and killed, Officer Thomas Shea, assigned to predominantly Black South Jamaica, killed ten-year-old Clifford Glover. Although he was acquitted by a jury with one Black woman on it, the ghetto rumor, acknowledged in white sections of the City, is that no white police officer can ever be convicted in Queens for the murder of a Black person. However, when his departmental trial was held, the evidence developed there made it clear that Glover was murdered without excuse. The hearing officer said that both Shea and his fellow-officer, Walter J. Scott, "thought deceit . . . could extricate them." It was found that Scott and Shea were "the hunters, not the hunted." During the trial Shea was asked whether or not he could tell the difference between a ten-year-old boy and a full-grown adult robbery suspect, especially at a distance of only three feet. Shea's reply is an eloquent testimonial to how death from official sources lurks in the streets of every ghetto for Black youth. He said the only thing he saw was "the color of" Glover's skin.

Officer Scott, in lying to support Shea's story, said, at one point, that he was nearly 500 yards away from the spot where the fallen body of young Glover was. However, the following, quoted from the opinion and recommendation of Trial Commissioner Philip Michael,[2] gives blood-stained drama to the value white police officers place upon Black life:

> Another point that illustrates Scott's false testimony is the remark at 5:04:50, as recorded on the tape transcription, "die you little fuck." Scott denies making this comment. But only Scott had access to the walkie-talkie. Scott admits the walkie-talkie transmissions on either side of this remark were his.

> It must be assumed that Scott, while waiting for help to arrive, inadvertently left his walkie-talkie on and it captured his senseless utterance.

Establishment Attitude: "I Give Up"

As though the police are not enough of a menace in genocide aimed at Black youth, there is the problem of narcotic addiction and the reaction of the courts and the prisons. Instead of being treated as an in-

---

[2]From the *New York Journal of Crime and Justice*, September 27–October 11, 1974.

duced illness requiring a search for cures, the illness is treated as a crime and the human beings who suffer from addiction are buried in prisons, more or less alive. . . .

In the June 1975 edition of *Psychology Today,* there is an article entitled "The Blackboard Penitentiary." It is tough, the two authors say, to tell a high school from a prison. I disagree. Our young Blacks learn more in prison than they do at many of our urban schools.

For more than twenty-one months, I sat in the Youth Part of the Criminal Court, presiding over the progress reports of young offenders who had been removed from the criminal process and were then in programs of counseling. A shockingly large proportion of the Black young men were unable either to read or write, although close questioning revealed that they had gone as far as the eleventh grade and sometimes had even been graduated. And, in flight from this kind of criminal neglect, these young Blacks have taken to the streets for the necessities of their lives. True, these men are truants, but should they be arrested by truant officers and treated as criminals? Of course not. As Marian Wright Edelman put it, speaking of the millions of children not in school and "special classes as holding pens," it is crazy to convict a child of truancy and expel him from school. "You find out why he doesn't come to school and try to help him so he'll come back." The schools, she says, suffer the same dismal disease as the courts, for as the schools throw out our children with impunity, the administrators of the schools abuse the purpose of learning. "Expediency and efficiency in administration have somehow become more important than educating the children. . . ."

James Q. Wilson, burdened with the prestige and credentials of a Harvard professorship, has just published a book entitled *Thinking About Crime.* He announces his belief that the causes of crime are *not* identifiable and, thus, are not subject to the discovery of a cure. In consequence of this thesis of surrender by an intellectual, he says that the judiciary has been too soft with offenders and he has proposed that society must get tough by isolating and warehousing those convicted of a crime. But, when he says that "wicked people exist," he deliberately elects to ignore the very wicked people who entrap so many minority young into a criminal situation, such as the police and those custodians of our Black children who deprive them of hope and thereby create a desperate census which has given up on society itself ever becoming rehabilitated.

Perhaps one of the most poignant and tersely stated comments on the inequities which dictate the adoption of a criminal mentality for survival is the one posed by a Black survivor of Attica and its deadly rebellion. He said, "How the hell we gonna be *re*habilitated, when we ain't never been *ha*bilitated in the first place?"....

Judges should be subjected to intensive screening before being allowed to take their preconceived notions about Black humanity to the bench. They should also be exposed to Hispanic values and culture, so as to know something about the people they face in such large numbers, other than what a policeman's hearsay complaint says or what an assistant district attorney has dictated.

And if this is ever to happen, it means that young Blacks, now with the vote at the age of 18, must not abandon the system to their tormentors but mount a concentrated struggle for recognition of themselves as human beings. Young Blacks must also get into the law and its support agencies, if ever the law is to reflect any of the changes they wish to see. There is need for physical agitation as well as intellectual revolution and the struggle must never be abandoned, lest we abandon it to those whose Black bourgeois standards are no less repressive than those of the majority.

The greatest goad to Blacks to take up the law as a career is found in a Constitution which makes no promises to groups or classes, but only to individuals. The base acts of the law are distinct and different from the ideals of justice. Under slavery, we had law but no justice. Under a police state which, like an edict from ancient kings, says that our young must be wiped out, it becomes an honor to be a part of a struggle for change. If there is justification for a Black Children's Crusade, there is even more justification for their parents to give them a noble precedent.

45

Pages from the Life of a
Black Prisoner, No. 4, 1971

FRANK E. CHAPMAN JR.

Frank Chapman had been corresponding with the editors of Freedomways
since 1964. His earlier article, "Science and Africa," was published in Freedomways, *Vol. 6, No. 3 (1966) in a special section on prison writings.*

To enter prison at the age of 19 is no extraordinary event for thousands of young Black people in the Ghetto—it merely happens every
day. The day I entered the Missouri State Penitentiary was November 3, 1961. To me it wasn't just another day because I entered those
gray walls with a sentence of life and fifty years for murder and armed
robbery. Elsewhere I have told the story of how this came about, so
here I will tell about my experience in prison and my current effort
to secure my freedom.

I was brought to prison in a train along with fifty other inmates.
When we arrived at the train station, we were picked up by a bus
which transported us inside the prison. Upon arrival we were all
taken past an iron gate into a large room. We were lined up and told
to take off all our clothing. After we were all naked, the guards told
us to bend over so they could inspect our rectums, then we were told

to open our mouths so they too could be inspected. After this ordeal we were all given a pair of overalls and taken into another room to be photographed and fingerprinted. All this took several tedious hours.

We arrived at prison at noon. However, for the foregoing reasons, we were not assigned and taken to cells until around 6 o'clock in the evening. The cells were just large enough to accommodate two men and were about 7 ft. wide and 11 ft. long, and 10 ft. high with one set of double-decker bunks. They were located in a building called the "Reception Diagnostic Center." We were to be kept here for about thirty days before being released into the general prison population.

During my thirty days in "Reception" I brooded quite a lot about what life could be like if I were in prison. Jail is not something one can adjust to overnight. However, the most disgusting part of my stay in "Reception" was having to sit in a room and listen to the prison officials lecture about the prison rules and codes of conduct. At one such lecture the warden said, "In here every son-of-a-bitch has to shift for himself, so if one of you young fresh punks go out there playing tough and get a knife hung in you, don't come crying to me. This is a penitentiary for *men!*" We knew nobody cared whether we lived or died in here so the warden's remarks only added insult to injury.

While in "Reception" I also talked with a caseworker. He asked me what did I want to do while in prison. I replied, "Get an education." The caseworker wanted to know why I wanted an education. My answer sort of shook him up. I said, "I think my coming here is the greatest mistake I ever made in life and if I can't learn from it, then there is no purpose in me living." He asked me did I want to live. To me the question seemed very silly so I refused to answer. I just sat there and gave him a bitter stare. After a moment or two, he said, "I think you are a very bitter young man." He was right. I was bitter but I still wanted an education and I wanted to know if he could help me. The interview ended on this note: "Be a good boy, Chapman, bring us ten or maybe fifteen years, and maybe you'll go free on parole. I'll tell the classification board you want to go to school."

When I went up before classification for assignment to the general population, they assigned me to the garbage detail. I protested stating that I wanted an education. I was told, with arrogance, that I would be a garbage worker and if I didn't like that, I could be disciplined.

In 1961 there was only one cell block in the general population for Black inmates and it was called A Hall. A Hall is a tall gray stone medieval looking structure that was built about 133 years ago. Black inmates were housed in here and forced to live with roaches, rats, and six men to a cell—only big enough to accommodate two men. In the winter we would nearly freeze, and in the summer the heat was always intolerable. I was forced to live in A Hall for nearly four years, and these were some of my most miserable years in prison.

When I first hit population I worked on the garbage detail for about sixty days. During this period I wrote letters to the educational director, requesting that I be assigned to the school. Finally I was called down to the school and given a Stanford Achievement Test; shortly thereafter I was enrolled as a student in the 8th grade.

In school I studied hard and made good grades. But I couldn't find in school an education that would give me my purpose in life, so I would go to the prison library and check out books on philosophy. Most of these books were too deep for me but I would get a dictionary and try to read them anyway.

One day while browsing in the library a white prisoner who worked in the library asked me if I wanted to read a very good book. I said yes and he gave me *Les Misérables* by Victor Hugo. This book told the most moving story of human oppression I had ever read. In reading it I was moved to tears and anger on several occasions. When I finished this book, I asked myself over and over again: "Why, why does man have to suffer such abuse and persecution at the hands of his fellows?" I did not know, yet I swore that before I die I would have the answer, no matter the cost. . . .

46

The Death Penalty:
Continuing Threat to
America's Poor, No. 1, 1971

LENNOX S. HINDS

Lennox Hinds was director of the National Conference of Black Lawyers in 1970.

The United States Supreme Court will rule momentarily on the constitutionality of the death penalty in the case of *Jesse Fowler v. North Carolina.* . . .

Throughout this country's history, lynchings, bombings, burnings, rapes and murders against Black, Brown and Red people, have been disregarded by federal law enforcement agencies as "outside their jurisdiction," while they have initiated and encouraged illegal surveillance of our struggles as rebellious minorities, controlled by constitutionally acceptable armed forces. Racist application of state criminal law enforcement continues to select Black and poor people for arrest, prosecution, conviction, imprisonment and death, no differently in 1976 than in 1876.

On June 29, 1972, when the Supreme Court declared that "the imposition and carrying out of the death penalty . . . constitutes cruel and unusual punishment in violation of the Eighth and Fourteenth Amendments," 600 persons were waiting on death row in 32 states for the opinion that would determine if they would be hung, gassed or electrocuted (*Furman v. Georgia, U.S. 408* [*1972*] *238*). . . .

In 1944, Gunnar Myrdal reported in *An American Dilemma* that "The south makes the widest application of the death penalty, and Negro criminals come in for much more than their share of the executions." Bald statistics confirm his view and the frequency of this discrimination, but it is not confined to the South.

Constitutional due process requires that the judicial functions of trial and sentencing be conducted with fundamental fairness. The application of the death penalty in rape and murder cases (since 1930, 99 percent of all executions have been for these crimes) is clear and unmistakable. Since 1930, 3,859 persons have been executed in the United States. Of these, 2,066 or 54 percent were Black. During these years Blacks were about one-eleventh of the population. For the crime of murder, 3,334 were executed—1,630 or 49 percent were Black. For rape, a total of 455 have been executed, all but two in the south—405 or 90 percent were Black. (*See National Prisoner Statistics* [1969].)

The Supreme Court in the (5–4) opinion in *Furman v. Georgia* (1972) came one vote away from sending the 600 to their deaths. Only Justices Douglas and Thurgood Marshall dealt squarely with the racism in the application of capital punishment. The three others in the majority opinion were more disturbed by its lack of efficacy in deterring crime. Douglas identified the way in which the death penalty is a tool in the hands of those in power when he said:

It is "cruel and unusual" to apply the death penalty—or any other penalty—selectively to minorities whose numbers are few, who are outcasts of society, and who are unpopular, but whom society is willing to see suffer though it would not countenance general application of the same penalty across the board.

Justice Thurgood Marshall was equally unequivocal on the class and race assumptions on which the application of the death penalty was based.

It . . . is evident that the burden of Capital Punishment falls upon the poor, the ignorant, and the underprivileged members of society. It is the poor and the members of minority groups who are least able to voice their complaints against Capital Punishment. Their impotence leaves them victims of a sanction that the wealthier, better represented, just-as-guilty person can escape. So long as the capital sanction is used only against the forlorn, easily forgotten members of society, legislators are content to maintain the status quo because change would draw attention to the problem and concern might develop.

The shaky majority in the *Furman* case did not resolve the blood lust for the death penalty as a facile, politician's solution to public concern with crime and violence. In the four years since the *Furman* decision, 31 state legislators have reinstated the death penalty, redrafted to "satisfy" the majority opinion, Supreme Court's objections to the prior laws. (Capital Punishment is cruel and unusual in the constitutional sense, or denies the equal protection of the laws, if it can be established that it is imposed and executed in a manner that discriminates against Blacks or other racial minorities or the poor in violation of the Eighth and Fourteenth Amendments. The *Furman* court divided on this common ground. Justice Douglas, Marshall and Stewart based their objections to the death penalty on that reasoning. There was no firm consensus on any aspect of the five-man majority opinion, but certain elements were touched upon by all. The majority agreed that the death penalty is a cruel and unusual punishment because it is imposed under no clear standards; that the Eighth and Fourteenth amendments should bar legislatures from imposing sanctions which, as administered, serve no valid social purpose; that the death penalty is unpredictably used. All members of the court with the exception of Justice Rehnquist personally opposed capital punishment.)

As of March 1, 1976, 450 people were on Death Row, including 6 women, 320 Blacks, 136 whites, 8 Native Americans and 9 Chicanos—75 percent non-white, almost all with appointed counsel (the surest index to a poor defendant). Ninety of those condemned are in North Carolina alone, where death may be the penalty for arson and burglary as well as murder and rape. The seven other states with the greatest number of prisoners on Death Row are: Florida, 50; Georgia, 32; Ohio, 29; Louisiana, 27; California, 26; Oklahoma, 22; Texas, 21.

The 450 Black, Brown and poor people are sitting it out in Death Row awaiting a new Supreme Court decision in *Fowler v. North Car-*

olina which will be argued in a Supreme Court without Justice Douglas. The appeal, if lost, will result not only in their deaths, but the reinstatement on state and federal levels of the legalized lynchings that characterized the years before the *Furman* decision. . . .

We at the National Conference of Black Lawyers, whose daily work takes us into the courts of this country, know that the face on the target of the criminal law is Black, Brown, Red and poor. We know, as all Black people know without reading statistics, that our chances of being arrested, convicted, sentenced, imprisoned and executed are disproportionately high.

We know that the worst and most dangerous criminals are rarely the ones executed. The death penalty is applied randomly at best and discriminatorily at worst. It violates the constitutional guarantees of the equal protection of the laws because it is imposed almost exclusively against racial minorities, the poor, the uneducated—persons who are victims of selective prosecution, overt discrimination in the sentencing process and who cannot afford sophisticated legal defenses.

Statistical studies support what our impressions tell us. In Pennsylvania it has been shown that only the defendant's race explains the fact that among persons convicted of felony murder and sentenced to death, most whites will eventually have their sentences commuted to life imprisonment, and Blacks will not. (Wolfgang, Kelly and Nolde, J., *Criminal Law, Criminology and Political Science*, [1962].) In New Jersey, juries tended to bring in the death sentence for more Blacks convicted of felony murder than they did for whites convicted of the same crime. (Wolf in *Rutgers Law Review* [1964].)

The most thorough statistical proof of racial bias in capital punishment has been compiled in the study of rape convictions. "Blacks convicted of rape are disproportionately frequently sentenced to death compared with whites. . . . We are now prepared to assert that a significantly higher proportion of blacks are sentenced to death upon conviction of rape . . . because they are black . . . and the victims were white" (Wodifgeng, "Capital Punishment," *Hearings Before Subcommittee No. 3, Committee on the Judiciary, House of Representatives, 92nd Congress, 2nd Section* [1972], pp. 178–179). . . .

Mindless reliance on the death penalty, never a deterrent to crime at any time in any country, obscures the pathological, economic and social conditions which foster crime and distracts our society from the changes needed to deal with it. Execution irrevocably deprives a person of the benefits of new law or new evidence; and most obviously, it brutalizes the society that practices it.

We lawyers may argue in the highest court by every means possible, but it will not be attorneys who shall vanquish this new move toward legalized racism. As in the past, it will be the people of this country telling those in power clearly and unmistakably that the legalized death penalty must join chattel slavery and other badges and indicia of racism in the blood-stained pages of the American experience as legal lessons to be learned from, and not perpetuated, in our next hundred years.

PART FIVE

Pioneers of Black Studies

ERNEST KAISER
An editor of Freedomways

W.E.B. Du Bois was the great forerunner in Black scholarship. His doctoral dissertation at Harvard, *The Suppression of the African Slave Trade to the United States of America, 1638–1870,* was published in 1896 as volume one in the Harvard Historical Studies series. In 1899 he turned from history to sociology with *The Philadelphia Negro: A Social Study*, and in 1903 he published a collection of essays, *The Souls of Black Folk*. James Weldon Johnson said, "This book *[Souls]* had a greater effect upon and within the Black race in America than any other single book published in this country since *Uncle Tom's Cabin.*"

C.L.R. James said in an essay for *Freedomways*, "Dr. Du Bois wrote on the American slave trade, on Black urban life and on the Black community in the rural South. Modern European critics recognize that in American historical scholarship he initiated a method which has profoundly influenced all succeeding American writers on history and sociology."

James continued, "Always the intellectual pioneer, he startled American historians by his audacious revaluation of the historical role of John Brown. His *Black Reconstruction* is one of the finest books of history ever . . . published on the American continent."

In 1935 his research on the Reconstruction period culminated with *Black Reconstruction in America, 1860–1880.* This book defends the role of African Americans and Radical Republicans during the Reconstruction and repudiates the widespread opinion of the period as a tragic era productive only of evil and corruption. *Black Reconstruction* and James S. Allen's *Reconstruction: The Battle for Democracy, 1865–1876* (1937) rescued this period from white historiography and forced American historians to reconsider their biased work on the Reconstruction.

Du Bois's works were part of the background for the Harlem Renaissance of the 1920s and early 1930s. Du Bois participated in this movement as the encouraging editor of the NAACP magazine *The Crisis* and also as a contributor to *The New Negro* (1925), edited by Alain Locke.

Du Bois had conceived of an *Encyclopedia Africana* to commemorate the fiftieth year of the Emancipation Proclamation (1913). He said that he became tired of finding excessive praise of white people in newspapers, textbooks, and history, but either no mention of dark people at all or disparaging or apologetic statements. So he decided that Africa must have a history and a destiny. One of his missions was to reveal this unknown past through his writing and research over the years.

At the University of Berlin, Du Bois, then 25 years old, dedicated himself to "work for the rise of the Negro people" since "their best development means the best development of the world; to make a name in science, to make a name in literature and thus to raise my race." All of his great physical resources, his many and prodigal talents, and the work of his long and fruitful life he devoted unstintingly to the uplift of all peoples of African descent. The editors of *Freedomways* tried to continue what Du Bois and other African American writers had already begun.

47

Conference of *Encyclopedia Africana*, No. 4, 1963

W.E.B. DU BOIS

Dr. Du Bois delivered this talk at the University of Ghana, December 15, 1962. In 1961 Kwame Nkrumah, the president of the new nation of Ghana and a leader of the anticolonial movement in Africa, had invited W.E.B. Du Bois to live in Ghana and complete work on the African Encyclopedia.

I wish first to express my sincere thanks to those of you here who have accepted the invitation of our Secretariat to participate in this Conference and thus assist us in the preparatory work which we have undertaken for the creation of an *Encyclopedia Africana*.

Had there been any doubts in your minds of the importance of African Studies, I am sure the papers and discussions of the past week have dispelled them. The wide attendance at the First International Congress of Africanists attests to the almost feverish interest throughout the world in the hitherto "Dark Continent."

It remains, therefore, for me only to lay before you the importance of an *Encyclopedia Africana* based in *Africa* and compiled by *Africans.*

You have noted from letters cited in our Information Report, the most gratifying endorsement from scholars in all sections of the world of the general aims of this work. Some of you, however, ask if an *Encyclopedia Africana* at this time is not premature. Is this not a too ambitious undertaking for African scholars to attempt? Is there enough scientifically proven information ready for publication? Our answer is that an *Encyclopedia Africana* is long overdue. Yet, it is logical that such a work had to wait for independent Africans to carry it out.

We know that there does exist much scientific knowledge of Africa which has never been brought together. We have the little known works of African scholars of the past in North Africa, in the Sudan, in Egypt. Al Azhar University and the Islamic University of Sankore made large collections; *Presence Africaine* has already brought to light much material written in the French language. We can, therefore, begin, remembering always that an encyclopedia is never a finished or complete body of information. Research and study must be long and continuous. We can collect, organize and publish knowledge as it emerges. The *Encyclopedia* must be seen as a living effort which will grow and change—which will expand through the years as more and more material is gathered from all parts of Africa.

It is true that scientific written records do not exist in most parts of this vast continent. But the time is *now* for beginning. The *Encyclopedia* hopes to eliminate the artificial boundaries created on this continent by colonial masters. Designations such as "British Africa," "French Africa," "Black Africa," "Islamic Africa" too often serve to keep alive differences which in large part have been imposed on Africans by outsiders. The *Encyclopedia* must have research units throughout West Africa, North Africa, East, Central and South Africa which will gather and record information for these geographical sections of the continent. The *Encyclopedia* is concerned with Africa as a whole.

It is true that there are not now enough trained African scholars available for this gigantic task. In the early stages we have need of the technical skills in research which have been highly developed in other parts of the world. We have already asked for and to a most gratifying degree been granted the unstinted cooperation and assistance of the leading Institutes of African Studies outside Africa. Many of you who have gathered here from distant lands can, and I believe will, make valuable contributions to this undertaking. And you can assist us in finding capable African men and women who can carry the responsibilities of this work in their own country and to their people. For it is African scholars themselves who will create the ultimate *Encyclopedia Africana*.

My interest in this enterprise goes back to 1909 when I first attempted to launch an *Encyclopedia Africana* while still teaching at Atlanta University in Georgia, U.S.A. Though a number of distinguished scholars in the United States and various European countries consented to serve as sponsors, the more practical need of securing financial backing for the projected *Encyclopedia* was not solved and the project had to be abandoned. Again, in 1931, a group of American scholars met at Howard University and agreed upon the necessity of preparing an Encyclopedia of the Negro—using this term in its broadest sense. There was much organization work and research done in the preparation, but once again, the undertaking could not be carried through because, money could not be secured. Educational foundations had doubts about a work of this kind being accomplished under the editorship of Negroes. We are deeply grateful to the President of Ghana and to the Government of this independent African State for inviting us to undertake this important task here where the necessary funds for beginning this colossal work are provided. After all, this is where the work should be done—in Africa, sponsored by Africans, for Africa. *This Encyclopedia will be carried through.*

Much has happened in Africa and the world in the last twenty years. Yet, something of what I wrote in the *Preparatory Volume of the Encyclopedia of the Negro,* which was published in 1945, will bear repeating now:

Present thought and action are all too often guided by old and discarded theories of race and heredity, by misleading emphasis and silence of former histories. These conceptions are passed on to younger generations of students by current textbooks, popular histories and even public discussion. Our knowledge of Africa is not, of course, entirely complete; there are many gaps where more information and more careful study is needed; but this is true in almost every branch of knowledge. Knowledge is never complete, and in few subjects does a time arrive when an encyclopedia is demanded because no further information is expected. Indeed, the need for an encyclopedia is greatest

Dr. W.E.B. Du Bois, Augusta Strong, and Esther Cooper Jackson at Kennedy airport, New York City, 1961, as Dr. Du Bois leaves to live the last years of his life in Ghana.

when a stage is reached where there is a distinct opportunity to bring together and set down a clear and orderly statement of the facts already known and agreed upon, for the sake of establishing a base for further advance and further study.

For these reasons and under these circumstances it would seem that an *Encyclopedia Africana* is of vital importance to Africa as a whole and to the world at large.

48

Negroes in the American Revolution, No. 2, 1961

SHIRLEY GRAHAM DU BOIS

Shirley Graham Du Bois remembered that as a child she read, with others, the Declaration of Independence and never forgot "that all men are created equal and endowed with certain inalienable rights." She became a lifelong student of American history.

Beginning in 1771 and for two decades thereafter, the Fifth of March was commemorated as Independence Day in America. Not until after all states had ratified the Constitution and the Union was firmly established was the Fourth of July substituted for general celebration. Even then, particularly in New England, the Fifth of March continued to be a day of oratory recalling the beginning of the struggle for Independence. Because on March 5, 1770, occurred the Boston Massacre, designated [by] Daniel Webster as: "From that moment we may date the severance of the British Empire." And in oration, poetry and song the name Crispus Attucks, a Negro, was hailed as the first to die for American independence. Schoolboys recited the verse carved as inscription on the monument to the four victims:

> Long as in Freedom's cause the wise contend,
> Dear to your country shall your fame extend;
> While to the world the lettered stone shall tell
> Where Attucks, Caldwell, Gray and Maverick fell.

This summer of 1961, Negroes in America are being told they are "pressing too hard." Attorney-General Kennedy asks for a "cooling-off period." Heads shake and one hears that "stirring up trouble only hinders progress." "All in good time!" "Not too fast! NOT TOO FAST!" So goes arguments against any agitation waged by Negroes in their efforts to attain first-class citizenship in the United States.

Acknowledged white supremacists do not bother even to pay lip service to the Constitution or to decisions of the Supreme Court. They would make no distinction between youthful, idealistic Freedom Riders and desperate, hardened Negro soldiers driven to armed mutiny. But many honest liberals and friends of the Negro are confused. They believe that Negroes have made "marvelous progress" in this country and that the nation as a whole has done much for the "uplift" of these "unfortunate descendants of slaves." They deplore violence in "backward Southern communities" but check it off as the work of "ignorant rabble." They point to the many advantages given Negroes. "Negroes must be grateful for all we have done for them." Some discreetly question whether or not the Negro is actually ready to assume "all the responsibilities inherent in full citizenship."

Such thinking reflects the woeful ignorance of national history prevalent in the United States today. Omitted from the history books is the fact that Negroes were in the original struggle for independence, that Negroes fought and died and were decorated in the revolutionary armies and that free Negroes exercised the privileges of citizenship under the earliest Articles of Confederation. We may be proud that our President tells Mr. Khrushchev that the United States led the world in revolution. But, accepting this premise raises a question: Just how long does liberation take?

Let us go back ninety-nine years to August 14, 1862. Union armies of the North were faring badly. In Washington, Frederick Douglass begged Abraham Lincoln to recruit Negro soldiers. "Let us fight!" he pleaded. "Give us arms and we'll bring down the slaveholders!" In Boston, on this sultry afternoon, George Livermore arose to present a paper to the assembled Massachusetts Historical Society. Mr. Livermore prefaced his reading with a few remarks:

In this time of our country's trials; when its Constitution and even its continued national existence, is in peril, loyal men are laying aside their chosen and accustomed private pursuits and devoting themselves, heart and hand, to the common cause. As true patriots, then, we members of the Massachusetts Historical Society, should do something more than comply, as good citizens, with all the requirements of the Constitution and laws: we must study, in the light of history, and by the traditions of those who originally founded and at first administered the Government, the fundamental principles on which it was based, and the paramount objects for which it was established. Having done this, it may not be amiss for us to offer the results of our historical researches to others not having the leisure or the opportunity to investigate for themselves.

Documents from Past

Mr. Liverman then delivered his paper on "The Opinions of the Founders of the Republic respecting Negroes as Slaves, as Citizens, and as Soldiers." At the close of this reading, the Rev. R. C. Waterston, Acting Secretary, presented to the Society a letter from their venerable and senior member, the Honorable Josiah Quincy, heartily endorsing "the purpose of Mr. Livermore to collect and publish documents on the subject of Slavery and Negro Soldiers originating from the great men who were guides of public affairs at the time of the American Revolution. I should regard such a publication as useful and desirable and shall be happy to aid Mr. Livermore in his purpose."

It followed that Mr. Livermore's extensive paper was published that same year by John Wilson & Son of Boston. And I am now able to present some of its findings to the readers of FREEDOMWAYS.

When the thirteen American colonies rebelled, twenty per cent of the total population, some 600,000 people, were Negroes. Of this number about 150,000 were free Negroes. These free Negroes were scattered along the eastern seaboard with concentrations in New York, Boston, Philadelphia and Baltimore. The majority were slaves, most of them in the area from Maryland to Georgia.

The United States had scarcely come into being before Thomas Jefferson sadly predicted that the status of the Negro would be "the rock upon which the Union would split." When some eighty years later southern states did secede this prediction was recalled by associates of Jefferson Davis. Alexander H. Stephens (Vice-President, as he was designated), in a speech delivered in Savannah, Georgia, on the 21st of March, 1861 declared:

> The new constitution (of the Southern Confederacy) has put at rest forever all the agitating questions relating to our peculiar institutions— African slavery as it exists among us and the proper status of the Negro in our form of civilization. *This was the immediate cause of the late rupture and present revolution.* Jefferson, in his forecast had anticipated this. . . . The prevailing ideas entertained by him, and most of the leading statesmen at the time of the formation of the old Constitution, were, that the enslavement of the African was in violation of the laws of nature; that it was wrong in principle, socially, morally and politically. Those ideas were fundamentally wrong. They rested upon the assumption of the equality of races. . . . Our new government is founded upon exactly the opposite ideas.

Answering the decision handed down by Chief Justice Taney in the celebrated Dred Scott case, Judge McLean of Ohio in 1856 wrote:

> Our independence was a great epoch in the history of freedom; and while I admit the Government was not made especially for the colored race, yet many of them were citizens of the New England states, and exercised the rights of suffrage when the Constitution was adopted; and it was not doubted by an intelligent person that its tendencies would greatly ameliorate their condition. Many of the states, on the adoption of the Constitution, or shortly afterward, took measures to abolish slavery within their respective jurisdiction; and it is a well-known fact, that a belief was cherished by the leading men, South as well as North, that the institution of slavery would gradually decline, until it would become extinct. The increased value of slave labor in the culture of cotton and sugar prevented the realization of this expectation. . . . On the same principles, white men were made slaves. All slavery has its origin in power and is against right.

Two or three incidents in the earliest conflicts with the British troops will show how ready the colonists generally were, not only to secure the Negroes' services as fellow-soldiers, but to honor them for their patriotism and valor.

We have mentioned the event referred to as the "Boston Massacre" when Crispus Attucks was killed. A further paragraph taken from Livermore's account:

> Three days after, on the 8th, a public funeral of the martyrs took place. The shops in Boston were closed; and all the bells of Boston and the neighboring towns were rung. It said that a greater number of persons assembled on this occasion than were ever before gathered on this continent for a similar purpose. The body of Crispus Attucks, the ex-slave, had been placed in Faneuil Hall, with that of Caldwell; both being strangers in the city. Maverick was buried from his mother's house in Union Street; and Gray, from his brother's in the Royal Exchange Lane. The four hearses formed a junction in King Street; and there the procession marched in columns six deep, with a long file of coaches belonging to the most distinguished citizens, to the Middle Burying-ground, where the four victims were deposited in one grave; over which a stone was placed with inscription.

At the battle of Bunker Hill, on the memorable 17th of June 1775, Negro soldiers stood side by side and fought bravely with their white comrades. It was reported that the shot which brought down Major Pitcairn, of the British marines was fired by Peter Salem, a Negro. At the time of the battle, the artist John Trumbull, then acting as adjutant, was stationed with his regiment in Roxbury and saw the action from that point. It is a significant fact, and pertinent to our present research, that, among the limited number of figures which he introduced on the canvas of his famous painting of the Battle of Bunker Hill, more than one Negro soldier can be distinctly seen.

Records of Gallantry

One Negro soldier who participated in the battle of Bunker Hill was formally called to the attention of the Massachusetts legislature in a petition signed by some of the principal officers, less than six months after the event. The subscribers beg leave to report that "under our observation, we declare that a Negro man called Salem Poor, of Col. Frye's regiment, Capt. Ames' company, in the late battle at

Charlestown, behaved like an experienced officer, as well as an excellent soldier. To set forth particulars of his conduct would be tedious. We would only beg to say, in the person of this said Negro centres a brave and gallant soldier." Fourteen officers, including three colonels signed this document.

A single passage from George Bancroft's "History of the U.S. (Vol. VII. p. 421) throws further light on the condition of the army in respect to Negro soldiers, at the time of the battle of Bunker Hill:

> Nor should history forget to record, that as in the army at Cambridge, so also in this gallant band, the free Negroes of the Colony had their representatives. For the right of free Negroes to bear arms in the public defense was, at that day, as little disputed in New England as their other rights. They took their place, not in a separate corps, but in the ranks with the white man; and their names may be read on the pension-rolls of the country, side by side with those of other soldiers of the Revolution.

Says Herbert Aptheker in his *The American Revolution* (Chapter XIII, p. 225):

> Negroes from every state fought in the Revolutionary Army. Indeed, in the case of several states—Maryland, New York, Connecticut, Rhode Island, Massachusetts and New Hampshire—one would have difficulty in naming many towns or cities from which Negroes did *not* enlist. A good example is Connecticut (which contained about 6,500 Negroes in 1774) whose records were kept particularly well, and show Negro volunteers from at least 47 different localities, from Ashford to Woodstock, from Branford to Waterbury, from Canaan to Winchester. Even for Georgia there is conclusive proof that at least five Negroes from that state fought against the British, for records are extant of the manumission of all five as rewards for their service. One of these, Austin Dabney, was not only freed, but, in addition, having conducted himself—said the legislative act of emancipation—'with a bravery and fortitude which would have honored a freeman,' he was awarded an annual pension of $96, and given 112 acres of land. At least one South Carolina Negro, John Eady, also distinguished himself in the Revolutionary Army and was rewarded with freedom and land. . . .

At the beginning of the war, it appears to have been customary for free Negroes to be enrolled with white citizens in the militia. In many instances, slaves also took their places in the ranks with freemen. The inconsistency, however, in using as soldiers in any army, raised for securing national liberation, those held in bondage was apparent. The Massachusetts Committee of Safety resolved that "the admission of any persons, as soldiers into the army now raising other than Freemen reflects dishonor on this Colony; and that no slaves be admitted into this army upon any consideration whatever."

The Reverend Dr. Hopkins of Newport, R.I., addressed himself to "The Honorable Continental Congress" on this subject with the argument:

> God is so ordering it in his providence, that it seems absolutely necessary something should be speedily done with respect to the slaves among us, in order to our safety, and to prevent their turning against us in our present struggle, in order to get their liberty. Our oppressors have planned to gain the blacks, and induce them to take up arms against us, promising them liberty on this condition, . . . The only way to prevent this threatening evil is to set the blacks at liberty ourselves by some public acts and laws, and then give them proper encouragement to labor, to take arms in the defense of the American cause, as they shall choose.

Many slaves were set free that they might become soldiers. Their skill and bravery were never called in question. There does not, however, appear to have been, at that time, any special legislation sanctioning the employment of Negroes as soldiers. It is a significant fact that the principal opposition to Negro soldiers came from those colonies where there was the least support for the Revolution and the least disposition to furnish a fair or equal quota of white soldiers. "Indeed, the Continental Congress, in March 1779, adopted a resolution urging Georgia and South Carolina, for the sake of saving the cause in those areas, to permit the enlistment of 3,000 Negroes. Both states refused and hinted that they would withdraw from the struggle before agreeing to such a proposition. Maryland in 1780 passed laws permitting slaves and free Negroes to be recruited as soldiers. New York, in accordance with an act passed in March, 1781, raised two regiments of slaves, all of whom enlisted with the understanding that loyal service for the war's duration would bring emancipation" (Aptheker's *The American Revolution,* page 224).

Negroes were with Anthony Wayne when he captured the fort at Stony Point, New York; Negroes were rewarded for important spying activity—thousands served as regular soldiers in the American Revolutionary Army and many thousands more served that army as teamsters, cooks, guides and what were then called pioneers—or are known today as combat engineers.

And so the successful struggle came to an end with the signing of the Treaty of Paris in 1783 and the United States of America was recognized before the world. Gradually, but persistently the great landowners of the South extended their hold on the new nation. Virginia, not Massachusetts, became the "cradle of liberty" and the signing of Thomas Jefferson's Declaration of Independence was deemed the more proper date for oratory than a "street brawl" which took place in Boston. And as cotton began to replace tobacco on the plantation, all talk of emancipating the slaves became unpopular. For the Negro, the bright vision of the nation he had helped to bring to birth began to fade. . . .

49

Black/Indian Origins of the Fight for Democracy, No. 2, 1984

WILLIAM LOREN KATZ

William Loren Katz, the author of numerous works of scholarship, is a specialist in the history of relationships of Native Americans and Black Americans and author of Black Indians: A Hidden Heritage.

. . . Were Roanoke, Jamestown or Plymouth the first foreign settlements on North American shores, or merely the first English ones? What the textbooks fail to mention is that in 1526, less than two generations after Columbus' 1492 landing, a settlement was founded in South Carolina at or near the mouth of the Pedee River. Six decades before Roanoke, eight decades before Jamestown and almost a century before Plymouth, Lucas Vasquez de Ayllon, a Spanish official, was pursuing his New World dream with about 500 Spanish men and women and about 100 enslaved Africans. His effort is overlooked, perhaps, because most North Americans prefer to believe their heritage began with the arrival of English-speaking people governed by British law, not Mediterranean types and black Africans. Or perhaps Ayllon's settlement is neglected because of its unusual fate and the subsequent history of its black survivors—an important American dialectic in the wilderness.

Several years before his expedition reached these shores, Ayllon's plans suffered from strategic and portentous blunders. A captain he sent to survey the landing site and build friendly relations with the native inhabitants teamed up instead with a notorious slave-trader. Abandoning his mission of charting a landing site and making friends, the captain sailed back to Santo Domingo with his disreputable cohorts and about 70 Native Americans they had seized as slaves. To his credit, Ayllon had a royal commission headed by Diego Columbus free the captives, but they were not returned home for years, if ever. However, to make amends with the decimated native society, Ayllon again sent off the fellow who started all the trouble in the first place. He also retained one captive, Francisco Chicora, for his personal use and trained him as his guide.

In the wake of this record of kidnapping and double-dealing, Ayllon made plans to found a prosperous colony on the North American mainland. In early June 1526, he set sail with three large vessels bearing his potpourri of colonists, slaves, supplies, physicians, three Dominican missionaries and about 80 to 100 horses. Though mishaps dogged their efforts—they landed on the wrong coast, lost a ship and Chicora deserted—the voyagers eventually reached their destination.

For his colony of San Miguel de Guadalupe, Ayllon selected a low, marshy area and initiated black slavery in the United States with his command that the Africans begin building the settlement homes. But the colony was not to endure. Illness and starvation wiped out the Spanish like flies, and those who lived fell into bitter disputes. Compounding the problems, an icy winter blew in before everyone could be housed.

The Native Americans viewed the quarrelsome foreigners with suspicion and disdain. These were the people who had carried off their relatives in chains, and now they had returned with Africans in chains. Moreover, the culture gap was enormous: the newcomers hailed from a country in which the nobility, two percent of the population, owned 95 percent of the land, in which exploitation of land and labor were rife; the Native Americans in the vicinity of San Miguel shared huge weather-insulated pine homes, measuring 20 by 300 feet, that slept 300 people each. Although the Dominican priests kept the Europeans from enslaving the natives, suspicion remained high.

By October, less than six months after he founded San Miguel, Ayllon succumbed to disease. Bereft of their leader, the Spaniards divided into warring factions, while the Africans, according to later testimony, committed acts of sabotage aided by Native Americans.

In November, the colony's fifth and weakest month, the Africans rebelled and fled to the natives in the woods. The surviving 150 Spaniards, unable to face the freezing winter without their labor supply, packed up and shipped out for Santo Domingo.

The first settlement installed by foreigners on U.S. soil, San Miguel, foundered, not least because it could not withstand the propulsion toward liberty of its African members. But even as that European-dominated coastal society collapsed, the Africans, joining with their Native American allies in the interior created a new community. There in South Carolina, two and a half centuries before the Declaration of Independence, two dark-skinned peoples exalted the principles of freedom. As the first to establish a settlement of any permanence in North American that included people from overseas, they qualify as our true ancestors.

The refugees from San Miguel and their Native American soul mates proved that our vaunted democracy did not march into the wilderness with buckled shoes and British accents. Rather, it began spontaneously in the hinterland among two peoples who understood profoundly what freedom is and is not. To this day, they have not found their way into our history courses because they were not white, not European, not Christian, nor did they draw up a "Mayflower Compact" neatly setting forth their plan of governance. They merely put into practice the concept that all people are created equal and are entitled to life, liberty and the pursuit of happiness.

Those inclined to mourn, symbolically, the pioneers of Roanoke Island, Jamestown or Plymouth, can take heart from the brave heritage bequeathed us by the African freedom-fighters who revolted in San Miguel and the Native Americans, with chestnut bows and quivers of skin, who understood their plight and took them in as sisters and brothers. Here is a story worthy of being ranked with the proud traditions established by other fighting Americans at Lexington, Concord and Valley Forge.

50

A Review of *The Crisis of the Negro Intellectual,* No. 1, 1969

ERNEST KAISER

Harold Cruse's book The Crisis of the Negro Intellectual *continues to be on the required reading lists of many college courses. The following excerpts are from the review Ernest Kaiser wrote for* Freedomways.

. . . Cruse's problem [in *Crisis of the Negro Intellectual*] is an old one. After breaking ideologically with the Left and Marxism, he searched desperately for an ideological alternative or critique of Marxism. But answering Marxism which synthesized originally the German philosophy, English economics and French socialism of the 19th century and has been modified and brought up-to-date by later Marxist thinkers and writers is no easy task for anyone no matter how formidable his learning and scholarship. Cruse also wants to blame someone for the plight of the Negro people. . . . Unable to oppose his real American oppressors, . . . he blames the Marxists or Communists and the Negro people themselves for the Negroes' plight and lets the capitalists off the hook. But being an intellectual, he has to have an elaborate rationale for this. . . .

The rise of mass cultural communications (radio, TV, film industries, advertising combines, electronic recording and computer industries, highly developed telecommunications, etc.) changes capitalism, says Cruse. Whoever controls the cultural apparatus, he says, controls the destiny of the country and everything in it. Although Marshall McLuhan is never mentioned, this is obviously a variation on or an extension or exaggeration of McLuhan's *Understanding Media: The Extensions of Man* (1964) which fills in all of the many details and ramifications. . . .Cruse thinks that economic and political power must come through a correct, basic cultural approach. . . . This is his general thesis. His economic emphasis is on cooperatives instead of trade unions. He wants to reform capitalism and avoid class warfare. When he applies this thesis to Negroes, he changes it somewhat to cultural nationalism or the politics of culture. All Negro thought throughout history to the present is divided into integrationist and separatist or nationalist. Interpreting history as basically cultural nationalism, Cruse doesn't have to deal with the socioeconomic factors of different periods with different cultural problems and on different levels. Everything is simplified but rigid. Douglass, Du Bois, NAACPers, the civil rights workers, Rev. King, et al., are all integrationists; Martin R. Delany, B. T. Washington, Garvey, Elijah Muhammad and today's Black nationalists are separatists. Negroes should have followed the separatists instead of the integrationists. That's the basic Negro trouble. Also E. F. Frazier and Du Bois's emphasis upon cooperatives should have been heeded. But Cruse can't see that U.S. Negroes have always struggled for integration and carried on various economic and cultural self-help activities at the same time throughout their history with varying degrees of emphasis. Cruse also says that Negro intellectuals failed to act on the Negro cultural revolution of the 1920's, the Harlem Renaissance, and that that's where the troubles of the last 40 years began. Communism blinded the Negro intellectuals of the 1920's. This is Cruse's basic theory. . . .

Cruse attacks Paul Robeson as naive and politically limited. Robeson was a pretty good columnist for his newspaper *Freedom* and his book *Here I Stand* (1958) has important political chapters. Let Cruse, who says that Robeson never called for direct action in his writings, read again chapter five of *Here I Stand* titled "The Power of Black Action." Here Robeson goes beyond the non-violent, direct action of early SNCC and CORE and calls on Negroes to defend their lives and property against mobs as well as participate in mass demonstrations, organize boycotts and go on strike. Mass action, says Robeson, in political life and elsewhere, is Negro power in motion. He also calls for unity of all Negro organizations in struggle with unified dedicated, independent Negro leadership.

Robeson always championed Negro culture in his speeches and writings. He was Mr. Negro Culture himself, singing Negro folk songs and spirituals; always preoccupied with and struggling for African and American Negro culture.

Cruse can't really deal with FREEDOMWAYS beyond the first few beginning issues. . . . He accuses FREEDOMWAYS of avoiding domestic issues by carrying material on Africa at a time when African independence struggles were at their height in the early 1960's and had to be dealt with as part of our struggle. FREEDOMWAYS also published Ossie Davis's "Purlie Told Me!" and Jim Williams's "The Need for a Harlem Theatre," two articles on building a Black theatre. The Davis article is attacked; the Williams article is ignored. Richard Moore's "Africa-Conscious Harlem" article in FREEDOMWAYS is also attacked. But Moore's record of activities and many writings stand for themselves and tell his story. FREEDOMWAYS has published many searching articles and critiques on the Negro question and Negro culture of the 1960's; it has summed up, drawn conclusions and pointed the way forward—an important task. Its support is broadening and increasing and its influence is growing rapidly.

Cruse's statement that minority Jewish nationalism is more successful than majority Anglo-Saxon nationalism is absurd and anti-Semitic. His treatment of Negro-Jewish relations is away off. Israel and some of the Jews there are tied up with imperialism in Africa and should be opposed. But Cruse would rather fight them than the main imperialists who are American WASPs. Carey McWilliams, in his book *Brothers Under the Skin* (1951), calls Jews a trading, marginal minority while the Negroes are a working, subordinate minority. Jews as a group are not the Negroes' enemy; the power elite which includes some Jews is. Negroes and Jews as groups have some competition and rivalries for jobs, housing, businesses in the ghetto and the like in a competitive capitalist society. Cruse attacks James Baldwin's early 1948 *Commentary* article on Negro-Jewish relations and ignores Baldwin's different "Negroes Are Anti-Semitic Because They're Anti-White" (*New York Times Magazine,* April 9, 1967).

Cruse also attacks West Indians and Africans and oversimplifies everything by ignoring the economic imperialism that still exists in the independent countries of both the West Indies and Africa. . . .

Cruse is so mean-spirited, so vengeful, such a misanthrope, hating almost everybody and everything, so bent on trying to destroy people if he can; his writing is just so much invective and vituperation reiterated over and over ad nauseam. He makes up or rewrites history as he goes along to fit the points he wants to make. He distorts, exaggerates and reads something sinister and covert into ordinary, often routine things.

Cruse calls repeatedly for a politics of culture, but nowhere in this 595-page book does he develop a cultural critique on Negro literature, art and drama within American culture; a critique, he says, a nationalist program must have. He asks instead that Afro-American nationalists do this while he pours out empty, cloudy, metaphorical rhetoric ("until this is done . . . without this or that") which is like beating a dead horse. In fact, he rejects with scorn all attempts of Marxists to bring a social and cultural philosophy to bear in the field of culture.

He attacks the Marxists unmercifully while, ironically, he is using Marxist terminology and Marxist concepts (however incorrectly and without ever admitting this) throughout the book to beat liberals and Negro civil rights advocates over the head. But almost all Cruse knows about capitalism, he learned from the Marxists. In fact, without Marxist terminology and concepts plus some C. Wright Mills, this book would not have been possible. And Cruse has the unmitigated gall to say that Marxism dulls Negro intellectuals and limits their social imagination.

Finally, Cruse, being a would-be playwright and an intellectual or critic, narcissistically elevates the Negro playwright and the critical intellectual to complete independence at the top of the political and social heap. How to get up there is really Cruse's crisis of the Negro intellectual. . . .

The Negro playwright develops, as Shakespeare did, by being closely associated with and writing for a Negro people's theatre. And both the Negro playwright and the Negro intellectual or critic must have a clear social philosophy in order to develop—something more than the vague cultural apparatus stuff of C. Wright Mills or the nebulous cultural nationalism of Harold Cruse. This is a very confusing, disorienting, dangerous book since Cruse, posing as a know-it-all, voluble super-critic, seems, to many who cannot see through his tricks and one-upmanship at all times, to have the answers for everything. The trouble with what Cruse is advocating is best exemplified by his book: Cruse is always analyzing Negro programs in a vacuum, never as programs, demands or developments that grow out of the Negro people's struggles.

PART SIX

Culture and the Cause of Black Freedom

RUBY DEE

An editor of Freedomways

My earliest recollection of *Freedomways* is of a time before it was actually published. I was in the living room in the home of Dr. Du Bois and Shirley Graham Du Bois in Brooklyn Heights. Among those few present were Esther and Jim Jackson, John O. Killens, Ossie, me—and I wish I could remember who else besides W.E.B. Du Bois, Doctor, The Great One, on a recliner, in house slippers, smoking his one cigarette for the day. Minds were moving over and around an idea whose time had arrived. I had interjected some kind of unnecessary protective remark about women. There was a momentary caring but puzzled silence, and Esther, I believe, incorporated my profound observation into some comment that got things back on track. A year or so later, many of the artists who helped found the journal and were a part of the collective that produced *Freedomways* attended the opening event at the Hotel Martinique in 1961 where it was launched.

Over the years, I have interpreted the works of a number of the Black women writers who appear in this anthology. On Broadway, I played the role of Ruth, the wife of Sidney Poitier's Walter Lee

Younger in Lorraine Hansberry's *A Raisin in the Sun*. In Alice Childress's drama *The Wedding Band*, I was Julia, the lover of Herman, a white baker in trouble. On a public television series titled "With Ossie and Ruby," we featured many of the writers and poets we love, including writers published in this anthology: Nikki Giovanni, and the Pulitzer Prize winners Gwendolyn Brooks and Alice Walker. This collection from *Freedomways* highlights the extraordinary flowering of these and other Black women writers.

The editorial "Culture and the Cause of Black Freedom" in the Spring 1962 issue pointed to the important social function of Black writers and artists in expressing the reality of Black life and aspirations. A hallmark of *Freedomways*'s editorial view was that literature, poetry, drama, and music could contribute to liberation struggles. Each poem and short story of the writers featured here proves the truth of this, for each work has a political theme and at the same time succeeds as art.

In this, *Freedomways* continued the tradition of uniting art, politics, and social experience that dated back at least to the Harlem Renaissance movement and the magazine *The Crisis* under Dr. Du Bois. Among the selections included in this anthology are recollections of the Harlem Renaissance that Langston Hughes and Arna Bontemps wrote for *Freedomways*. The superb example of art and political activism, *"Ode to Paul Robeson"* by Nobel Prize–winning poet Pablo Neruda, also graces these pages. Another Nobel laureate poet, Derek Walcott, had works published in the journal some thirty years before receiving the award.

For many years I have admired the work of master percussionist Max Roach, who wrote the *Freedom Now* suite. His article on jazz in this collection protests "the rape of the Black jazz musician." Abbey Lincoln, singer and interpreter of the blues and so much more, celebrates other great Black women singers in her article. I am proud also that my life has touched the work of Alex Haley and John O. Killens, both of whom are represented here.

Freedomways was a unique journal in the freedom movement in that it recognized, promoted, and celebrated the arts and many artists as part of the struggle. It declared, in effect, that the arts define us, put us as a species in perspective, and locate us in the cosmos. *Freedomways* contributed to the cultural life of the United States and helped clarify and pinpoint its political achievements.

51

The Negro Woman in American Literature, No. 1, 1966

ALICE CHILDRESS, PAULE MARSHALL, and SARAH E. WRIGHT

Paule Marshall, Alice Childress, and Sarah Wright spoke at the conference "The Negro Writer's Visions of America" held at the New School for Social Research in New York City in 1965. The women on this panel were pioneers in criticizing the degrading and stereotypical portrayals of women in American literature. Alice Childress was the author of the novel A Hero Ain't Nothin But a Sandwich *and the play* A Wedding Band. *Sarah Wright is a poet and novelist. Her classic* This Child's Gonna Live *has recently been reissued. Paule Marshall is author of the award-winning novel* Brown Girl, Brownstones *and a collection of short stories,* Soul Clap Hands and Sing, *among other works.*

Sarah E. Wright

I am convinced that most American men, and unhappily, far, far too many of our Afro-American men, are walking around begging for a popular recognition of what is fictitiously called "manhood," a begging which takes the form of attacks on women launched from many different directions.

It is for this reason (since men are the most prolific producers of literature) that we have so much slop concerning women in the popular literature and advertisements of our day.

One can hardly pick up a book which does not advertise naked, or suggestively naked women on the cover. Now women for the most part do not slink around naked or in flimsy negligees unless they are adolescent and uninformed about what makes the world go around.

One can hardly pick up a book and read anything about the thoughts of women regarding the conditions of the world unless there are sexual innuendoes and overtones coming through first and foremost. As most of the authors with whom I am acquainted would have it, a woman does not have non-sexual preoccupations. She has been reduced, according to one of the most commercially successful films of recent times, into being, and I quote, "Pussy Galore."

The popular musical literature of our time is in a supreme state of chaos. The reduction of women in song to mere sexual animals is at the point beyond which it can go no further.

A virtual wilderness of the human mind exists with respect to what it is to be a woman, a mother, a responsible-minded citizen, a creator of significant and humanly meaningful work, a thoughtful person.

Mothers are treated as stranglers; as people who eternally refuse to "cut the navel cord" even if the child grows up to be one hundred. It is no news to any women of my acquaintance that this is not so. A mother's womb and the intelligence which guides the womb is utterly glad when the child is freed from it. For almost every minute that she carries a child, feels that child nursing on the foods that she has eaten the nights and days of life which transpired before, feeling that child nudging and kicking for life, she is in a state of anxiety for her own safety, as well as that of the baby's. Most mothers do not refuse to cut the navel cord. They are happy to be freed of the child and, I am sure, from the signs of pre-delivery kicking, the child is glad to be freed of the mother. And this is true in the years of childhood and adolescence as well. So much for the "strangling mother" scene.

The stern and fearsome grandmother is another "way out" scene which ought to be abandoned. The grandmothers whom I know are for the most part kind and sometimes overly indulgent. They forgive easily, they talk far more kindly than most people I know; they love graciously and with good judgment. They love with experience in the ways of loving. They are most susceptible to learning. They are people who have achieved humanity. They are usually not "wits" or jokers, as I understand much of our popular literature to say. They are life understood, life lived through many a trial and many an error and many, many successes in the ways of being human beings. They are lovers, not correctors. They are at peace because of the conditioning given by the sense of loving.

If you look at the way most women, and I give particular stress to Afro-American women, being as they are in our society generally on the lowest rung of the ladder, if you look at the way women are treated in literature (mostly produced by men), you can begin to wonder why they are readers at all, and why particularly, they are producers of literature.

However, there are some of us who come through as producers, as well as readers. I for one have a very limited reading experience, but I am a writer. There are women among us who in spite of economic enslavement in various forms, in spite of being in the condition of Afro-American enslavement, are both readers and writers. Some of these women you will meet today. . . .

Alice Childress

I agree that the Negro woman has almost been omitted as important subject matter in the general popular American drama, television, motion pictures and radio, except for the constant, but empty and decharacterized faithful servant. And her finest virtues have been drawn in terms of long suffering, with humility and patience.

Today, the Negro woman's faults are sometimes pointed out, that she is too militant, so domineering, so aggressive, with son, husband and brother, that it is one of the chief reasons for any unexpressed manhood on the part of the Negro man in America.

There must be some truth in this charge. The mother in James Baldwin's *Amen Corner* attempts to restrict her son and husband to her passive and withdrawn way of life, but fails. The husband abandons her and seeks to find himself in music. He returns home to die, then advises the son she has raised to break free of her gentle domination. The son leaves home.

In Lorraine Hansberry's *A Raisin in the Sun,* the strong, loving mother so dominates the home that she restricts her children and infringes upon the rights of her son as a man.

In Louis Peterson's *Take a Giant Step,* a Negro mother tries to separate her son from his black heritage in order to shield him from the realities of life.

All Negro writers have written, first, about that strong, matriarchal figure. I did in a one-act play, *Florence,* and in *Trouble in Mind.*

But now we frequently hear that strength has taken femininity away from her with the end result that she is the main culprit in any lack of expressed black manhood, and that she has been masculinized in the process.

Certainly this is too easy and too misleading a conclusion. We know that most alien visitors are guaranteed rights and courtesies not extended to at least one-fifth of America's citizens. They are entitled to travel, without restriction, reside in hotels, eat at restaurants and enter public and private places closed to Americans who have built up the country under bondage and defended it under a limited and restricted liberty.

But the American Negro woman has been *particularly* and deliberately oppressed, in slavery and up to and including the present moment, above and beyond the general knowledge of the average American citizen.

After the Emancipation, the white South was faced with a dilemma. How could it protect itself against the legal claims of slaveowners' half-Black children? Some of them were the only offspring of a white master. Many Black women had been purchased to fulfill the role of wives, but most were used as sexual outlets under degrading circumstances and none had the privileges of consent or refusal concerning the use of her body. She was forced to bear children and her offspring belonged legally, not to her, but to her owner-master.

There were many Black men who were resentful of being named father to the white slaveowners' children and eager to escape the additional bondage of an enforced family set-up.

There were also some cases of whites who wished to acknowledge their colored children and leave property to them. Laws were passed, declaring what percentage of "Black blood" made a human being all Black, and thus no responsibility to their white parents.

To spare white men the responsibility of support claims, and to avoid Black men challenging in court the paternity of some fair-complexioned child, the white South took action against the Negro woman.

State after state passed legislation declaring that all children born to Black women during slavery shall be known as the legitimate children of *their mothers only*.

In the first generation of "freedom," the Black woman was abandoned, not only by the white father-owner, but by any Black man faced with acknowledging children bred by the slave-master, or by other Black men, since women were mated by the owners with various men, to bring forth various kind of offspring. Mated for strength, endurance, size, color, and even docility.

With one stroke of the pen, she was told that no man, Black or white, owed her anything, and her children were disinherited of all property rights. Her brothers, her father, male cousins, all family ties had been sold, resold, scattered, and so lost that she was, in the majority of cases, without family of any kind.

In so-called freedom, she could now seek a Negro husband. A man who, like herself, was jobless, without education, and doomed to petition for basic human rights and needs for the next century, and God knows how many more years past that century mark of 1963.

The white South and much of the North destroyed reconstruction efforts and passed laws designed to subjugate and keep the ex-slave in a state of ignorance. He was not allowed to attend schools, churches, parks, libraries, and most certainly, not the concert halls or theaters.

Two hundred years of outlawing the use of African languages has divorced Africans from their folk stories, songs, ritual ceremonies, even the ability to pass on crafts and handiwork.

The Negro was ridiculed; he was emancipated in rags and tatters. Cartoonists lampooned his appearance; vaudeville performers blackened their faces and made mocking, comic characters of "Mandy" and "Sambo."

The mainstay of television and movies has ever been the fist fight scene; the hero fights the villain for mistreating or manhandling a defenseless woman. How many times have you seen these men fighting for the honor of a Negro woman? How many guns have been fired for *her* protection? How many detectives have rescued *her* in the nick of time?

She came out of bondage with the burden of the white and the black man's child. Her former master passed laws absolving him of all moral and financial obligation to his children, and she has to feed, raise and educate them by her own effort.

And today, the slave owners' acknowledged children fight to keep their own, as well as ours, out of the school and out of the voting booth.

Writers be wary of those who tell you to leave the past alone and confine yourselves to the present moment. Our story has not been told in any moment.

Have you seen us in any portrayal of the Civil War? *Gone With the Wind* is not our story. And our history is not gone with the wind; it is still with us. . . .

Facing the world alone makes a woman strong. The emancipated Negro woman of America did the only thing she could do. She earned a pittance by washing, ironing, cooking, cleaning, and picking cotton. She helped her man, and if she often stood in the front line, it was to shield him from a mob of men organized and dedicated to bring about his total destruction.

The Negro mother has had the bitter job of teaching her children the difference between the White and Colored signs before they are old enough to attend school. She had to train her sons and daughters to say "sir" and "ma'am" to those who were their sworn enemies.

She couldn't tell her husband "a white man whistled at me, or insulted me, or touched me," not unless she wanted him to lay down his life before organized killers who strike only in anonymous numbers. Or worse, perhaps to see him helpless and ashamed before her.

Because he could offer no protection or security, the Negro woman has worked with and for her family. She built churches, schools, homes, temples and college educations out of soapsuds and muscle.

It seems a contradiction for a woman to be degraded by law, and by popular opinion which was shaped and formed by that law, and yet also take her rightful place as the most heroic figure to emerge on the American scene, with more stamina than that shown by any pioneer.

Finally, I would like to say, today we hear so much about the *new Negro*. As though we never breathed a protest until a few years ago.

But the story of the old Negro has not been told.

Denmark Vesey, Francis Watkins Harper, Monroe Trotter—if their true stories were told, there would not be so many school drop-outs.

Who wants to sit in a classroom and be taught that he is nobody?

The Negro woman will attain her rightful place in American literature when those of us who care about truth, justice and a better life tell her story, with the full knowledge and appreciation of her constant, unrelenting struggle against racism and for human rights.

Paule Marshall

As I see it, and it is a very subjective view on my part, the person we are talking about, the Negro woman, has been until recent times almost non-existent in the prose literature of the country.

This is not to say that some creature which has been passed off as the Negro woman hasn't appeared in stories and novels written by both white and Negro writers since the earliest beginnings of the country's literary history; but I contend that, by and large, the figure which emerges even upon the most cursory examination of these works, is a myth, a stereotype, a fantasy figure, which has very little to do with the Negro woman in reality.

In other words, the black woman as portrayed, has suffered the same unhappy fate as the black man. She has in a sense been strung up on two poles and left hanging. At one end of the pole, there is the "nigger wench"—sensual, primitive, pleasure seeking, immoral, the siren, the sinner. Her type was perhaps best summed up by Gertrude Stein in her description of Rose in the story "Melanctha." "Rose," Miss Stein wrote, "a real black, well-built, sullen, stupid, child-like, good-looking Negress," who had, in Miss Stein's words, "the simple, promiscuous immorality of the black people."

At the other end of the pole, we find that larger than life figure, the Negro matriarch, who dominates so much of fiction—strong, but humble, devoted, devoutly religious, patient—a paragon of patience, if you will—wise beyond all wisdom, the saint, the mammy, the great wet nurse of the society, and the country deep within the recesses of its psyche longs to return to her ample breasts.

We see her in the early novels of Thomas Nelson Page, in *Gone with the Wind*. She is Berenice out in the kitchen in *Member of the Wedding* and William Faulkner's Delsey trudging up the stairs with the hot water bag for Mrs. Compson. She has become an almost legendary figure. She endures.

Now, I am not saying that there is anything wrong in writing about sinners or saints, matriarchs or wenches, black or white. All is grist for the novelist's mill. But what is wrong, glaringly and inexcusably wrong, is that the Negro woman as a character in the fiction, has been confined largely to these two categories. Moreover, to compound the crime, she is seldom realized as a valid character in these two categories; by this I mean she is denied the complexities, the contradictions, the ambiguities that make for a truly rich and credible character in fiction. The reason for this is simple and yet complex, and it has to do with the history of this country, a history grounded in slavery. The purpose ... was to deny the Negro woman her humanity. For if she was less than human, all sorts of crimes could be committed against her and go unpunished. She could be exploited in the fields and kitchens, her body freely used, her children taken from her, her men castrated before her eyes, and yet in the mind of white America this abuse, this outrage, was somehow not serious.

The use of the Negro woman as an embodiment of myths and fantasies that have ... much to do with the troubled and repressed conscience has over the years reached so far down in the national psyche that not even the best of the white writers have escaped it.

52

Paul Robeson, No. 1, 1971

GWENDOLYN BROOKS

Gwendolyn Brooks won a Pulitzer Prize for poetry in 1950. She was the first African American to receive a Pulitzer Prize.

That time
we all heard it,
cool and clear,
cutting across the hot grit of the day.
The major Voice.
The adult Voice
forgoing Rolling River,
forgoing tearful tale of bale and barge
and other symptoms of an old despond.
Warning, in music-words
devout and large,
that we are each other's
harvest:
we are each other's
business:
we are each other's
magnitude and bond.

53

Prologue, No. 1, 1972

AUDRE LORDE

Audre Lorde was a Black feminist poet and professor of literature who wrote about her Caribbean heritage in Cables of Rage *and other works.*

Haunted by poems beginning with I
Seek out those whom I love who are deaf
to whatever does not destroy
or curse the old ways that did not serve us
while history falters and our poets are dying
choked into silence by icy distinctions
their death rattles are blind curses
and I hear even my own voice becoming
pale strident whispers
At night sleep locks me into an echoless coffin
sometimes at noon
I dream
there is nothing to fear;

now standing up in the light of my father sun
without shadow
I speak without concern for the accusations

that I am too much or too little woman
that I am too black or too white
or too much myself
and through my lips come the voices
of the ghosts of our ancestors
living and moving among us
Hear my heart's voice as it darkens
pulling the old rhythms out of earth
that will receive this piece of me
and a piece of each one of you
when our part in history quickens again
and is over:

Hear
the old ways are going away
and coming back
pretending change
masked as denunciations and lament
as a choice
between eager mirrors that blur and distort us
in easy definitions until our image
shatters along its faults
while the other half of that choice
speaks to our hidden fears with the promise
that our eyes need not seek any truer shape—
our face at high noon particular and unadorned—
for we have learned to fear/ the light from clear water/
might destroy us
with reflected emptiness or a face without tongue
with no love or with terrible penalties
for any difference
and even as I speak remembered pain is moving
shadows over my face
my own voice fades and
my brothers and sisters are leaving.

Yet when I was a child
whatever my mother thought would mean survival
made her try to beat me whiter every day
and even now the color of her bleached ambition

forks throughout my words
but I survived
and didn't I survive! confirmed, and
teaching my children where her errors lay
etched across their faces between the kisses
that she pinned me with asleep
and my mother beating me
as white as snow melts in the sunlight
loving me into her blood's black bone
the house of all her secret hopes and fears
and my dead father whose great hands
weakened in my judgment
whose image broke inside of me
beneath the weight of failure
helps me to know who I am not
weak or mistaken my father
loved me alive to grow and hate him
and now his grave voice joins hers
within my words rising and falling
Are my sisters and brothers listening?

The children remain
like blades of grass over the earth and
all the children are singing
louder than mourning
all their different voices sound like a raucous question
but they do not fear the blank empty mirrors
they have seen their faces
defined in a hydrant's puddle
before the rainbows of oil obscured them
and now my mother survives
through more than chance or token
yet she will read what I write
with embarrassment
or anger, and little understanding.

My children do not need to relive my past
its strength or its confusion
nor care that their holy fires may destroy
more than my failures

Somewhere in their landscape past noon
I shall leave a dark print
of the me that I am and who I am not
etched in a shadow of angry and remembered loving
and their ancestor ghosts will move
whispering through them
with me none the wiser
for they will have buried me
either in shame or in peace.

And the grasses will still be singing.

54

Rites of Passage, No. 3, 1970

AUDRE LORDE

to MLK Jr.

Now rock the boat to a fare-thee-well.
Once we suffered dreaming
into the place where the children are playing
their child's games
where the children are hoping
knowledge survives if
unknowing
they follow the game
without winning.

Their fathers are dying
back to the freedom of wise children playing

at knowing
their fathers are dying
whose deaths will not free them
of growing from knowledge
of knowing
when the game becomes foolish
a dangerous pleading
for time out of power

Quick
children kiss us
we are growing through dream.

55

The Lion in Daniel's Den, No. 1, 1971

NIKKI GIOVANNI

A professor of English for many years, Nikki Giovanni is the author of Racism 101 *and* Selected Poems of Nikki Giovanni.

(for Paul Robeson, Sr.)

on the road to damascus
to slay the christians
saul saw the light
and was blinded by that light
and looked into the Darkness
and embraced that Darkness
and saul arose from the great white way
saying "I Am Paul
who would slay you

but I saw the Darkness
and I am that Darkness"
then he raised his voice
singing red black and green songs
saying "I am the lion
in daniel's den
I am the lion thrown to slaughter"

do not fear the lion
for he is us
and we are all
in daniel's den

56

For Beautiful Mary Brown: Chicago Rent Strike Leader, No. 2, 1971

JUNE JORDAN

A professor of African American studies, June Jordan is the author of Poetry of the People: A Revolutionary Blueprint *and* Civil Wars: Selected Essays *and many other works. She composed the lyrics and libretto for the opera* I Was Looking at the Ceiling and then I Saw the Sky.

All of them are six
who wait inside that other room
where no man walks but many
talk about the many wars
Your baby holds your laboring arms
that bloat from pulling
up and down the stairs to tell
to call the neighbors: We can fight.

She listens to you and she sees
you crying on your knees or else
the dust drifts from your tongue and almost
she can feel her father standing tall.

Came to Chicago like flies to fish.
Found no heroes on the corner.
Butter the bread and cover the couch.
Save on money.

Don't
tell me how you wash hope hurt and lose
don't' tell me how you
sit still at the windowsill:

you will be god to bless you
Mary Brown.

57

Rock Eagle, No.4, 1971

ALICE WALKER

A contributing editor of Freedomways, *Alice Walker published her early short fiction and criticism as well as poetry in the journal in 1968.*

In the town where I was born
There is a mound
Some five feet high
That from the ground
Seems piled up stones
In Georgia
Insignificant

But from above
The lookout tower
Floor
An eagle widespread
In solid gravel
Stone
Takes shape
Below

The Cherokees raised it
Long ago
Before westward journeys
In the snow
Before the
National Policy slew
Long before Columbus knew

I used to stop and
Linger there
Within the cleanswept tower stair
Rock Eagle pinesounds
Rush of stillness
Lifting up my hair
Pinned to the earth
The eagle endures
The Cherokees are gone
The people come on tours
And on surrounding National
Forest lakes the air rings

With cries
The silenced make
Wearing cameras
They never hear
But relive their victory
Every year
And take it home
With them

Young Future Farmers
As paleface warriors
Grub
Live off the land
Pretend Indian, therefore
Man
Can envision a lake
But never a flood
On earth

Alice Walker, 1976. Photo by Bernard Gotfryd.

So cleanly scrubbed
Of blood

They come before the rock
Jolly conquerors

They do not know the rock
They love
Lives and is bound
To bide its time
To wrap its stony wings
Around
The innocent eager 4-H Club.

58

Facing the Way,
No. 4, 1975

ALICE WALKER

the fundamental question about revolution
as lorraine hansberry was not afraid to know
is not simply whether i am willing to give up my life
but if i am prepared to give up my comfort:
clean sheets on my bed
the speed of the dishwasher
the washer/dryer
and my gas stove
gadgetless
but still preferable to cooking out of doors
over a fire of smouldering roots
my eyes raking the skies for planes
the hills for army tanks.
paintings i have revered stick against my walls
as unconcerned as saints
their perfection alone sufficient for their defense.
yet not one life line thrown by the artist
beyond the frame
reaches the boy whose eyes were target

for a soldier's careless aim
or the small girl whose body napalm
a hot bath after mass rape
transformed
or the old women who starve on muscatel
nightly
on the streets of new york.
it is shameful how hard it is for me to give them up.
cease this cowardly addiction
to ease
to art that transcends time
beauty that nourishes a ravenous spirit
but drags on the mind whose sale would patch a roof
heat the cold rooms of children. replace an eye.
feed a life.
it does not comfort me now to hear
thepoorweshallhavewithusalways
(christ should never have said this:
it makes it harder than ever to change)
just as it failed to comfort me
when I was poor.

59

The Abduction of Saints, No. 4, 1975

ALICE WALKER

As it was with Christ, so it is with Malcolm
and with King.
Who could withstand the seldom flashing smile,
the call to dance among the swords and barbs
that were their words? The men leaning from
out the robes of saints,
good and wholly kind? Though come
at last to both fists clenched and Voice
to flatten the ears
of all the world.

You mock them who divide and keep score of what
each man gave. They gave us rebellion as pure love: a beginning
of the new man.

Christ too was man rebelling. Walking dusty roads, sweating
under the armpits. Loving the cool of evening beside the ocean,

the people's greetings and barbequed chicken; cursing under
his breath the bruise from his sandal and his donkey's
diarrhea.

Don't let them fool you. He was himself a beginning of the new
man.
His love in front. His love and his necessary fist, behind.
(Life, ended at a point, always falls backward into what little
was known of it.)

But see how this saint too is hung defenselessly on walls, his
strong hands pinned: his pious look causes us to blush, for him.

He belongs to Caesar.
It is because his people stopped to tally and to count: Perhaps
he loved young women too much? Did he wear his hair a bit too
long, or short? Weren't the strategies he proposed all wrong,
since of course they did not work?

It is because his people argued over him. Denounced each other
in his name. When next they looked they hardly noticed he did
not look himself.

Who could imagine that timid form with Voice like thunder
to make threats, a fist enlarged from chasing merchants? That
milkwhite cheek, the bluebell eye, the cracked heart of plaster
designed
for speedy decay.

Aha! said a cricket in the grass (ancient observer of distracted
cross examiners);
Now you've seen it, now you don't!

And the body
was stolen away.

60

My Early Days in Harlem, No. 3, 1963

LANGSTON HUGHES

One of the leading lights of the literary movement the Harlem Renaissance, Hughes shares with Walt Whitman the honor of being the most translated of American poets.

On a bright September morning in 1921, I came up out of the subway at 185th and Lenox into the beginnings of the Negro Renaissance. I headed for the Harlem YMCA down the block, where so many new, young, dark, male arrivals in Harlem have spent early days. The next place I headed to that afternoon was the Harlem Branch Library just up the street. There, a warm and wonderful librarian, Miss Ernestine Rose, white, made newcomers feel welcome, as did her assistant in charge of the Schomburg Collection, Catherine Latimer, a luscious café au lait. That night I went to the Lincoln Theatre across Lenox Avenue where maybe one of the Smiths—Bessie, Clara, Trixie, or Mamie—was singing the blues. And as soon as I could, I made a beeline for *Shuffle Along*, the all-colored hit musical playing on 63rd Street in which Florence Mills came to fame.

I had come to New York to enter Columbia College as a freshman, but really why I had come to New York was to see Harlem. I found it hard a week or so later to tear myself away from Harlem when it came time to move up the hill to the dormitory at Columbia. That winter I spent as little time as possible on the campus. Instead, I spent as much time as I could in Harlem and this I have done ever since. I was in love with Harlem long before I got there, and I still am in love with it. Everybody seemed to make me welcome. The sheer dark size of Harlem intrigued me. And the fact that at that time poets and writers like James Weldon Johnson and Jessie Fauset lived there, and Bert Williams, Duke Ellington, Ethel Waters, and Walter White, too, fascinated me. Had I been a rich young man, I would have bought a house in Harlem and built musical steps up to the front door, and installed chimes that at the press of a button played Ellington tunes.

After a winter at Columbia, I moved back down to Harlem. Everywhere I roomed, I had the good fortune to have lovely landladies. If I did not like a landlady's looks, I would not move in with her, maybe that is why. But at landing work in New York, my fortune was less than good. Finally, I went to sea—Africa, Europe—and then a year in Paris working in a nightclub where the band was from Harlem. I was a dishwasher, later bus boy, listening every night to the music of Harlem transplanted to Montmartre. And I was on hand to welcome Bricktop when she came to sing for the first time in Europe, bringing with her news of Harlem.

When I came back to New York in 1925 the Negro Renaissance was in full swing. Countee Cullen was publishing his early poems, Aaron Douglas was painting, Zora Neale Hurston, Rudolph Fisher, Jean Toomer and Wallace Thurman were writing, Louis Armstrong was playing, Cora la Redd was dancing, and the Savoy Ballroom was open with a specially built floor that rocked as the dancers swayed. Alain Locke was putting together *The New Negro*. Art took heart from Harlem creativity. Jazz filled the night air—but not everywhere—and people came from all around after dark to look upon our city within a city, Black Harlem. Had I not had to earn a living, I might have thought it even more wonderful than it was. But I could not eat the poems I wrote. Unlike the whites who came to spend their money in Harlem, only a few Harlemites seemed to live in even a modest degree of luxury. Most rode the subway downtown every morning to work or to look for work.

Downtown! I soon learned that it was seemingly impossible for black Harlem to live without white downtown. My youthful illusion that Harlem was a world unto itself did not last very long. It was not even an area that ran itself. The famous nightclubs were owned by whites, as were the theatres. Almost all the stores were owned by whites, and many at that time did not even (in the very middle of Harlem) employ Negro clerks. The books of Harlem writers all had to be published downtown, if they were to be published at all. Downtown: *white*. Uptown: *black*. White downtown pulling all the strings in Harlem. Moe Gale, Moe Gale, Moe Gale, Lew Leslie, Lew Leslie Lew Leslie, Harper's, Knopf, *The Survey Graphic*, the Harmon Foundation, the racketeers who kidnapped Casper Holstein and began to take over the numbers for whites. Negroes could not even play their own numbers with their own people. And almost all the policemen were white. Negroes couldn't even get graft from themselves for themselves by themselves. Black Harlem really was in white face, economically speaking. So I wrote this poem:

Because my mouth
Is wide with laughter
And my throat
Is deep with song,
You do not think
I suffer after
I have held my pain
So long?

Because my mouth
Is wide with laughter
You do not hear
My inner cry?
Because my feet
Are gay with dancing,
You do not know
I die?

Harlem like a Picasso painting in his cubist period. Harlem—Southern Harlem—the Carolinas, Georgia, Florida—looking for the Promised Land—dressed in rhythmic words, painted in bright pictures, dancing to jazz—and ending up in the subway at morning rush time—*headed downtown*. West Indian Harlem—warm, rambunctious, sassy, remembering Marcus Garvey. Haitian Harlem, Cuban Harlem, little pockets of tropical dreams in alien tongues. Magnet Harlem, pulling an Arthur Schomburg from Puerto Rico, pulling an Arna Bontemps all the way from California, a Nora Holt from way out West, a Charles S. Johnson from Virginia, an A. Philip Randolph from Florida, a Roy Wilkins from Minnesota, an Alta Douglas from Kansas. Melting pot Harlem—Harlem of honey and chocolate and caramel and rum and vinegar and lemon and lime and gall. Dusky dream Harlem rumbling into a nightmare tunnel where the subway from the Bronx keeps right on downtown; where the money from the nightclubs goes right on back downtown; where the jazz is drained to Broadway; whence Josephine goes to Paris, Robeson to London, Jean Toomer to a Quaker Meeting house, Garvey to the Atlanta Federal Penitentiary, and Wallace Thurman to his grave; but Duke Ellington to fame and fortune, Lena Horne to Broadway, and Buck Clayton to China.

Before it was over—our New Negro Renaissance—poems became placards: DON'T BUY WHERE YOU CAN'T WORK! Adam Powell with a picket sign: me, too. BUY BLACK! The Stock Market crash. The bank failure. Empty pockets. *God Bless the Child That's Got His Own*. Depression. Federal Theatre in Harlem, the making of Orson Welles, WPA, CCC, The Blue Eagle, Father Divine. In the midst of the Depression I got a cable from Russia inviting me to work on a picture there. I went to Moscow. That was the end of the easy days of Langston Hughes in Harlem.

61

Langston Hughes: He Spoke of Rivers, No. 2, 1968

ARNA BONTEMPS

The multitalented Arna Bontemps was a poet, novelist, essayist, and dramatist as well as a teacher and librarian. He had been a member of the Harlem Renaissance and a close friend of Langston Hughes for many years.

Even a dependable memory sometimes plays tricks, and often enough I have had to call mine to task. This has never been true, I hasten to add, when the subject was the life and works of Langston Hughes. Even his adolescent poems were unforgettable. His personal history, as one picked it up from fragments in newspapers and magazines, had begun to read like a legend long before he finished college.

I seem to be the member of the Harlem literary group of the twenties elected to hold in trust a certain legacy of recollections, and the first of these is that he was our bellwether in that early dawn. The first poems by Langston that I read appeared in the *Crisis* in the summer of 1924. That magazine had been publishing articles, stories and poems by him for several years, but being away at a college that did not subscribe to such periodicals, immersed in the reading of the

"Chief American Poets" and collections of British poetry of the Victorian era, I had missed the earlier Hughes works as well as most of the other American Negroana of the period. Lines like "We have tomorrow/Bright before us/Like a flame" and "I am waiting for my mother/She is Death," as they appeared in those months, struck me with such surprise, seemed so quietly disturbing, they immediately convinced me I had been missing something important, something I needed.

But I was rushing away to New York as I made the discovery, and it was not 'til I arrived in Harlem that I was able to go to the Public Library and look up back issues of the *Crisis* and *Opportunity* and other periodicals hospitable to the work of Langston Hughes and his contemporaries of that period. I did not have to be told, as I browsed, that I had been short-changed in a significant area of my basic education. So many lights began flashing all around me, I could not fail to get the message. I eagerly set about trying to correct the omissions and perhaps repair some of the damage to dreams and aspirations that should normally have flourished in school and college days.

That winter I met Langston himself. He returned to Harlem from seafaring and sojourning, and the word was passed up and down the Avenues that the Poet was back. He had been seen. I heard it first from one of the librarians in the 135th Street Branch of the New York Public Library. Then I heard it in a rather strange way in the parsonage of the Salem Methodist Church on Seventh Avenue. I had gone there by appointment to meet another young poet whose foster father was the church minister, and it was the Rev. Cullen who opened the door to me. Without even pausing to speak to me, he spun around and shouted up the steps toward the second floor, "Countee! Countee! Come here! Langston Hughes is back."

In a sense I considered this my official welcome, under mistaken identity, into the Harlem literati. I promptly explained the situation and introduced myself, but these two friends of Langston remained cordial (albeit let down) and assured me that they could not tell one of us from the other by sight, so much did we look alike in those years. A night or two later Countee and I were both included in a small group invited to the apartment shared by Regina Anderson Andrews, the librarian, and Ethel Ray Nance, an editorial secretary in the office of either the *Crisis* or *Opportunity*, welcoming the real Langston Hughes home and listening to his reading of some of the poems he had written aboard the ships on which he worked and more recently in the kitchen of the Grand Duke night club in Paris.

One of the poems he read that night won the first *Opportunity* poetry prize soon thereafter and then became the title poem for *The Weary Blues,* his first book. A few weeks later Langston sent me from Washington, D.C., manuscript copies of these and other unpublished poems in which I had expressed interest. So it becomes an enormous satisfaction to one who has watched his bibliography grow over an arch of more than forty years to see it now compiled in manuscript form and awaiting publication.

It would be much too casual to merely observe that Hughes has been prolific. He has been a minstrel and a troubadour in the classic sense. He has had no other vocation, and he lived by his writing since that winter evening we met in Harlem late in 1924 or early in 1925. Naturally, the lean years and the full years considered, this has required versatility. Hughes has worked competently in all the literary forms. As a man of letters he has done what needed to be done: poems, song lyrics, librettos; short stories, novels, sketches, articles; plays, pageants, revues; autobiographies, books for children, and adult nonfiction. But nothing he has written has been out of tune with his first poems. Almost any biographical piece about him could appropriately be called "The Negro Who Spoke of Rivers." And his repeated use of the word *soul* in the refrain of his first widely published poem represents the first extension of this word into its current connotations, indicating a kind of "Negro" quality in certain areas of American self-expression and culture.

62

An Old Woman Remembers, No. 3, 1963

STERLING A. BROWN

A literary historian, poet, and educator, Sterling Brown was a leading authority on African American literature.

Her eyes were gentle; her voice was for soft singing
In the stiff-backed pew, or on the porch when evening
Comes slowly over Atlanta. But she remembered.
She said: "After they cleaned out the saloons and the dives
The drunks and the loafers, they thought that they had better
Clean out the rest of us. And it was awful.
They snatched men off of street-cars, beat up women.
Some of our men fought back, and killed too. Still
It wasn't their habit. And then the orders came
For the milishy, and the mob went home,
And dressed up in their soldiers' uniforms,
And rushed back shooting just as wild as ever.
Some leaders told us to keep faith in the law,
In the governor; some did not keep that faith,
Some never had it: he was white too, and the time

Was near election, and the rebs were mad.
He wasn't stopping hornets with his head bare.
The white folks at the big houses, some of them
Kept all their servants home under protection
But that was all the trouble they could stand.
And some were put out when their cooks and yard-boys
Were thrown from cars and beaten, and came late or not at all.
And the police they helped the mob, and the milishy
They helped the police. And it got worse and worse.

"They broke into groceries, drug-stores, barber shops,
It made no difference whether white or black.
They beat a lame bootblack until he died,
They cut an old man open with jack-knives
The newspapers named us black brutes and mad dogs,
So they used a gun butt on the president
Of our seminary where a lot of folks
Had sat up praying prayers the whole night through.

"And then," she said, "our folks got sick and tired
Of being chased and beaten and shot down.
All of a sudden, one day, they all got sick and tired.
The servants they put down their mops and pans,
And brooms and hoes and rakes and coachman whips,
Bad niggers stopped their drinking Dago red,
Good Negroes figured they had prayed enough,
All came back home—they'd been too long away—
A lot of visitors had been looking for them.

"They sat on their front stoops and in their yards,
Not talking much, but ready; their welcome ready:
Their shotguns oiled and loaded on their knees.

"And then
There wasn't any riot any more."

63

A Letter from Brooklyn, No. 3, 1964

DEREK WALCOTT

A native of the Caribbean, Derek Walcott won the Nobel Prize for literature in 1992.

An old lady writes me in a spidery style,
Each character trembling, and I see a veined hand
Pellucid as paper, traveling on a skein
Of such frail thought its thread is often broken;
Or else the filament from which a phrase is hung
Dims to my sense, but caught, it shines like steel,
As touch a line, and the whole web will feel.
She describes my father, yet I forget her face
More easily than my father's yearly dying;

Of her I remember small, buttoned boots and the place
She kept in our wooden church on those Sundays
Whenever her strength allowed;
Grey haired, thin voiced, perpetually bowed.

'I am Mable Rawlins,' she writes, 'and know both your parents';
He is dead, Miss Rawlins, but God bless your tense:
'Your father was a dutiful, honest,
Faithful and useful person.'
For such plain praise what fame is recompense?
'A horn-painter, he painted delicately on horn,
He used to sit around the table and paint pictures.'
The peace of God needs nothing to adorn
It, nor glory nor ambition.
'He is twenty-eight years buried,' she writes, 'he was called home,
And is, I am sure, doing greater work.'

The strength of one frail hand in a dim room
Somewhere in Brooklyn, patient and assured,
Restores my sacred duty to the Word.
'Home, home,' she can write, with such short time to live,
Alone as she spins the blessings of her years;

Not withered of beauty if she can bring such tears,
Nor withdrawn from the world that breaks its lovers so;
Heaven is to her the place where painters go,
All who bring beauty on frail shell or horn,
There was all made, thence their lux-mundi drawn,
Drawn, drawn, till the thread is resilient steel,
Lost though it seems in darkening periods,
And there they return to do work that is God's.

So this old lady writes, and again I believe.
I believe it all, and for no man's death I grieve.

64

Poems of Agostinho Neto, No. 1, 1976

TRANSLATED BY MARGA HOLNESS

Agostinho Neto led Angola's anticolonial struggle for independence from Portugal and became the first president of the new nation in 1975.

We Must Return

To the houses, to our crops
to the beaches, to our fields
we must return

To our lands
red with coffee
white with cotton
green with maize fields
we must return

To our mines of diamonds
gold, copper, oil
we must return

To our rivers, our lakes
to the mountains, the forests
we must return

To the coolness of the *mulemba*
to our traditions
to the rhythms and bonfires
we must return

To the marimba and the *quissange*
to our carnival
we must return

To our beautiful Angolan homeland
our land, our mother
we must return
we must return
to liberated Angola
independent Angola.

Struggle

Violence
voices of steel in the sun
setting fire to a landscape already hot

And dreams
dispersed
against a wall of bayonets

A new wave rises
and longings dispersed
over unburied bodies

And a new wave rises for the struggle
and yet another and another
until there remains of violence
only our pardon

65

Eventide, Kumasi, No. 2, 1970

KEITH E. BAIRD

Keith Baird was a contributing editor of Freedomways *and is a linguist and teacher.*

How suddenly the evening falls
At the end of the sun's theophany!
Here where splendour calls to splendour
In myriad modalities of colour, shade and tone
To celebrate the wonder that is Africa
'Tis fitting that evenfall be sudden,
Sudden like the curtain that in its ruffling closure
Marks the finale, sends the spectators home . . .
In Africa the evening falls
Almost silently, like a benediction.

City Hotel, Kumasi
July 16, 1969

66

We Are of the Same
Sidewalks, No. 3, 1980

LORRAINE HANSBERRY

Lorraine Hansberry is best known for her play (later made into a film) A
Raisin in the Sun, *which won the New York Drama Critics Circle Award in
1959. She was the first Black writer and the youngest dramatist to receive this
award. The quintessential committed artist, she sacrificed neither her art nor
her political beliefs. In this tribute to the painter Charles White, a fellow committed artist, she brings clarity to the complex subject of art's relationship to the
people. It was originally published in 1961 as the foreword to the catalogue of
the ACA Gallery's Charles White exhibition.* Freedomways *also published
Hansberry's speech against McCarthyism, "A Challenge to Artists."* Hansberry
died from cancer in 1965, at thirty-four years of age.*

Those of us who suspect that much of contemporary art cannot sustain or even allow a philosophical base or boast a technical standard
which can be practiced and perfected—that it is apparently outraged
by the most ancient and wisest of all human questions: "What does it
mean?"—have become a strong-minded lot. The emperor's new
clothes have not, somehow, captured our imagination.

Yet, it is not, nor has it ever been, easy to go against the grain of fashion; it is dreadfully uncomfortable to have the sole umbrella on the beach; to seem to be the fool of fools who cannot perceive what the eager legions cheering the emperor and his masterful tailoring clearly "see." It is not easy and it is not comfortable but now and again, the rewards are infinite.

We all know that to stand in certain of today's galleries or museums and dare ponder aloud quite what that painting yonder, the one made up of the vast, solid, palette-applied crimson field, with the three asymmetrical purple dots, *means*, is to make some people cough behind their fists and roll their eyes while the more tolerant of such confident cliques explain that it doesn't have to mean anything, it merely has to be; that, furthermore, it is really all a matter of space relationships and linear organization; which, moreover, despite the fact that it was poured from a can, really required immeasurable skill, profundity and vision, etc.

One can only suppose that if Mark Twain yet moved among the living he would draw from all of it a fine, fat lot of double talk for some of his greatest satirical monologues. Lacking his golden wit to fit the situation, most of us can only despair, for beyond the latent humor lies something horrible and grotesque: the far-flung ideas of our time that seem to insist that between the psychotic and the rational no boundary can be said to truly exist; that, also, those two or three thousand years of human thought, energy, imagination, study and labor that went into the evolution of art since cave-folk sought valiantly to render nature were all a waste of time.

No matter how they are written or painted, those are horrible and destructive ideas and one must despair for any culture which directly or indirectly embraces them. In the meantime, we who long for the perpetuation of genuine art, who despise its violation and the frauds saddled upon it, are moved to cherish the artists who hold fast to the legacies of the great historical achievement in art. Consequently, we celebrate and salute the ever-deepening humanism and art in the work of an artist such as Charles White.

For if it is true that the consumer of representational art is almost outcast in the present cultural climate, it is a simple thing to imagine what must be the ordeal of the artist who eschews the current vogues. I personally learned in my own art student days, as well as the early aspiring-writer times, that there was virtually no field in the arts where "fashion" did not find the vigorous emotions of common folk "sentimental"; where the wonder of their speech as they actually spoke it and made it work for them was not held "crude"; where the lively assertion of their mannerisms and clothes was not found "quaint." Exposure to "true sophistication" was supposed to teach the developing creative artist that "Street Vendor," "Mother and Child," "Fisherman," "Woman Weeping," "Child Laughing" and all such themes, like passion itself, were, as a matter of course, maudlin and pedestrian. One absorbed such wisdom from those who could also, smilingly, over a drink, find joy in someone's remark that the paintings of Rembrandt constituted "black pits." I do not intimately know the personal history of Charles White. I do not know at what point in his development as a man and artist his own particular resistance was brought to bear against the many faces of absurdity and sterility in this particular age and culture. But I can surmise certain aspects of it. For we are of the same sidewalks and acres of "rocking store-front churches." Like him, I drew breath hearing certain music, watched by certain eyes, chastised and comforted again by certain voices. Like him I came to adolescence in a ghetto encased within it a multitude of black folk who endured every social ill known to humankind: poverty, ignorance, brutality and stupor. And, almost mystically, beside all of it: the most lyrical strengths and joys the soul can encompass.

One feels that the memories of that crucible, the Chicago Southside, must live deep within the breast of this artist; live and compel him through his mighty gifts, to such fulfillment as this present show. For what now explodes from his boards is a monumental essence of a people; the winged cheeks, the comforting-chastising eyes, the willful jaws set to book, song and ancestral reawakening: *"Mayibuye Afrika!"*

Year after year it has been possible to watch the incalculable growth of Charles White which has now let fall away the once deep-seated tendencies to poster-urgency, then, later, to architectural and not quite human, if always arresting, angularity. The humanity of a vision has utterly taken command and, wedded as it is to the drawing tools of a master craftsman, the result is that beauty of statement, that totality which, in art, defines man everywhere and the indomitable nobility of his potential.

Lorraine Hansberry (from the estate of Lorraine Hansberry).

67

Lorraine Hansberry:
On Time! No. 4, 1979

JOHN OLIVER KILLENS

John Oliver Killens wrote the novels Youngblood *and* And Then We Heard the Thunder *and* The Great Black Russian, *a novel based on the life and times of the Afro-Russian poet Alexander Pushkin. Killens was a founding member of the* Freedomways *collective. This essay appeared in the* Freedomways *special issue "Lorraine Hansberry: Art of Thunder, Vision of Light."*

At a writers conference at Howard University sponsored by the Institute for the Arts and the Humanities in April of 1976, Sister Toni Cade Bambara said, "The responsibility of a writer representing an oppressed people is to make revolution irresistible." Several decades before, the great Paul Robeson had said, "An artist must elect to fight for freedom or for slavery. . . . I have made my choice. I had no alternative." To immodestly quote myself from a book of essays entitled *Black Man's Burden,* I wrote: "Every time I sit down to the typewriter, every line I put on paper, I'm out to change the world, to capture reality, to melt it down and forge it into something entirely different."

How does one evaluate the life of the late Lorraine Hansberry, as a Black person, as a Black woman, as a human being? How is she to be evaluated literarily, politically, historically?

Did Lorraine Hansberry take upon herself the responsibility "to make revolution irresistible"? Did she recognize the battle lines, freedom or slavery? Did she choose sides?

To me, Lorraine Hansberry was a one-woman literary warrior for change—qualitative and fundamental change. She was, moreover, a Pan-Africanist. In her plays *A Raisin in the Sun* and *Les Blancs,* she expressed, through character development and dramatic situations, a oneness with the African peoples and their struggles for liberation. This is certainly the meaning of Asagai, the young, articulate African student in *Raisin*. And it is the entire meaning of *Les Blancs,* which endorses change *and* revolution. Lest there be any misunderstanding, however, it should be emphasized that Lorraine was a consummate artist. Her writing is not agit-prop. Her characters are flesh and blood people who possess all the flaws and fears and foibles and aspirations and courage that lie restive in human beings. The situations she placed them in are believable and recognizable. She knew that the Western notion of "art for art's sake" is an unadulterated myth, and that art can be a weapon to liberate the people.

I remember Lorraine Hansberry when she first came to New York from her native Chicago. I remember her as a brilliant young woman when she worked with Louis Burnham for Paul Robeson's newspaper, *Freedom.* We engaged in many dialogues and shared many concerns about the world, about its movement in the direction of fundamental change and how the change would affect Black people. The question that would always come up was what role should the artist play in bringing this change about? Those days were a profound learning experience for all of us *Youngbloods,* a time when I was working with Dr. Alphaeus Hunton and Mr. Robeson and Dr. W.E.B. Du Bois in an organization known as the Council on African Affairs. Our offices were in the same building the *Freedom* office was in on 125th Street in Harlem.

We had many lively discussions about the state of the world and the nation, and especially about the condition of the Afro-American people. It was a time of great excitement, when we took our convictions into the streets, a time of boycotts, of demonstrations and mass meetings at Rockland Palace and the Golden Gate Ballroom, of street meetings on the corner of 125th Street and Seventh Avenue in front of Michaux's book store which boasted of containing "A Hundred Thousand Facts About the Negro." We were part of all that along with Paul Robeson, Adam Powell, Benjamin Davis! It was a time when so many of us young warriors matriculated in the University of the Streets. Robeson was an inspiration to us all. By his example, he taught us the true meaning of manhood and womanhood and, especially, of commitment. In the arts, he was our patron saint. Who was Lorraine Hansberry?

One could safely say, in retrospect, that Lorraine Hansberry was a Pan-Africanist with a socialist perspective. Let me be even bolder. In my view, Lorraine was a Black nationalist with a socialist perspective. Her world view combined a commitment to Black liberation with an equally fierce commitment to the demise of capitalism. I think she knew that the contradiction was more apparent than real. As an artist, she saw the paradox and irony of every human being's sojourn on this earth, especially where Black Americans are concerned. The ancestors of most Americans came to these shores seeking freedom, while most of our ancestors came in chains. There is the terrible paradox, the national contradiction. I think she saw contradictions as the very spice of life, and dialectics as the method one uses to go about resolving the contradictions.

A Black nationalist with a socialist perspective? Have not all the revolutions of the 20th century been about national liberation? And haven't they all been socialist revolutions—Russia, China, Cuba, Vietnam?

Her double commitment was explicit and implicit in everything she wrote, in every lecture and every statement. As with Robeson and Malcolm, her nationalism had an internationalist context that is reflected in a statement by one of her African characters in *Les Blancs*. Tshembe tells the white man, Charlie Morris:

> I shall be honest with you, Mr. Morris. I do not "hate" all white men— but I desperately wish I did. It would make everything infinitely easier! But I am afraid that, among other things, I have *seen* the slums of Liverpool and Dublin and the caves of Naples. I have *seen* Dachau and Anne Frank's attic in Amsterdam. I have seen too many raw-knuckled Frenchmen coming out of the Metro at dawn and too many pop-eyed Italian children to believe that those who raided Africa for three centuries ever "loved" the white race either.[1]

---

[1] *Les Blancs: The Collected Last Plays of Lorraine Hansberry*, Random House, pp. 102–103.

Lorraine believed that the road to socialism is through national liberation, just as the literary road to universality is through local identity. Many critics said of *Raisin* that it is "universal," that it isn't
specifically about Blacks. "It is about people. It could be about anybody." But a play that could be about anybody would most probably
be about nobody at all. Lorraine was very clear on this point when
she said in an interview

> One of the most sound ideas in dramatic writing is that in order to cre-
> ate the universal, you must pay very great attention to the specific. . . .
> In other words, I have told people that not only is this a Negro fam-
> ily. . . . It is specifically South Side Chicago. . . . So I would say it is def-
> initely a Negro play before it is anything else.[2]

One of the most important qualities of Lorraine Hansberry was
that she cared. She cared about the whole damn human race. Her
caring is expressed eloquently in *The Sign in Sidney Brustein's Window*, when her protagonist says:

> Is that all you can ever say? Who cares, who cares? Let the damn bomb
> fall, if somebody wants to drop it, 'tis the last days of Rome, so rejoice
> ye Romans and swill ye these last sick hours away! Well, I admit it. I
> *care!* I care about it all. It takes too much energy *not* to care. Yesterday
> I counted twenty-six grey hairs in the top of my head—all from trying
> *not* to care.[3]

Lorraine unquestionably identified herself with the aspirations of
the people of the so-called Third World (which I prefer to call the
First World, since even racist anthropologists grudgingly concede
that civilization first began in Africa and Asia). She was always there
with Fanon's "wretched of the earth," her anti-fascist vision of liberation embracing all of the oppressed regardless of race, color or eth-
nicity. Ahead of her time? I think not. As Sister Betty Shabazz once
said of her husband, Malcolm, Lorraine was not ahead of her time—
she was *on* time. Too many of the rest of us were lagging far behind
the times.

---

[2] *To Be Young, Gifted and Black*, New American Library, p. 128.
[3] *A Raisin in the Sun/The Sign in Sidney Brustein's Window*, New American Library, p.
247.

In a historic Town Hall forum entitled "The Black Liberation Movement and the White Backlash," she called for "a basic change of society" and called upon the white liberal to "stop being a liberal and become an American radical." She also said she'd never heard of Negroes booing the name of John Brown and noted that "the vantage point of Negroes is entirely different [from the rest of the nation]."[4]

Lorraine Hansberry was an extraordinarily articulate young Black woman, committed to the struggle and very fast on the draw. Indeed, literarily and intellectually, she was one of the fastest guns in the East—and her gun was for revolution and for change. She was a humanist; she was anti-slavery (meaning she was anti-capitalist). The pity of it, and the loss to us, is that she was with us for so terribly short a period. Who knows to what heights this courageous falcon might have soared!

---

[4] *To Be Young, Gifted and Black,* op cit., pp. 247–249. (Speech on *Lorraine Hansberry Speaks Out: Art and the Black Revolution,* Caedmon Records.)

68

The Once and Future Vision
of Lorraine Hansberry,
No. 4, 1979

ALEX HALEY

Alex Haley, author of The Autobiography of Malcolm X *and the novel* Roots, *wrote this essay for* Freedomways' *special issue focusing on Lorraine Hansberry's life and works.*

> *For me, this is one of the most affirmative periods in history. I'm very pleased that those peoples in the world whom I feel closest to: the colonial peoples, the African peoples, the Asian peoples are in an insurgent mood, and are in the process of transforming the world, and I think for the better. I can't quite understand pessimism at this moment; unless, of course, one is wedded to things that are dying out, which should die out, like colonialism, like racism.*[1]

---

[1] *Lorraine Hansberry Speaks Out: Art and the Black Revolution* (record album). NY: Caedmon Records. 1972. (Caedmon TC 1352)

These words of our late sister, Lorraine Hansberry, were not spoken during the late 1960's explosions within such American urban ghettos as Watts, Detroit and Harlem. Nor was she protesting the Cambodian bombings of 1972. Instead, the year was 1959 and Sister Lorraine was expressing herself in an interview on "60 Minutes." Matching tone for tone the acerbic quality of host Mike Wallace's voice, she was responding to his comment that her play *A Raisin in the Sun* ended on an affirmative note.

Especially when one reflects upon the 1959 date, one is aware that Hansberry's entire corpus of work was characterized by her singular penchant for sensing signs of change in the air, and by her ability to make accurate forecasts that were years in advance of a mass acceptance. We have but to recall that during the decade following the statement quoted above, the Civil Rights Movement, first surfacing in Southern isolation, crescendoed into national and even international significance along with other diverse causes which, collectively, saw an unprecedented number and social range of Americans taking up the banners of protest.

Now, on the threshold of 1980, the historical adage again rings clarion true that "every revolution devours [many of] its own." The toll has been heavy on many drained by exposure to Watergate, inflation and recession. Indeed, not a few have fallen by the wayside, disheartened and lacking faith. The ennui that characterized the Eisenhower years parallels in many ways the apathy of today, which certainly would have sorely frustrated and displeased Hansberry. For she envisioned a world in which good men and women face injustice boldly, and lift their voices to combat it. Throughout her creative lifetime, she served as a model for us all, using as her weapons her verbal articulateness and her powerful pen.

For instance, in a most gripping dramatic example of the triumph of man over his circumstances, in *A Raisin in the Sun,* Walter Lee Younger stretches to the full height of his manhood. A Black man who has been systematically disenfranchised, Walter develops a burning need to surmount the poverty of his life. When his dream to own a liquor store vanishes with the money remaining from an insurance policy, Walter will surely crawl back into the hole of his ghetto apartment—we *think*. But not only are we surprised, we are enlightened by the new dimensions that are revealed in Walter, when he musters the internal strength to inform the white Mr. Lindner that he and his family *will* resist all obstacles, that they *will* move into the white middle-class neighborhood.

With a similarly characteristic Hansberry stroke, in *The Sign in Sidney Brustein's Window,* one of her best plays, she helps us to examine the question of faith. A product of the post-war intellectual malaise that found expression in Sartre and Camus, Sidney Brustein has adopted the philosophy of apathy. He no longer thinks he has the energy to devote to politics. But in the end, he—and we—find his commitment to be so strong that despite his wife's desertion and the suicide of a young sister-in-law, he stands firmly against injustice in an affirmation of life. He becomes "a . . . fool who believes that death is waste and love is sweet and that the earth turns and men change every day and that men wanna be better than they are . . . and that hurt is desperation and desperation is energy and energy can *move* things. . . ."

In *Les Blancs,* Hansberry assigns to Tshembe Matoseh the conflict of racial identity versus personal identity. An African intellectual, English-educated, he returns to his homeland only to find it divided by the struggle for independence. Having left behind his English wife and London's creature comforts, and both attracted and repulsed by what he sees in his native Africa, he wishes he could forget the homeland ties but finds that he simply cannot. Ultimately, he discovers that his "two identities" are as one—inextricably intertwined; that it is equally impossible to divorce himself either from the moral rectitude of independence or from his conscience as an intellectual, and he joins the band of rebels as their leader.

The list of Hansberry's contributions is lengthy, but one thing in particular has always struck me as unique, perhaps due to my own special interest in this subject. She wasn't the *first* Black writer to illuminate the relationship between the American Black and Africa (that credit belongs to the Harlem Renaissance writers), but she was the first to *popularize* the notion. Merely by the force of *A Raisin in the Sun*'s success, she helped to dispel the myth of the "cannibal" African with a bone in his hair. Her educated African character, Asagai, was certainly the first time a large audience had seen and heard an African portrayed as carrying himself with dignity and as being, moreover, a primary spokesman for sanity and progress. It must also have been the first time a mass audience had ever seen a Black woman gracefully don African robes or wear an "afro" hairstyle.

In *Les Blancs,* Hansberry forthrightly states her position on the question of colonialism. At a time when Algeria had exploded and Kenya was in turmoil, she dramatized the African quest for independence. And despite the then unpopularity of her thinking, she supported the concept of self-rule.

Although her works were attended by protest, Lorraine Hansberry was no utopian sentimentalist. She didn't blindly worship one group to indict another. Rather, in her passionate understanding, she treated all of her characters equally. Mr. Lindner, in *A Raisin in the Sun,* is not a cardboard reactionary but a human being whom years of socialization have made racist. His sweat and his voice betray his nervousness over his mission to bar the Youngers' entry into his community. He tries, albeit comically, to justify his presence, explaining that his "welcome committee" deplores the violence that has occurred in some areas over integration. When he makes his pathetic offer to purchase the Youngers' new home at a profit to them, we almost pity his ignorance.

Conversely, just as she avoided creating stereotyped villains, Hansberry fleshed out her heroes with sometimes unflattering humanity. Sidney Brustein's drunken debauch when his wife leaves him; Walter Lee's cruelty to his wife, stemming from his frustration at being deprived of his manhood; Tshembe Matoseh's ambivalent desire to bury his head in the sand and avoid involvement in the independence movement signal Hansberry's understanding of the struggles that engulf and frustrate individuals—and which drive humanity.

And yet, Hansberry never gave up hope that eventually, however clumsily, people could solve their social conflicts. "I think that the race of man is obviously worth saving, ridiculous as it can be."

Lorraine Hansberry's death in 1965 came within a month of the assassination of Malcolm X, when I was just completing *The Autobiography of Malcolm X.* I had personally been in her company but once, briefly, among others at her home. Some months before, I had heard that she was ill, next that she was very ill, and then one morning I read in the paper that she was in a hospital, failing. I went there; none but her family was being admitted, and so I put my name on the list with the names of others who had also just felt we should come there where she was.

I feel now that, were she still among us, in her gentle and yet firm way she would still beckon us to persist, to have faith, and to continue to work for a better world. The final words of Sidney Brustein, trying to make sense out of the loss of his sister, are the most fitting testament for *our* sister:

> That is the first thing: to let ourselves feel again. . . . Then tomorrow we shall make something strong of this sorrow.[2]

---

[2]*A Raisin in the Sun/The Sign in Sidney Brustein's Window.* New American Library, p. 318.

69

At the Emmy Time!
No. 1, 1980

RUBY DEE

Ruby Dee, actress, playwright, and author, was a contributing editor of Free-domways. *Ruby Dee and her husband Ossie Davis coauthored their autobiography,* With Ossie and Ruby: In This Life Together *and other works.*

I took my body to the affair, but my head stayed home. Looking around at the people in the lobby, and later at those sitting nearby, nobody looked as if they really wanted to be there. Maybe, like me, they were hungry, headless and thinking of the feast to follow. Maybe, like me, they were wondering if they looked all right in case the cameras sneaked in. Was the dress all right, nothing falling or slipping or showing or melting or smearing? There was air conditioning; but it couldn't be on too high, I thought, because it might make too much noise and drown out the deathless prose hand-printed on huge cue cards just under the center camera. Don't be an ass all your life, Ruby, I told myself. This is HOLLYWOOD. The air conditioning apparatus is probably the latest thing to be thought of. After all, out of Hollywood comes the latest of everything not even remotely envisioned by little ol' Black ladies spawned from the bowels of New York. Keep cool, fool. Dab the dewdrops, chatter and smile. After all, you must have wanted to be here because here you are—almost.

I should have fueled my attention with a cup of black coffee. Oh, if only someone could knock me over the head with a two-hour mallet. You're a snob, Ruby. A lot of folks are having "a rilly good time."

Jealous, that's what you are. Jealous of HOLLYWOOD, of all the expensive talent, of tuxedos stuffed with world-renowned geniuses, of the fluttering, sparkling importances—jealous of the whole damned occasion. They let you in, didn't they? Nominated you for something, didn't they? It's their game; but they *are* good enough to let you think you belong—to let you play. So sit up. Smile in case a camera should catch you. The proceedings are not all dull, insipid, stupid, unfair or embarrassing. The youngsters handling things are "rilly cute." This is the 31st Annual Emmy Awards ceremony honoring the Creative Arts in Television. It is a most important occasion. It is one of the only games in town where the stakes are higher than a new car, a TV, a trip abroad or a million dollars. There are awards for aesthetic achievements. This is a time of highest recognition, this is—My God, I think they've just brought out about six Emmys at once. I wonder if they're massed produced. Bet there would be quite a market for counterfeiters here. I like it better when a gorgeous girl brings out one at a time. Then one can imagine that maybe only two or three are made in a day. I just bet there are Emmys backstage by the carton! Ruby! Pay attention! Don't forget, you stand a very good chance of winning one of these prizes for your very own. You want one now, don't you? Admit it!

"Have you thought about what you're going to say?" This from my assigned seat companion. "You're going to win, you know." Alarm turns to frenzy. Does he have some inside info? After all, he is on the board of the Academy of Television Arts and Sciences. Incipient psychosis sets in. Shall I talk about the economic plight of minorities? Shall I loosen things up and try to make a little joke? No, I shall talk about Blacks and the media. Thirty seconds. That's what somebody said should be the length of the responses.

But look at me. Look at the given condition. Black actress for over a quarter of a century, still waiting for the big break, tired of the neglect, the indifference to material of substance about Black people and I can only have thirty seconds! Well, I've got news for you! Maybe I'll say: I suppose that one of the proudest times in my life re-

Ossie Davis and Ruby Dee (photo by Kawame Brathwaite).

sulted from having introduced the executive producer of "Roots,"
David Wolper, to the idea of doing something with Alex Haley's proposed book. No. Maybe I'll begin: For many years, I've tried to
bring stories by Black Americans, especially, to the attention of producers because I believe that some of the finest writing in the world
is being done by such authors and by those from the Caribbean and
Africa. No, I've said that a lot and often and written about that too.
Actors. I'll talk about actors. One of the proudest and saddest times
in my life came as I watched "Roots II" and realized what a host of

very fine Black actors there are—most of whom I'd never seen. Where have they been? Where did they train and work to become so compelling? Where and when shall most of them perform again in such worthy roles? In these times of shoddy offerings, from whence shall come another such opportunity?! The material is there—the consciousness-raising material I mean—that puts art in a responsible context to these most challenging times. "We're up to your category. Got that speech ready?" asks Robert, my seat companion from the academy, sadistically. Cameras moving in. Sweat popping out. After all, Walter Cronkite had said it all—in effect, "Okay. You're doing okay, my fellow craftspeople. But not good enough." He'd said it at least twice in case we'd missed the point. The open-eyed sleepers had blinked. A realization of hearing something more than bullshit had rippled through the huge assemblage and rattled in my ear.

OUTSTANDING SUPPORTING ACTRESS IN A LIMITED SERIES OR A SPECIAL—and the winner is ESTHER ROLLE—for "Summer of My German Soldier." For Chrissakes, that role was just a '79 version of mammy. That was the most anti-Black, anti-Semitic, pro-Nazi piece, I didn't think a major network would have the nerve to produce it. I don't care if it *was* based on a real life story! Shoot! She was really superb in Maya Angelou's "I Know Why the Caged Bird Sings!" Why couldn't she have gotten the thing for that! She is an aware, gifted. . . . Relief overcomes me. I won't have to make a speech. Applause, applause. Applause for Esther Rolle. She comes on stage. I think she's crying. "Ladies and Gentlemen," she says in essence. "I really and truly didn't expect this. I really didn't. I don't know what to say." I, for one, feel for her. I believe her.

But in the wee hours, when the evening was all over and I was settling down to sleep, my head came sneaking back and it occurred to me: Robert Guillaume, superb singer and actor, won an Emmy for his role as Benson, the butler in "Soap," Esther won for the mammy role, and Marlon Brando won for his role as head of the American Nazi party. Such thoughts, of course, loused up the memory of "a rilly fine evening."

70

The Welcome Table: A Short Story, No. 3, 1970

ALICE WALKER

Alice Walker became a contributing editor of Freedomways *in 1974. In 1982 her novel* The Color Purple *received the Pulitzer Prize. Her other works include* The Temple of My Familiar *and* The Third Life of Grange Copeland.

> *I'm going to sit at the Welcome table*
> *Shout my troubles over*
> *Walk and talk with Jesus*
> *Tell God how you treat me*
> *One of these days!*
>
> —*Spiritual*

(for Sister Clara Ward)

The old woman stood with eyes uplifted in her Sunday-go-to-meeting clothes: high shoes polished about the tops and toes, a long rusty dress adorned with an old corsage, long withered, and the remnants of an elegant silk scarf as headrag stained with grease from the many oily pigtails underneath. Perhaps she had known suffering. There was a dazed and sleepy look in her aged blue-brown eyes. But for those who searched hastily for "reasons" in that old tight face, shut now like an ancient door, there was nothing to be read. And so they gazed nakedly upon their own fear, transferred; a fear of the Black and the old, a terror of the unknown as well as of the deeply known. Some of those who saw her there on the church steps spoke words about her that were hardly fit to be heard, others held their pious peace; and some felt vague stirrings of pity, small and persistent and hazy, as if she were an old collie turned out to die.

She was angular and lean and the color of poor gray Georgia earth, beaten by king cotton and the extreme weather. Her elbows were wrinkled and thick, the skin ashen but durable, like the bark of old pines. On her face centuries were folded into the circles around one eye, while around the other, etched and mapped as if for print, ages more threatened again to live. Some of them there at the church saw the age, the dotage, the missing buttons down the front of her mildewed black dress. Others saw cooks, chauffeurs, maids, mistresses, children denied or smothered in the deferential way she held her cheek on one side towards the ground. Many of them saw jungle orgies in an evil place, while others were reminded of riotous anarchists looting and raping in the streets. Those who knew the hesitant creeping up on them of the law, saw the beginning of the end of the sanctuary of Christian worship, saw the desecration of Holy Church, and saw an invasion of privacy, which they struggled to believe they still kept.

Still she had come down the road towards the big white church alone. Just herself, an old forgetful woman, nearly blind with age. Just her and her eyes raised dully to the glittering cross that crowned the sheer silver steeple. She had walked along the road in a stagger from her house a half mile away. Perspiration, cold and clammy, stood on her brow and along the creases by her thin wasted nose. She stopped to calm herself on the wide front steps, not looking about her as they might have expected her to do, but simply standing quite still, except for a slight quivering of her throat and tremors that shook her cotton-stockinged legs.

The Reverend of the church stopped her pleasantly as she stepped into the vestibule. Did he say, as they thought he did, kindly, "Auntie, you know this is not your church"? As if one could choose the wrong one. But no one remembers, for they never spoke of it afterwards and she brushed past him anyway, as if she had been brushing past him all her life, except this time she was in a hurry. Inside the church she sat on the very first bench from the back gazing with concentration at the stained glass window over her head. It was cold, even inside the church, and she was shivering. Everybody could see. They stared at her as they came in and sat down near the front. It was cold, very cold to them too; outside the church it was below freezing and not much above inside. But the sight of her, sitting there somehow passionately ignoring them, brought them up short, burning.

The young usher, never having turned anyone out of his church before, but not even considering this job as *that* (after all, she had no right to be there, certainly), went up to her and whispered that she should leave. Did he call her "Grandma," as later he seemed to recall he had? But of those who actually hear such traditional pleasantries and to whom they actually mean something, "Grandma" was not one, for she did not pay him any attention, just muttered "Go 'way" in a weak sharp *bothered* voice, waving his frozen blond hair and eyes from near her face.

It was the ladies who finally did what to them had to be done. Daring their burly indecisive husbands to throw the old colored woman out they made their point. God, mother, country, earth, church. It involved all that, and well they knew it. Leather bags and shoes, with good calfskin gloves to keep out the cold, they looked with contempt at the bloodless gray arthritic hands of the old woman, clenched loosely, restlessly in her lap. Could their husbands expect them to sit up in church with *that*? No, no, the husbands were quick to answer and even quicker to do their duty.

Under the old woman's arms they placed their hard fists (which afterwards smelled of decay and musk—the fermenting scent of onionskins and rotting greens). Under the old woman's arms they raised their fists, flexed their muscular shoulders, and out she flew through the door back under the cold blue sky. This done the wives folded their healthy arms across their trim middles and felt at once justified and scornful. But none of them said so, for none of them ever spoke of the incident again. Inside the church was warmer. They sang, they prayed. The protection and promise of God's impartial love grew more not less desirable as the sermon gathered fury and lashed itself out above their penitent heads.

The old woman stood at the top of the steps looking about in bewilderment. She had been singing in her head. They had interrupted her. Promptly she began to sing again, though this time a sad song. Suddenly, however, she looked down the long gray highway and saw something interesting and delightful coming. She started to grin, toothlessly, with short giggles of joy, jumping about and slapping her hands on her knees. And soon it became apparent why she was so happy. For coming down the highway at a firm though leisurely pace, was Jesus. He was wearing an immaculate white, long dress trimmed in gold around the neck and hem, and a red, a bright red cape. Over his left arm he carried a brilliant blue blanket. He was wearing sandals and a beard and he had long brown hair parted on the right side. His eyes, brown, had wrinkles around them as if he smiled or looked at the sun a lot. She would have known him, recognized him, anywhere. There was a sad but joyful look to his face, like a candle was glowing behind it, and he walked with sure steps in her direction as if he were walking on the sea. Except that he was not carrying in his arms a baby sheep, he looked exactly like the picture of him that she had hanging over her bed at home. She had taken it out of a white lady's Bible while she was working for her. She had looked at that picture for more years than she could remember, but never once had she really expected to see Him. She squinted her eyes to be sure he wasn't carrying a little sheep in one arm, but he was not. Ecstatically she began to wave her arms for fear he would miss seeing her, for he walked looking straight ahead on the shoulder of the highway, and from time to time looking upward at the sky.

All he said when he got up close to her was "Follow me," and she bounded down to his side with all the bob and speed of one so old. For every one of his long determined steps she made two quick ones. They walked along in deep silence for a long time. Finally she started telling him about how many years she had cooked for them, cleaned for them, nursed them. He looked at her kindly but in silence. She told him indignantly about how they had grabbed her when she was singing in her head and not looking, and how they had tossed her out of His church. An old heifer like me, she said, straightening up next to Jesus, breathing hard. But he smiled down at her and she felt better instantly and time just seemed to fly by. When they passed her house, forlorn and sagging, weatherbeaten and patched, by the side of the road, she did not even notice it, she was so happy to be out walking along the highway with Jesus.

She broke the silence once more to tell Jesus how glad she was that he had come, how she had often looked at his picture hanging on her wall (she hoped he didn't know she had stolen it) over her bed, and how she had never expected to see him down here in person. Jesus gave her one of his beautiful smiles and they walked on. She did not know where they were going, someplace wonderful she suspected. The ground was like clouds under their feet, and she felt like she could walk forever without becoming the least bit tired. She even began to sing out loud some of the old spirituals she loved, but she didn't want to annoy Jesus who looked so thoughtful, so she quieted down. They walked on, looking straight over the treetops into the sky and the smiles that played over her dry windcracked face were like first clean ripples across a stagnant pond. On they walked without stopping.

The people in church never knew what happened to the old woman; they never mentioned her to one another or to anybody else. Most of them heard sometime later that some old colored woman fell dead along the highway. Silly as it seemed it appeared she had walked herself to death. Many of the Black families along the road said they had seen the old lady high-stepping down the highway; sometimes jabbering in a low insistent voice, sometimes singing, sometimes merely gesturing excitedly with her hands. Other times silent and smiling, looking at the sky. She had been alone, they said. Some of them wondered aloud where the old woman had been going, so stoutly that it had worn her heart out. They guessed maybe she had relatives across the river some miles away, but none of them really knew.

71

The First Day
(A Fable After *Brown*):
A Short Story,
No. 4, 1974

ALICE WALKER

Stanley marched to the edge of the jungle, took a deep breath, then plunged in. The morning sun was already high in the September sky. The humid air drew a delicate film of perspiration to his brow. He walked a few yards across red burning sand and the perspiration ran into his eyes. It was very hot. He reached up timidly and loosened his collar. He was cramped in his clothes and as he breathed outward, his shirt, under the armpits and down along the ribs, strained inward against him. He was not dressed for the jungle, for he was wearing everything new. New white shirt, new blue suit, new black shoes, red socks and red tie. His shoes were hard and stiff; the starch in his shirt was beginning to melt into his skin.

Into such dense foliage and lush green grass Stanley had never been before. He was more used to plain dry sand and a barren view. He looked with apprehension at the gorgeous and riotous flowers around him, and his steps were cautious, quiet, and quick, on the soft springy floor of the woods. His attentive ears caught the sound of animals roaming about in the forest. Two of them bounded up to him. They began running to and fro on both sides of him. He kept walking. One of the animals, a small lion cub, snarled at him. The cub's father hit him across the eyes with his tail. Wiping at his eyes, Stanley began to run. Then he remembered something his mother had told him: that human beings should not show their fear of animals. If you don't let them know they scare you, she had said, you can walk right past them and they will not attack. Accordingly, Stanley deliberately slowed his pace, and when the big lion roared and his foul breath rolled out into his face, he pretended not to notice but stared and walked straight ahead.

He wished fervently that he had taken his father's gun, then he could send them all scattering. But he was just a small boy, and his father would never have allowed him to take the gun. His father had told him he must learn not to fear the jungle animals. He said if he was afraid of them he would never leave their yard, and would grow up to be a timid scared little man who jumped when anyone said "boo!"

He was going somewhere he had never gone before, and that made it hard; most of the animals running alongside him he had never seen before. He had been given direction how to get there. He had been told that the animals themselves would provide the surest guide; and it was true, all the animals of the jungle kept going by him. Some snarled fiercely, some barked, and some hit at him with their tails. Those with good teeth bared them, and he had to look away quickly or risk being tempted to run.

The closer he got to where he was going the more furious the animals became. A lioness who could not contain herself leapt forward and drove her claws down the side of his face. When the other animals saw the blood they began to prance around, sniffing at the blood and wanting more. Hesitantly, then boldly, because he did not want them to think he was afraid, Stanley took out his clean white handkerchief and wiped the blood away. But even after he put the handkerchief back into his pocket the red stripes kept dripping and his new white shirt was ruined.

But he had almost reached his destination. He walked up, up, up, while the animals pressed forward and gathered in behind him. A hyena bumped against him, almost knocking him over. She was mangy and thin, hungry-looking and smelly, laughing a crazy laugh. Stanley felt sick. The perspiration from his face fell in droplets down through the red tracks of the lioness' claws and rolled to the ground in noiseless scarlet splashes.

As he approached the opening through which he must pass, he was horrified to see a line of fat blue vultures standing shoulder to shoulder across it. He wondered if he had come so far for nothing. But he would not turn around now, nor could he, for behind him the animals had pressed fast and thick. Muttering and milling about, spitting and practically cursing with fury, the pack behind him began to advance. There was nothing for him to do but press forward.

Squaring his shoulders, and concentrating on his multiplication tables—which he had started to learn the summer before—Stanley pushed his way through. As he ducked under the wings of the vultures he felt a stunning crash at the back of his head and then a searing burn across the back of his neck. Once inside he did not turn to look back at them; he knew they stood pressed around the entrance, momentarily without a leader to follow in after him. His head hurt terribly, his knees felt weak. His clothes had been slashed and he was bleeding profusely from the nose.

There was no one inside to meet him. He stood limply against the long cool wall of the corridor, a small dark shadow beneath electric lights. He was all alone. Suddenly he began to cry. He wanted his mother. He wanted his father. He could not recall the correct sequence of his multiplication tables, and all thought except for peace and home deserted him. He was paralyzed by this first excursion away from home, and wanted arms around him.

But in the empty school building, which belonged to him too, there was no one; only a new, shiny white water cooler to offer him comfort. And suddenly, because he had never done so before, he was afraid to drink from it.

72

A Review of
God's Bits of Wood
by Ousmane Sembene,
No. 2, 1978

LOYLE HAIRSTON

Loyle Hairston was a contributing editor of Freedomways. *In each issue,* Freedomways *published a number of reviews of books that were of interest to activists in the freedom struggle.*

. . . Probably best known as a filmmaker, Ousmane Sembene is uncompromising in his opposition to any institution, social convention, idea or form of mysticism which corrupts or retards the liberation of African peoples. Moreover, he believes the destiny of a nation rests with the enduring struggles of ordinary people—God's bits of wood. This is a story about such people, long suffering but unbowed as they resist the humiliating hardships imposed by a foreign enemy.

Published several years ago and mostly ignored by mainstream critics, *God's Bits of Wood* tells the story of a railroad strike which takes place in an African country under French colonial rule. It is based on an actual strike which took place in what is now Senegal in 1947, several years before that country achieved independence. Essentially, it is the story of rudimentary class struggle in colonized Africa and how social awareness grows out of the dynamics of common struggle.

More specifically, the strike in *God's Bits of Wood* relates the impact of a prolonged work-stoppage upon the personal lives of the people directly involved, men, women and children. It causes class division among Africans to sharpen, old attitudes come into conflict with modern realities, but, more importantly, the collective will and spirit of the people are galvanized around an issue which painfully disrupts their lives. The strike is called for the usual reason—the men can no longer tolerate the ruthless exploitation of their labor by the French bosses.

There are those among them who doubt the wisdom of such a radical action. Mamadou Keita, the Old One, whose word is highly respected, acknowledges at the strike meeting that they are being robbed. He bemoans the fact that their "wages are so low there is no longer any difference between ourselves and animals." Still he cautions the men, reminding them of another strike that took place many years ago and was "only settled by deaths, deaths on our side." But his cautionary words are interrupted by one of the younger men, a leader of the strike.

"We're the ones who do the work," Tiemoko roars, "the same work the white men do. Why then should they be paid more? Because they are white? And when they are sick, why should they be taken care of while our families are left to starve? Because we are black? In what way is a white child better than a black child . . . a white worker better than a black worker? . . . If we want to live decently we must fight?"

The action begins with the spontaneous support of the people and grows into the organized resistance of the whole community. It sets in motion a politicizing process that will perceptibly raise the consciousness of the people, especially the women whose roles become central to winning the strike. Under the money economy imposed by colonialism their courage, perseverance and loyalty are thoroughly tested by the vindictive French authorities. Food and water resources are depleted, hunger and starvation threaten the children and the aged as the mechanism of colonial rule attempts to grind the people into submission.

The women move to the center of the novel's action, assuming responsibility for the well being of their homes while the men attend to the tactical affairs of the strike. Dire circumstances draw them into the strike action itself. With all their valuables sold or pawned and credit denied them by the local merchants, they still will not pressure the men into ending the strike. They manage to keep themselves and the children alive, while becoming active participants in the struggle against the French authorities. . . .

The author de-mythologizes Africa. With a keen eye for substantive detail, he gives the reader some fascinating insights into African sensibilities, and their particular ways of coping with the complexities of life. Outmoded social customs often hamper them from effectively combating the arrogant, ruthless European colonizer. They do not quite know how to rid their lives of these foreigners who have somehow installed themselves as lords and masters with little resistance.

But the harsh measures taken against them during the strike compel the people to draw some hard conclusions about their predicament. Their suffering awakens them to a larger issue, that of their subjugation itself. Whatever the outcome of the strike, the French authorities will no longer be able to command their loyalty and cooperation. Though under the control of the Europeans, the Africans are nevertheless hostile to their conquerors; therefore, culturally and psychologically they are never really conquered. . . .

There are flaws in the novel—too many characters, narrative sometimes episodic, tension not sufficiently sustained—but it succeeds nevertheless on the strength of the author's storytelling ability, social vision and aesthetic integrity. The writing is imbued with a sense of humanity and a revolutionary commitment to the liberation of the African spirit. Sembene obviously rejects the value system of those who gave the world colonialism, racism, imperialism and neocolonialism. . . .

73

Jazz, No. 2, 1962

MAX ROACH

The great percussionist's artistic commitment to the freedom struggle was evident in his jazz composition Freedom Now Suite, *composed in 1960 in honor of Dr. King.*

> *[Jazz:] A kind of music, generally improvised but sometimes arranged, achieving its effects by syncopation, heavily accented rhythms, dissonance, melodic variation, and particular tonal qualities of the saxophone, trumpet, clarinet, and other instruments. It was originated by New Orleans Negro musicians.*

This interpretation, taken from the *Encyclopaedia Britannica Dictionary* is, at best, only a surface explanation of this many spectrumed terminology. "Jazz," has never, except in very vague terms, been answered, as to its meaning, intent and content by its creators. This phenomenon (its never being answered), for all its intrigue, however, will not be delved into at this time. I mean to deal only with what the music, in actuality, is.

"Jazz" is an extension of the African chants and songs. It is an extension of the pain and suffering of those long, and too often, destinationless trips across the Atlantic Ocean, deep in the holes of those dark, damp, filthy, human slave ships, endured by chained, innocent, Black men, women and children. "Jazz" is an extension of the humiliations suffered by these same human beings while being sold as cattle or produce. It is an extension of the pain of the whip, the assaulter, the procurer, the "driva' man," the patrol wagons, the kidnapper, the sunup to sundown slave field and plantation. It is the extension of many, many lynchings, castrations, and other "improvisations" of genocide on these same Black men, women and children. "Jazz" is an extension of the Black man, "freed," who found himself still shackled to the same chain, all shined up, when he unwittingly ventured out into "their" free world of opportunity and wealth, only to be assaulted, whipped, murdered, and raped some more. The "Spiritual," "Race music," "Rhythm and Blues," "Dixieland," "Jazz" (and never, yet, any of the music named by its creators, but by the disdainful, master observer). "Jazz" is an extension of the Black artist being relegated to practice his or her craft, even today, under these intolerable, too similar, conditions.

This is why I say the white musician has never made a contribution of any consequence, is not making a contribution of any consequence, and will never make a contribution of any consequence to what is known to this society as "Jazz." The white man named the music, is intrigued by the music, has made billions of dollars from the music, and now would claim to be its collaborator in the authoring of the music.

There are, however, those white musicians who have come to the music respectfully and sympathetically, and elaborate, within the bounds of their emotional ability to identify with their Black brothers and humanity, on the music. To me, a contribution is a creation, and two mothers cannot give birth to the same child nor has it ever been so. "Jazz" is the indigenous music of the indigent Black man and woman. The musical instruments and theories on harmony preceded the Black man in this country, but it was, and is, the Black man's hell on earth, which he sublimated, and is sublimating into beauty that makes for the esthetic contribution, "Jazz." The music, in its emotional intensity, brilliance and drive, and extended harmonic and rhythmic frontiers, is indicative of where the "Negro" came *from* and *to* and foretells where he might go one day.

Because the connotation of the word, "Jazz," has gained stature in the eyes of the society and the world, and its original spelling (jass), abandoned, it has not changed its original emotional and social content, just as to be born Black has not changed in its punitive and despicable repercussions within the society that fosters repression. The music, consequently, is being misrepresented, distorted, misconstrued, and capitalized upon by others than its authors. (I, for one, do not feel called upon, nor obliged to let it pass so lightly.) Indeed, why should it be allowed to pass at all? For the sake of my children, and my children's children, I will not let it pass. Will we still be robbed and raped of our heritage? Is there to be no unclouded, "pure" legacy for mine? Can I have so little regard for all my years of "living," "learning," and *loving*? Has any man? All men are protective and jealous of the things they love, if they be "men."

The white musician, if he truly loves and respects the art form called "Jazz," will respectfully recognize its authors and bring whatever attitudes to the music he can, and will, honestly. The Black musician is not so bigoted and insensitive as to shut out his white brother, as he (the Black man) was and is still being shut out, as for example, in the "classical" concert stage, television, movies, "legitimate" theatre. (Though, in nearly all of these mediums, simulated "jazz" is being incorporated.) The shining crown of "Jazz" would be usurped.

To the white musician who screams, "crow-jim," I ask him to justify this terminology, if indeed he can, by explaining how Dave Brubeck, Stan Kenton, Gerry Mulligan, Shelly Manne, Stan Getz, Gene Krupa, Anita O'Day, Al Hirt, Benny Goodman, Chet Baker, Peggy Lee, Buddy Rich, Gil Evans, Bill Evans, Pete Rugolo, Andre Previn, Jack Teagarden, June Christy, to name a few who make a very healthy living, and enjoy much fame (state department tours to Africa, yet) compared to our small Black minority of an astronomical majority of very fine artists, who can boast of the kind of money the white artists are "privileged" to make. In what other society can an artist be so flagrantly plagiarized, ignored, and deprived and still be made the "heavy?" Would you see a man, finally allowed to produced, employ his proven rival, his dedicated rival, (in every walk of life) in preference to his brother and commiserator, who is not only in complete emotional sympathy with him, and therefore more suitable and adequate for the job to be done, but who would be left with no job at all, if not for the consideration, dependence and *finally* opportunity of the "employer" who is in essence, himself? Can a man be so charged for licking his own wounds?

"Jazz" is persevering, in the face of all obstacle and humiliation, to paint some musical, bitter sweet picture that comes out of the experience, suffering, and love of the Black people of the United States. Until the white musician has been called upon to give and experience as much, and the same, he can not, in all honesty, claim the kind of affinity to the music he insists he has. Would you ask a man with heart trouble to describe a cancer? A man may die of both but one is infinitely more painful and less merciful than the other. Why not have two descriptions of sickness then? Heart trouble and cancer. Or would you be so ignorant of pain and so unsympathetic to its sufferer and humanity as to give a vague and untruthful diagnosis? Charlie Parker was a musical product of his experiences as a man. But he was a Black man, first, last, and always. No intellectual analysis or "understanding" of the man's experiences will work for a reproduction of the emotional tools of feeling he used. Each man must, by necessity, develop his or her artistic offering by use of the only emotional tools he has; his own, and his tools are shaped, and molded as an extension of his own unique emotional climate.

While the Black man, lover and creator of his contribution, "Jazz," a product that grosses billions of dollars yearly on an international scale, has been so nicely raped of the glory (monetary benefits, although he is quite often a "poll winner") of his achievement, he (the militant) has been accused of practicing racism, of being weird (the "classical" musician, on the other hand, is called "sensitive") of being bitter, has been placed in insane asylums, penal institutions (rather than hospitals), pressured into leaving the country altogether, beaten for standing on a street corner, murdered on the highways, graverobbed, preyed upon by socially outcast neurotic women and others. His plight can only be compared to the Harlem plebian.

The royal family of "jazz" is a joke. No other "Duke" (Ellington) has ever reigned so nobly and gotten such ill and paltry compensation. No other "Count" (Basie) has been so ignobly used. No other "Lady" (Holiday) has died so friendless and under such dire circumstances (and in jail, yet). No other "Pres" (Lester Young) has been so ill-abused or condemned to die so tortuously. No other "King" (Cole) has been so ignobly detested by sight. Since our artistocracy is held in such low esteem, can the plebian hope for God to save us?

74

Black Women Singers-Artists, No. 1, 1966

ABBEY LINCOLN

Abbey Lincoln is a noted blues singer and a stage and film actress. This essay was part of a panel discussion, Black Writers' Visions of America, held at the New School for Social Research in New York City in 1965.

Since the masculine and feminine principles do not and never have been entities unto themselves, but the one interdependent upon the other, and the two reflections, one to the other, I will deal with the African-American image in music, as seen from the viewpoint of the feminine component.

The African-American woman is the most significantly creative and widely imitated singer-artist, in the world today. She has set the pace and still sets the pace for the creative singer of contemporary African-American music.

The Black woman of the United States of America has emerged as a symbol of depth, vitality, strength and sincerity. Her influence and womanliness has been heard and felt throughout the world, in the concert halls, on the vaudeville stage, on Broadway, in the intimate night club and by way of the prosperous recording companies, who have much for which to thank her.

She has told of the glorious and enduring love she has for her man as evidenced by the great stylist and innovator, lovely Miss Billie Holiday, who was a poet as well as a singer. She gave us:

Hush now, don't explain. Just say you'll remain.
I'm glad you're back, don't explain.
You know that I love you and that love endures
All my thoughts are of you for I'm so completely
yours. Hush now, don't explain.

The Lady, Billie Holiday, revealed her retiring disposition and impish modesty in "Billie's Blues."

Some men like me cause I'm happy.
Some cause I'm snappy.
Some call me honey, others think I've got money.
Some tell me, Billie, you're built for speed.
When you put that all together, makes me everything a good man
needs.

She sang of the importance of economic independence when she co-authored the classic, "God Bless the Child."

Them that's got shall get,
them that's not shall lose,
So the Bible says, and it still is news.
Mama may have, Papa may have,
but God bless the child that's got his own,
that's got his own.

And Miss Holiday sang of murder, and lynching, and the sweet scent of magnolias, and the stench of burning flesh of Black bodies, and of a strange and bitter fruit, in a song she helped create, entitled, "Strange Fruit."

The compassionate trailblazer, Miss Bessie Smith, poet and singer, described the Harlem rent parties, and the fight to keep body and soul together in a white and hostile society in the blues ballad, "Gimme a Pig Foot and a Bottle of Beer." She told of the despera-

tion and the distorted way of life her people suffered in the song
"Black Mountain Blues."

> Down in black mountain a child will smack
> your face.
> Babies cryin' for liquor and all the birds
> sing bass.
> On black mountain, can't keep a man in jail.
> If the jury finds him guilty, the judge'll
> go his bail.

She told of the rampant vice and political corruption in the Harlems
throughout this country. In the year 1928, Bessie Smith wrote and
recorded a song entitled "Poor Man's Blues."

> Rich man rich man, open up your heart and mind.
> give the poor man a chance, help these hard, hard times.
> While you livin' in your mansion, you don't know what
> hard times mean.
> Poor workin' man's wife is starvin', you wife is livin'
> like a queen.
> Listen to my pleadin', I can't stand these hard times long.
> They'll make a man do something that you know is wrong.

The image of the female African-American in music is one of the
realist. The man she sings of is a flesh and blood man, a man with
positive and negative aspects, of a give and take relationship, of responsibilities to that relationship and of the resulting rewards. She
has not demanded that he be the "ideal man." Recognizing her own
human frailties, she candidly acknowledges his, and loves him none
the less for all that.

The image of the female African-American in music is one of the
responsible citizen. Her songs tell of a way of life, of the joy and pain
of being Black in racist America. Her portrayals of life's experiences
are functional and act as "equipment for living." Her songs are
preparations for what to expect in the business of living in the U.S.A.

The Black female singer-artist is the sophisticated woman who
couldn't and cannot look away from injustice and degradation. To
racist America, she has been a secretary, a record keeper, a positive
catalyst. The school of hard knocks teaches her political and social

awareness. Generously and artistically, she passes on the information as she sees it. She has sung the white poet's ballad of the Black man. It was no accident that Gershwin's *Porgy* was a cripple, without legs. It was no accident that Harold Arlen's *Cabin in the Sky* featured a song called "Happiness is just a *thing* called Joe." It has been no accident that the hostile, racist-oriented white poet could find no excellence or worth to portray in the Black man. It has been no accident that the white poet has *always* portrayed the Black male image as a Step'n Fetchit, ne'er do well, Joe, irresponsible and helpless. Still there was always that certain something that had to be conceded, and that was that the "Negro" woman loved her man . . . that he was the source of her fulfillment and happiness. There's a lot to be said for a man who can inspire that kind of vilification on one hand and so much devotion on the other.

The life and talents of the revered and beloved Mahalia Jackson is a monument to Black feminine virtue and morality. Her profound treatment of the African-American "spiritual" has made her immortal, and her rendition of the great Duke Ellington composition is a masterpiece.

> Lordy Lord of love, God Almighty, God above,
> Please look down and see my people through.
> I believe the sun and moon that shine up in the sky.
> When the day is grey I know it's clouds passing by.
> Up from dawn till sunset, men work hard all day,
> Come Sunday, oh come Sunday, that's the day.

75

Will Jazz Survive?
Thoughts on the State of
the Great American Art,
No. 4, 1983

PLAYTHELL BENJAMIN

Playthell Benjamin is a writer, journalist, and publicist. The following are excerpts from an extensive article he wrote for Freedomways.

The genre of musical expression popularly known as jazz is a modern, complex form of instrumental music grounded in the blues idiom and created by African American artists. Notwithstanding the late Marshall McLuhan's contention that the commercial is an indigenous American art form, or the rather extravagant claims made for abstract expressionist painting, jazz is without question the great North American contribution to fine art. No other art form embodies so many of the best ideals and characteristics to which North American civilization aspires. Jazz is democratic, values individual freedom, promotes innovation, and reflects the complex rhythms of a machine age sensibility. These rather pedestrian observations should be all too obvious to our cultural commentators and music critics. But alas, there is none so blind as he who will not see.

Actually, the failure to award jazz its proper status in North American culture, more than being a failure of aesthetic assessment, reflects a deeper cultural quandary: the ongoing North American identity crisis. This crisis is buttressed by the intellectual enslavement of the cultural commissars to a doctrine Afro-American critic and cultural historian Albert Murray has properly called "the folklore of white supremacy," which seeks to deny the influence of Black folk on U.S. culture in spite of the fact that Africans and their descendants have participated in "the making of America" since before the arrival of the Mayflower. . . .

. . . the U.S. musical theater has long been in love with Afro-American music and dance, albeit in white face. Indeed, one could argue that a major feature of the history of U.S. show business is the wholesale expropriation of Black cultural ingredients by white performers, who then went on to fame and fortune.

The list of white performers who built artistic careers by plagiarizing Black material is long, containing the names of some of the most illustrious of white America's pantheon of show business immortals. Al Jolson, Eddie Cantor, Vernon and Irene Castle, Paul Whiteman, Benny Goodman, Gene Kelly, Blood, Sweat, and Tears, the Beatles, the Bee Gees, and Elvis Presley are only a few. The wholesale pillage of Black America's creative storehouse has proceeded at full speed for well over a century and a half and continues today unabated. Adding insult to injury, the typical response of white America's cultural arbiters is to ignore or deny the existence of this phenomenon. And the odd man out in the game, the Afro-American artist, whose gifts have enriched everyone else, remains a struggling and neglected figure on the fringes of the nation's vast cultural industry.

It was this state of affairs that led the great writers, dancers and comedians, George Walker and Bert Williams, to name their act, "Two Real Coons." When they first got together in San Francisco in 1894, there were so many white acts in blackface, they felt the need to advertise the fact that they were the real deal. The most imitated U.S. composer at the turn of the century, Scott Joplin, was driven to insanity and an early grave by the anguish and stress of watching white composers grow rich from his ideas while he remained in poverty—a fact that was overlooked when he was posthumously awarded the Pulitzer Prize during the Scott Joplin craze a few years ago. One could argue that the reason Joplin received this belated acclaim is because Marvin Hamlisch used his music as the basis for the soundtrack of the popular film, *The Sting*. Langston Hughes gave poetic expression to this condition in his poignant lament, "You've taken my blues and gone."

The other arm of the broadcast industry, radio, has traditionally given a much greater hearing to the art of jazz and the Afro-American musician than television has. However, jazz made its entrance into radio through the back door and not without protest. For in the early days of the 20th century when commercial radio was born, European classical music alone was deemed suitable for the public airways. In this period, not only was most Black music confined to special labels known as "race records," but even the instrument that was to eventually emerge as the dominant voice in Afro-American instrumental music, the saxophone, was held in suspicion. Moreover, the first jazz recording made was not of a Black band. In 1917, a group of Southern white musicians having the audacity to call themselves "The Original Dixieland Jazz Band" issued the first recording of New Orleans style jazz, commonly referred to as Dixieland. Thus, most of the American and European public first heard this early Black style from white musicians. This development set a pattern in the recording, distribution and promotion of Afro-American musical creations that manifestly favors the white musician to this very hour.

With the growth of a serious jazz audience and the development of FM radio, Black jazz was widely heard in special media markets. But even this development is presently endangered. Due to the hypersensitive attitude of station managers and programmers to the Arbitron ratings, a stampede toward format changes in radio has occurred in recent years, bringing us, for example, to the present state of jazz radio in New York City. For several decades now, New York has been regarded by both musicians and critics as the jazz capital of the world, yet today there is not a single commercial station devoted to the broadcasting of this musical form.

The last commercial station to program jazz as its basic format was WRVR, which now programs country and western music exclusively. . . .

One must question whether jazz can remain a viable art form if left to the ravages of the commercial marketplace. Because classical art forms do not generally attract a mass audience, they require public subsidies or private philanthropy in order to survive. The problem is that the U.S. cultural establishment has resisted the inclusion of jazz in its definition of Fine Art.

Around the question of how jazz is critically assessed hover all the thorny issues of race and class relations, along with the issue of how these factors influence the character of U.S. culture. In our art is reflected the true character of our national spirit, and what our social relations look like when translated into the language of art reveals the true perception we have of ourselves as a nation and culture. North American music by itself confirms that the creative energy and vision informing indigenous art forms derive, fundamentally, from the people who came to these shores from Africa. In other words, the Black presence has had an enormous impact on U.S. art forms. Yet those who function as the recognized interpreters of these art forms perennially avert their eyes from this fact, armed to the teeth as they are with critical standards that derive solely from the European experience.

To admit the influence of Blacks on U.S. music requires recognition of a creative intelligence in Black folks, the denial of which is central to "the American way of life." Even among the handful of white cultural commentators who do recognize the artistry of jazz, most would deny that it is a creation of Afro-Americans. Addressing the attitude of these critics, historian and veteran commentator on jazz, Frank Kofsky remarked, "If they are in the jazz world proper, they will tend to deny that, whatever else jazz may be, it is first and foremost a Black art—an art created and nurtured by Black people in this country and out of the wealth of their historical experience."

Speaking of the general attitude of his fellow white Americans in regard to jazz Kofsky writes, "On the other hand, if they are not a part of the jazz milieu, white Americans will automatically and virtually without exception assume that jazz is Black—though not an art—and therefore, though this may go unstated, worthy of no serious treatment or respect." The preeminent example of this attitude is the refusal of the Pulitzer Committee to award Duke Ellington the prize for continued excellence in U.S. music in 1965, a time when Ellington had been an orchestra leader and composer for over 40 years. From this rejection of a quintessential American musical genius, we can well imagine how the Pulitzer Committee and similar cultural arbiters view the art he represented. While North American pundits have refused to come to terms with the magnitude of Ellington's achievement, many European critics have long celebrated his artistry, as evidenced by the distinguished British music critic Constant Lambert's statement, reported in the *New York Times* in 1934:

> The real interest of Ellington's records lies not so much in their color, brilliant though it may be, as in the amazingly skillful proportions in which the color is used. I do not only mean skillful as compared with other jazz composers, but as compared with so-called highbrow composers. I know of nothing in Ravel so dexterous in treatment as the varied solos in the middle of the ebullient "Hot and Bothered," and nothing in Stravinsky more dynamic than the final section. The combination of themes at this moment is one of the most ingenious pieces of writing in modern music.

Even in the best of times, funding for jazz programs constituted a miniscule portion of the budget of the National Endowment for the Arts. While annual grants to symphony orchestras totaled millions of dollars, funding for jazz projects came to less than half a million dollars in 1980. Needless to say, the Reagan administration, being no friend of the arts in general, is certainly no friend of jazz.

Ambivalent about their national identity, the Euro-American elite lavishes resources on institutions that perpetuate European music, while the great U.S. art struggles to survive. Interestingly, contempt for the products of U.S. culture, engendered by a low estimation of the creative possibilities afforded by the American experience, surfaced years ago regarding another art form in the attitude of T.S. Eliot, who despaired over the "poverty" of U.S. culture. Likewise, Henry James found it incredible that Nathaniel Hawthorne could actually produce novels in the wilderness of North America. Both felt it necessary to emigrate to Europe in order to find an environment sufficiently rich in the ingredients essential to the creation of great literature. Fortunately, not all U.S.

artists adopted so pessimistic a view of the potential of the American cultural inventory.

The historical record will verify that the first group of artists to create a fine art form that is quintessentially North American were Afro-American musicians, who drew liberally from a rich musical heritage that included spirituals, work songs, hollers, country blues, city blues, ragtime and gospel to establish a classical tradition that made no apology to the traditions of Europe. Indeed, it was the lack of self-conscious intimidation by the achievements of European culture that allowed the Black musician to discover the process by which intellect and alchemy continue to transform folk art into fine art. Afro-American historian Nathan Huggins writes, in his brilliant *Harlem Renaissance,* "Everywhere they looked they found white men mimicking them, trying to master their blue notes, their slurs, their swing, their darting arpeggios, their artistic concept. It was as if Black jazzmen from the very beginning sensed that they were creating an art and the whole world would have to find them the reference point for critical judgment."

Unlike European classical music, in which technique is often pursued as almost an end in itself, in jazz, technical mastery of an instrument is only the starting point. The object of jazz performance is not to faithfully render the notated musical ideas of a composer but to express one's own attitude towards a musical idea as one experiences it at the moment. Thus, improvisation, not composition, is the most valued attribute in the art of jazz. In the classical European tradition, the instrumentalist is subservient to the composer; but the Afro-American classical instrumentalist seeks to overthrow the tyranny of the composer, whose role in jazz is to set the theme and parameters of the musical repartee.

The character of all art forms reflects the life experience of the people who create them. The classical music of Europe developed under the patronage of the church, state and aristocracy, many compositions being commissioned by princes, queens, bishops and other members of the ruling elite. Accordingly, the music projects a formal etiquette that prizes rigid organization, hierarchy, and strict adherence to prescribed rules. By contrast, the central value in the North American classical music created by Black people is freedom of expression. This is not surprising, for the dominant theme in Black American history is the struggle for freedom, and the values of group cooperation and individual dignity are central to that struggle. Consistent with this ongoing pursuit of freedom, the ultimate artistic expression of Black Americans is a music that is both highly collective yet profoundly personal. This desire for personal expression in group activities can also be observed in Afro-American popular dance styles, as well as in the structure and liturgy of much of the Black church. For the jazz instrumentalist, then, it is not enough to be a competent ensemble player; one must also be able to stand alone as an effective soloist.

Beyond this, the serious jazz artist is never satisfied until he is able to speak with a unique voice on his instrument. If one thinks of any of the great jazz instrumentalists, each has a distinct style or sound. Pianists Willie "the Lion" Smith, Errol Garner, Thelonious Monk, Bud Powell and McCoy Tyner all have personalized sounds that are immediately recognizable. This is equally true of alto saxophonists Charlie Parker and Cannonball Adderley. It should be obvious that at least as many thousands of hours of intense study and practice are required for this level of achievement as are required to perform European classical music. (Max Roach recalls a pertinent bit of advice from Charlie Parker: "You should know your instrument so well that it becomes like another part of your body.") Furthermore, the jazz instrumentalist must know something of composition for he must combine the creative and interpretive functions in his artistry.

Uninformed about the jazz tradition and about the African American experience that produced and informed it, and having proclaimed the inferiority of Black people for centuries, the Euro-American cultural establishment is indisposed to accept any product of Afro-Americans as serious art. Hence, they can deny financial support for jazz based on the argument that it represents little more than popular entertainment. Apparently, they are unimpressed by the fact that the music of Bud Powell and Thelonious Monk commands no greater a popular following than that of Bach or Beethoven, or by the fact that many jazz artists, past and present, are also fine interpreters of European classical music. . . .

Another great danger to the survival of jazz is the decline of an Afro-American audience, reflecting the alienation of contemporary Black Americans from a tradition that is the most sophisticated artistic response to the U.S. experience and that mirrors their identity.

This decline suggests that a profound change has perhaps occurred in the collective sensibility of Black America. In the language of jazz one hears the articulation of a wide range of attitudes, ideas and values. The wit of Lee Morgan, the humor of Dizzy Gillespie, the revolutionary thunder of Max Roach, the ascetic religious devotion of McCoy Tyner, the academic precision of Hubert Laws, the abstract expressionism of Ornette Coleman, and the mystical musings of John and Alice Coltrane are all part of the lexicon of jazz. Does the rejection of the jazz tradition imply a dulling of these sensibilities, especially among the youth who devotedly listen to mechanically produced dance music? One thing is certain: Commercial music, with its lack of complexity and monothematic concerns, can never convey the subtlety and texture of human emotion one hears in jazz, nor can it pose the intellectual challenge offered by jazz. For these reasons, Black youth are missing out on an important part of their heritage. As for aspiring young musicians, the wealth and celebrity associated with success in popular music are leading many of them to avoid the difficult challenge of jazz improvisation, to opt, instead, for a career in which knowledge of five chords is sufficient for success. Thus is the jazz tradition being subverted at the source.

It would seem that if anyone were to recognize the value of jazz and celebrate its achievement it would be the Black bourgeoisie. After all, here is a splendid example of the Black creative intelligence at work, a discipline that sets the highest standards of excellence and requires years of devoted study to master. Yet, much of the Black middle class remains oblivious to the dimensions of this achievement. The problem has to do, in part, with many middle class Blacks having succumbed to materialistic philistinism to the extent that neither the soaring staccato attacks of Freddie Hubbard nor the moods of an Ellington tone poem excite or delight them. No, only a steel gray Mercedes 450 XL can really turn them on. Miseducation and cultural insecurity are in the picture too. Indoctrinated in the idea that fine art music is synonymous with the European classics, many members of the Black bourgeoisie may be ambivalent when confronted with the finest fruit of their own tradition—jazz. In an essay, Amiri Baraka describes the tremendous struggle that had to be waged, as late as 1957, against the administration of Howard University in order to hold a jazz concert, with the dean of the Music School becoming apoplectic when it was suggested that the concert be held in the Fine Arts building.

Underlying the hostile attitude towards jazz displayed by earlier generations of Black academics was an embarrassment about certain aspects of jazz history, which they felt tended to reinforce the stereotypical image of Black folks as immoral creatures given to licentiousness and debauchery. They were hesitant about regarding jazz as serious, representative, Afro-American art because of its association with brothels in its early development, with bars and cabarets throughout its history, and the addiction of some of its most gifted innovators to alcohol and drugs.

However, it is important to realize that a different attitude prevails among contemporary Afro-American academics. There are many Black scholars today engaged in efforts to define and preserve the jazz legacy and its antecedents, such scholars as Professors Ortiz Walton, Roland Wiggins, Ann Southern, Fred Tillis, David Baker, J. R. Mitchell, Archie Shepp, Bob Cole, Portia Maultsby, A. B. Spellman, Albert Murray and Amiri Baraka. Moreover, there has been a healthy interest in jazz on the part of Black creative intellectuals dating back to the very beginnings of the jazz tradition. Paul Laurence Dunbar and James Weldon Johnson were both great lovers of the music.

The meter and style of the poetry of Sterling Brown and Langston Hughes consciously refer to the blues tradition, and Albert Murray argues that Ralph Ellison's *Invisible Man* can be seen as an extended blues. . . . But, alas, all of this is of little consequence to the majority of bourgeois Blacks, who are indifferent to the entire range of serious Afro-American art.

The ultimate tragedy is that these attitudes deprive Black jazz artists of their logical patrons. For one of the most important roles of the educated and affluent classes in an ethnic group is to subsidize the advancement of group expression by patronizing their important artists. Confused in their values and lacking a coherent concept of Black expression, bourgeois Blacks are spending millions annually on synthetic, anesthetic music while relative economic deprivation and artistic obscurity are prompting even jazz virtuosos to abandon that genre for commercial careers. (Herbie Hancock, Wayne Shorter, George Benson, Ramsey Lewis, Roy Ayers and Stanley Turrentine are all presently lost to Mickey Mouse music.)

The final nail in the coffin of jazz could be the dearth of opportunities for young aspirants to participate in jam sessions, which have been the main classrooms of instruction for developing musicians. The centrality of the jam session to the evolution of jazz artistry is verified by the testimony of a long line of musicians including Jelly Roll Morton, Scott Joplin, Billy Taylor, Mezz Mezzrow, Max Roach, and Dizzy Gillespie. Much of the early ragtime, musical theater, and large ensemble styles were worked out in places like the Old Marshall Hotel on West 53rd Street and the Clef Club Uptown, and one of the most exciting movements in modern art, the be-bop revolution, was largely developed in Minton's Playhouse. Significantly, all of these establishments were Black-owned and operated. So affluent Afro-Americans, please note: You have an exceedingly valuable role to play that requires neither extensive musical education nor control of the music industry.

76

Martin Luther King: A Personal Tribute, No. 1, 1972

HARRY BELAFONTE

Harry Belafonte, the internationally famous performing artist, was a trusted adviser and friend of Dr. Martin Luther King Jr. The following is excerpted from a tribute to Dr. W.E.B. Du Bois and Dr. King that Belafonte delivered at the Freedomways *annual W.E.B. Du Bois Cultural Evening, January 30, 1972.*

On all levels of life and as each day unfolds, respect for Dr. Martin Luther King Jr. grows impressively, and the essence of this respect is the fact that he had deeper insights than most of us have appreciated. It is not mere poetry to call him prophetic. The accuracy of his prophecies is almost uncanny.

By the early 1950's, history had endowed him with a sense of the precise moment that Black people were ready for mass action, ready for its risks, and ready for its responsibilities. At a time when there was only limited, essentially timid, activity, except for those acts solely confined to the courts, Dr. King realized that Blacks were ready to do battle on a series of fronts and to do it defiantly, proudly and militantly in massed ranks. Although he was himself unique and incomparable, even among the foremost of leaders, he was not a believer in elitism. He knew that the power of the isolated intellectual had great limitations. He perceived that only in joining individual brilliance with the strength and steadfastness of the masses can a movement of transforming power be achieved. Thus he brought the people into the making of their own history.

Following his early dramatic triumphs, Dr. King brooded. For he recognized that dismantling segregation was in and of itself not enough. He understood that racism with all of its bestiality was only one of the aspects of the forces that were and are destroying mankind. In the face of this truth, he saw that it was necessary to consolidate centers of power that represent the thrust for liberation. Earlier than others he saw the potential in electoral activity, not on a token scale, but involving millions of Black people, poor whites, Chicanos, students, and women. So he fought for the ballot. However, he did not fall into the trap of posing electoral activity against other forms of direct action. He favored both and felt Black people could do both simultaneously. Before his brutal assassination, he was able to see partial fulfillment of his struggles in the election of Black Mayors, Sheriffs, Congressmen and State Legislators. Today there are approximately 2,000 Black elected officials—when Dr. King began his work there were less than 300. . . .

The absence of Dr. King speaks so profoundly. Not just to those of us who were close to him and loved him dearly, but to the entire family of man in this glorious, exciting, and enormously painful time in history when it is mandatory that like the Phoenix we rise from the ashes of decay and darkness and continually complain, and complain, and complain loudly until that day when with resistance, rebellion, organizing and rebuilding unified by truth and the knowledge that our cause is just man will find himself wrapped in a new day of love, justice and eternal brotherhood.

Afterword

DAVID LEVERING LEWIS

David Levering Lewis is author of the Pulitzer Prize–winning biography W.E.B. Du Bois: Biography of Race, 1868–1919, Vol. 1; Prisoners of Honor: The Dreyfus Affair, *and* The Race to Fashoda: Colonialism and African Resistance, *among other works.*

"This is a good world and a good time in which we were born," the editors of the inaugural issue of *Freedomways* announced. Their optimism takes us back to a time before the Ice Age of reaction, a long-ago interval of exhilarating possibilities in which the underprivileged, the poor, the powerless, and the best of the progressives pushed to the forefront of the nation's history. Across the stepping stones of racial justice that could have led in time to the high ground of economic democracy marched the hosts of Blacks and browns and whites mobilized in the wake of *Brown v. the Board of Education.* Martin Luther King Jr.'s epic debut in Montgomery, Alabama, had come six scant years before the first issue of *Freedomways.* Little Rock, the South's redneck rerun of Fort Sumter, had come but four years earlier. In Atlanta, wave after wave of orderly students from the four historically Black colleges defied the city's Jim Crow ordinances and went to jail, their ringing manifesto, "An Appeal for Human Rights," catching the attention of the nation a year before the upbeat *Freedomways* editorial. In Raleigh, North Carolina, that same year, Ella Baker, the godmother to the civil rights movement, jump-

started the Student Nonviolent Coordinating Committee—
"Snick"—at a historic meeting of some 200 sit-in students at Shaw
University.

And then, in the spring of 1961, as bus caravans of Black students
invaded what many called the belly of the beast while world headlines
recorded the mayhem visited upon them in Anniston and Montgomery, Alabama, the élan of those remarkable events inspired and
emboldened the editors of *Freedomways*. Who but the most politically cynical or morally corrupt wished to decry the cascading mo-
mentum of the 1960s? Martin Luther King was wont to speak of the
seeming march to the Good Society as the work of the zeitgeist.
Politicians with a conscience or a simulacrum thereof claimed to be
legislating the beginnings of the Great Society. Angry young radicals,
impatient with the pace of everything, marched to the mantra of "nation time." Upon closer examination, these prescriptions for civil
rights and social justice would be shown to have very different mean-
ings, some of them not necessarily compatible. Most subscribers to
Freedomways (many of them scarred veterans of the sectarian Left,
savvy activists of the labor movement, and disabused loyalists of civil
rights) would have been keenly alert to the dissonances of the era and
would have kept their analytical balance, even as they worked for and
prudently contemplated the ascendancy of their social and economic
ideals.

What the magazine offered readers, issue after issue, was a record
of splendid things achieved and evidence of the validity of things aspired to. Jimmy McDonald's "A Freedom Rider Speaks His Mind"
was a bit of both—achievement and aspiration—as was Whitney
Young's "What Price Justice?" Kwame Nkrumah's UN address on
the Congo seemed to foretell a united Africa and a defeated white
South Africa. Paul Robeson's "We're Moving' '63," his last public
statement, must have been as poignant for its "ol' man river" fidelity
to proletarian justice as it was a cautionary epitome of the malevolent
power of what might well have been called the military racial-indus-
trial complex. "Over a half million Negroes in the United States are
participating in organizations formed to do away with discrimination, segregation, and to demand full citizenship right," the editors
trumpeted in their first number. Truly, it seemed possible that those
rights of full citizenship were about to be achieved.

What *Freedomways* made patently clear, however, was that the fight
for full citizenship by people of color antedated the turbulence of the

1960s, that it had been unfolding before the electric moment when Rosa Parks refused her seat in the back of the bus and even before the watershed decision of *Brown v. Board.* Entries by W.E.B. Du Bois and Robeson, as well as King's magnificent Carnegie Hall tribute to the author of *The Souls of Black Folk* on the occasion of the latter's centennial, Pablo Neruda's grand salute to Robeson, along with James Baldwin's moving apostrophe to Lorraine Hansberry serve to contextualize the struggle, to give it what French historians used to call the *long durée.* Before King and Malcolm and Wilkins and Carmichael, James Farmer, H. Rap Brown, and Fannie Lou Hamer, there had been the Old Left when it was young with its interracialism, its Louis Burnhams and Ben Davises calling for economic empowerment of the poor, its civil libertarian precocity in the first hours of Scottsboro, and its pathbreaking Southern Negro Youth Congress.

Esther Cooper Jackson, the dominant editorial voice in the life of *Freedomways,* has chosen the revealing title for this collection mined from the magazine's rich output, "Prophets in Their Own Country." At the end of the twentieth century—the close of the American Century—the voices of the prophets who speak to us from this collection hardly command the respectful attention of mainstream America today. Forty years after *Freedomways'* opening editorial salvo, the ideals of these iconic personalities have receded from the general consciousness as first the Nixon New Federalism, then the Reagan Revolution, followed by the Clinton Evasion, have made the world safe for the Darwinian regime of unregulated capital. Du Bois and Robeson, Baldwin and Hansberry, Julius Nyerere and Louis Burnham remain problematic seers in this new order. I take it that the sobering, instructive, and politically crucial message of this valuable *Freedomways* collection is, nevertheless, that we would do well to learn to esteem those prophets who are unappreciated in their own countries.